ERIC VOEGELIN
AND THE GOOD SOCIETY

ERIC VOEGELIN
AND THE GOOD SOCIETY

JOHN J. RANIERI

UNIVERSITY OF MISSOURI PRESS

COLUMBIA AND LONDON

Library of Congress Cataloging-in-Publication Data
Ranieri, John J., 1956–
    Eric Voegelin and the good society / John J. Ranieri.
        p.   cm.
    Includes bibliographical references and index.
    ISBN 0-8262-1012-0 (alk. paper)
    1. Voegelin, Eric, 1901– .   I. Title.
    B3354.V884R36 1995
193—dc20   95–15371
                                                                  CIP

Text Design: Elizabeth K. Fett
Jacket Design: Kristie Lee
Typesetter: Connell Zeko
Printer and binder: Thomson-Shore, Inc.
Typefaces: Kabel, New Baskerville

Permission to quote from the following works of Eric Voegelin has been
granted by Louisiana State University Press: *Autobiographical Reflections,*
© 1989; *The Collected Works of Eric Voegelin:* vol. 12, *Published Essays, 1966–
1985,* © 1990, vol. 27, *"The Nature of the Law" and Related Legal Writings,*
© 1991, and vol. 28, *"What Is History?" and Other Late Unpublished Writings,*
© 1990; and *Order and History,* vol. 1, *Israel and Revelation,* © 1956, vol. 2,
The World of the Polis, © 1957, vol. 3, *Plato and Aristotle,* © 1957, vol. 4, *The
Ecumenic Age,* © 1974, and vol. 5, *In Search of Order,* © 1987. Permission to
quote from *The New Science of Politics,* © 1952, has been granted by the
University of Chicago Press. Permission to quote from *Anamnesis,* © 1978,
has been granted by the University of Notre Dame Press.

The University of Missouri Press gratefully acknowledges the support for
its ongoing work in the humanities provided by Seton Hall University.

> Certainly we shall rise, certainly we shall see and gladly, joyfully tell one another all that has been . . .
>
> —Dostoyevsky, *The Brothers Karamazov*

IN MEMORY OF

Augusto Lou
Noel Giles
DeVernon Jacobs
Edward N. West
Patricia McCombs
and my father, John Peter Ranieri

CONTENTS

ACKNOWLEDGMENTS

I am indebted to Professor Frederick Lawrence and to Professor Patrick Byrne, both of Boston College, for their advice and support during the writing of this book. Besides being fine scholars and teachers they are genuine philosophers, men whose lives are animated by the love of wisdom. I am grateful to them for their help, insight, and friendship.

To the Most Reverend Theodore E. McCarrick, Archbishop of Newark, I owe a debt of gratitude for granting me the time to pursue graduate studies in philosophy. Monsignors Richard Liddy and Joseph Slinger offered helpful advice and guidance throughout the process of writing the book.

Rev. Thomas R. Peterson, O.P., the President and Chancellor of Seton Hall University, has been most supportive, both during my graduate work and now that I am teaching. I also thank Monsignor Harold Darcy, Minister of the Priest Community at Seton Hall, for his sensitivity to the needs of priest faculty. Special thanks are due to the Provost of Seton Hall University, Dr. Bernhard Scholz, for his generous assistance in the publication of this book.

I am grateful to my colleagues in the Philosophy Department for their support and their interest in my work. In particular, the chairman of the department, Dr. David O'Connor, has encouraged and helped me at every step along the way.

A final word of thanks goes to the staff of the University of Missouri Press. In particular, I wish to thank Gloria Thomas for her careful editing of the manuscript, her suggestions, and her graciousness.

ERIC VOEGELIN
AND THE GOOD SOCIETY

INTRODUCTION

Looking back on his friendship with Alfred Schutz, Eric Voegelin observed that they both had been involved in an attempt to reach "some clarity concerning the experiences that motivate philosophical thinking." For neither man was this inquiry a merely academic exercise; how one resolved the issue in question had important practical implications:

> This question had preoccupied us ever since the beginning of our dialogue, but with the philosophical tools then available it was not possible to attain satisfactory insight into it. The starting point common to both of us was determined by our training in neo-Kantian methodology, and in particular by Husserl's phenomenology. Moreover, we had both learned from Max Weber that ideologies get you nowhere in the sciences, although we did not know by what methods to attack the problems dealt with by the ideologies, and indeed the problems of the ideologies themselves. Finally we had in common the project of designing, with the philosophical means at our disposal, a theory of social action and of political order. In regard to concrete efforts, however, our ways parted.[1]

According to Voegelin, Schutz continued to refine the phenomenological method in order to deal with these issues. He also believed that Schutz was "far more intent on tangible results." Voegelin was attentive to the very same concerns, but his path was to be different:

> Compared to Schutz's vigorous advance, my own beginnings were much more hesitant. My interests tended toward Platonic-Aristotelian Politics, and, as I studied the classics, I could not fail to remark that the presuppositions of their philosophizing on political order differed radically from those of phenomenology, although I was not able to conceive clearly the differences in the motivating experiences. . . . It

1. Eric Voegelin, "In memorium Alfred Schutz," 463.

1

was the New York conversations of 1943 that clarified for both of us the question we were pursuing in our different but parallel attempts: phenomenological philosophizing such as Husserl's is in principle oriented to the model of the experience of objects in the external world; classical philosophizing about political order is equally in principle oriented to the model of noetic experience of transcendent being.[2]

The preceding quotations illustrate several significant themes at the heart of Voegelin's project—attention to the experiences underlying philosophy, concern for developing a method by which these experiences could be explored and communicated, the need to deal with ideologies on their own level of philosophical sophistication, and the very practical concern that such analyses result in "a theory of social action and political order." Where Voegelin seems to have parted company with Schutz is in his emphasis on the classical sources of political philosophy, his recognition of the important role of "transcendent being" in the ancient philosophical tradition, and his criticism of the phenomenological method as the means by which to gain access to the experiences articulated by the classical philosophers.

What is also evident in these passages is the social and political orientation of Voegelin's approach. In other writings he made it equally clear that the motivation behind his work was the contemporary political situation. The triumph of communism in Russia, the rise of fascism and National Socialism, and the weakness of Western democracies in checking the spread of these ideologies were the catalysts that prompted his philosophical work.[3]

In confronting these problems, Voegelin realized that it would be necessary to recover the experiences of reality that found expression in the self-interpretation of every contemporary social and political order. The difficulty consisted in developing a conceptual framework and a philosophical method with which to gain access to these experiences. In an attempt to work through this dilemma, his early work consisted of a series of specialized studies, by means of which he tried to acquire the historical and philosophical knowledge necessary to deal adequately with the problems before him. Among these

2. Ibid., 464.
3. Eric Voegelin, *Autobiographical Reflections,* 24–25, 93; Eric Voegelin, "Autobiographical Statement at Age Eighty-Two," 116–17; Ellis Sandoz, *The Voegelinian Revolution: A Biographical Introduction,* 33–70.

earlier studies are *Ueber die Form des amerikanischen Geistes* (1928), *Rasse und Staat* (1933), *Die Rassenidee in der Geistesgeschichte von Ray bis Carus* (1933), *Der autoritaere Staat* (1936), and *Die politischen Religionen* (1938).[4]

The rise of National Socialism prompted Voegelin's interest in racial theory, with its biological and evolutionary implications. Voegelin was living in Vienna at the time, and he felt compelled to address these matters. His studies earned him the displeasure of the Nazi regime and eventually forced his emigration to the United States. On the level of theory he discovered that the more deeply he penetrated these areas, the more insistently questions concerning the ultimate ground of reality imposed themselves:

> You cannot proceed by logical analysis from one species to another without knowing where one species develops out of another. You can only say that in fact it does occur. You can go back within the biological sphere to the vegetative level pre-existing animal evolution and state the fact that there is an evolution on the level of the vegetative. And then you can go back to before the vegetative realm, to the material levels which are the basis for the evolution of the vegetative. The vegetative are the basis for the evolution of the animal realm and the animal realm ultimately of the human realm. You can do all that and still not know what happens. What is the original force that structures reality and imposes structure on reality?[5]

From these specialized studies Voegelin moved toward a treatment of these issues in terms of the evolution and development of ideas. He was commissioned in the early 1940s to write a history of political ideas, which coincided with his own interests at the time and eventually led to a dramatic reorientation in his approach:

> . . . When I came to America I was asked by Mr. Morstein-Marx at Harvard to write a brief history of political ideas for McGraw-Hill. I thought it was a good idea. One could do that. . . . I was interested in the subject matter; I worked with the sources. It was a mistake. I found out that the standard history of political ideas was George Sabine's, beginning with classical antiquity and working (with a few gaps in the middle ages) up to the modern period. Well, I found out

4. Voegelin, "In memorium," 464; Gregor Sebba, "Prelude and Variations on the Theme of Eric Voegelin," in Ellis Sandoz, ed., *Eric Voegelin's Thought: A Critical Appraisal*, 9–14; Thomas Heilke, *Voegelin on the Idea of Race: An Analysis of Modern European Racism;* Sandoz, *Voegelinian Revolution*, 44–70.

5. "Autobiographical Statement," 117–18.

that this procedure would not do, because besides the predominant classical ideas, there were also a few Christian ideas which did not just fall from heaven, but which were historically connected with the development of Judaism. And Judaism, too, did not just fall from heaven, but was connected with reactions of certain tribal groups to Egyptian surroundings and cosmological-imperial constructions. At that time the Chicago Institute of Oriental Studies and the development of the theory of empires and so on were flourishing, and I included that material. That material increased, and instead of a short history of ideas, all of a sudden there was a manuscript of several volumes. I worked myself all the way from the Chicago Oriental School on the oriental empires up through the nineteenth century. Then I arrived at Schelling and his philosophy of myth.

That brought the crash. Because Schelling was an intelligent philosopher, and when I studied the philosophy of myth, I understood that ideas are nonsense: there are no ideas as such and there is no history of ideas; but there is a history of experiences which can express themselves in various forms, as myths of various types, as philosophical development, and so on. One has got to get back to the analysis of experience. So I cashiered that history of ideas, which was practically finished in four or five volumes, and started reworking it from the standpoint of the problem of experiences. That is how *Order and History* started.[6]

Henceforth, Voegelin would occupy himself with an analysis of experiences. From this analysis there would develop a theory of human participation in reality, culminating, in later years, in a philosophy of consciousness.

What is important to remember when considering Voegelin's project is that his philosophy of experience and consciousness must never be understood apart from the social and political concerns from which it emerged. Voegelin was indeed a philosopher of consciousness, and, as a chronicler of the differentiation of consciousness, a philosopher of history as well. I would maintain, though, that these important and in many ways constitutive dimensions of his thought arise from that interest that he shared with Alfred Schutz, to develop "a theory of social action and of political order." In my reading of Voegelin I have found nothing that would cast doubt on the social and political motivation behind his work. Indeed, in its recovery and adaptation (as opposed to mere reiteration) of classical political wisdom, Voegelin's thought sheds a fresh light upon the question of

6. Ibid., 118–19. See also *Autobiographical Reflections*, 62–64.

what it is that constitutes a society as good and what this implies for an authentic understanding of practicality in social and political matters.

This work is written from the perspective that political and social concerns are at the heart of Voegelin's enterprise. This perspective shapes the manner of proceeding. For if it is true that Voegelin never turned away from these issues, and that they remained of central importance to his work, then his understanding of what it is that constitutes a good society and of the possibility of its realization is a matter of some importance. Throughout his career Voegelin wrestled with problems involving the relationship between the order of reality as known in consciousness and the concrete social orders created by human beings. The manner in which he articulated this problem may have changed over time, and the emphasis given to certain aspects of the problem may have shifted, but it was this relationship that remained at the center of his work. If, as he believed, contemporary social and political disorder could be traced to an ignorance of the structure of reality, then a proper understanding of reality and its relationship to society is of critical importance. The degree to which the members of a given society can understand the structure of reality and live in accordance with it is at the core of questions concerning societal authenticity and change. To what degree is any society capable of embodying the truth about reality, that is, the truth of order, in its institutions and practices? To what extent is such change possible at all? These are the questions I wish to consider in light of Voegelin's thought.

The first step involves situating Voegelin's thinking about society within the context of his understanding of reality as a whole. It is important to understand the broader contours of reality, so as to conceptualize a horizon within which to situate social reality. The first chapter will consider Voegelin's thought concerning the wider structure and movement of reality, and the consciousness by which that reality is apprehended. In the second chapter I will focus on the ways in which this knowledge of reality has differentiated and been articulated in various cultures over the course of history.

Having thus given an account of reality, consciousness, and its differentiations, we will be in a better position to discuss social reality. Society, as discussed in Chapter 3, is a composite of meanings and the institutions that embody those meanings. To investigate Voegelin's conception of social reality would be difficult without having first analyzed, as I do in chapters 1 and 2, reality as a whole and those differentiations of consciousness in terms of which societies orient themselves within reality.

In orienting themselves toward the encompassing reality in which they participate, societies are always in danger of failing to respond authentically. Derailment and deformation of existence are always possible. For Voegelin, the modern period offers ample evidence that instances of derailment far outnumber those of authentic attunement. Chapter 4 will consider these "eclipses of reality." The precariousness of attunement and the very real possibility of derailment mean that the struggle for order as it takes shape in various societies will consist of advances and regressions, breakthroughs and stagnation. To reflect upon the variety and diversity of response is to be confronted with the problem of history; for history, as Voegelin conceived it, has to do with this process of attunement and derailment as it emerges in society. Chapters 5 and 6, after introducing the notion of history, will trace the struggle for order as it manifested itself in the two societies in which the great noetic and pneumatic differentiations emerged: Israel and Hellas. In these two chapters the focus will be on a representative figure in whom the differentiation of consciousness led to a conflict with the society in which he lived. In the case of Israel we will concentrate on the prophet Isaiah and the prophetic critique of Israelite society; in the case of Hellas our attention will be focused on Plato and his reaction to a corrupt polis.

Having thus chronicled the difficulties of social attunement to the truth of order, the question to be considered will be to what extent the good society is realizable. Another way of framing the question is to ask to what extent Voegelin believed in the possibility of social/political change. Chapter 7 deals with this issue as Voegelin addressed it in his writings. The eighth chapter will be taken up with reflections on Voegelin's attempt at a "resolution" of the tension between the truth of order and its attempted social incarnation. I will consider there his formulation of this problem in *The Ecumenic Age* and the role that the Platonic notion of "vision" plays in its resolution.

While I believe that I have been attentive to the development of Voegelin's thinking on these issues, this book is not a chronological survey of his work. For the most part, I have concentrated on *Order and History* and subsequent writings. In these works Voegelin seems to have found the philosophical language he had been seeking. Admittedly, *The Ecumenic Age* represents a shift in his approach, but it is a shift to a viewpoint that still falls within the horizon of that analysis of experience and participation set forth in the preface and introduction of the earlier *Israel and Revelation*. Where I have discussed his earlier writings, it has been mainly to demonstrate that throughout his career, the condition of society was of tremendous concern to Voegelin, and that his later work represents a continuing therapeutic effort to reclaim the sources of authentic political community and to address the ills that beset us today.

O N E

REALITY AND CONSCIOUSNESS

Voegelin's conception of social and political change can be discussed only within the wider context of his thinking about reality and consciousness. For Voegelin, elucidation of the structures of reality and consciousness was an essential precondition for an authentic political or social theory. Reality and consciousness, together with language, form a "complex" whose structure gradually emerges through the differentiations of consciousness that constitute history. This chapter will focus on Voegelin's understanding of reality and consciousness; the following chapter will offer an account of the major differentiations of consciousness and their relationship to history. Once these broad contours of Voegelin's thought have been understood it will be possible to situate social reality within the larger complex. The first part of this chapter follows Voegelin in his meditation on reality and his attempts to clarify its structure. The second section deals with consciousness and its relationship to reality. The third section contains a brief account of language, symbolization, and reflective distance, concluding with some critical reflections.

REALITY

Near the very beginning of *Order and History* we find the following statement: "God and man, world and society form a primordial community of being." In a later essay this same community will be referred to as the "primordial field of reality."[1] A sense of participation

---

1. Eric Voegelin, *Order and History*, vol. 1, *Israel and Revelation*, 1; Eric Voegelin, "Equivalences of Experience and Symbolization in History," 126. As far as I can tell, Voegelin does not distinguish very carefully between the terms *being* and *reality*. The former term is more common in the earlier volumes of *Order and History*, while the latter term seems to be preferred in his later writings. The

marks the human experience of this primordial community: "Whatever man may be, he knows himself a part of being. The great stream of being, in which he flows while it flows through him, is the same to which belongs everything else that drifts into his perspective. The community of being is experienced with such intimacy that the consubstantiality of the partners will override the separateness of substances."[2]

Human beings are aware of themselves as participants in an ongoing drama of existence that they did not originate and that will continue when they are gone. To participate is to experience oneself as sharing in the reality that is common to all the partners within the community of being, to realize that the partners participate in each other within the whole, while at the same time recognizing that the partners are not identical. Participation is not a matter of choice; it is simply given, without the human being knowing the how or the why. Nor is participation merely a dimension of existence; Voegelin believed that participation, as experienced by human beings, *is* existence.[3] Participation is correlative with the reality in which it shares; the area covered by the term *reality* comes into view through participation: "Reality (a) is not a thing that man confronts but the encompassing reality in which he himself is real as he participates; real (b) are the 'things' that can be distinguished in the encompassing reality—the gods, men, and so on; real (c) is also the participation of things in each other within the encompassing reality."[4] In participation humans are aware of living within an encompassing whole even when that whole is not made the specific object of investigation. An implicit awareness of reality as a whole is always present as a background to human experiences of participation. There exists no readily available term with which to speak of the encompassing whole that embraces the partners in the community of being; in his later work Voegelin would simply refer to it as the "It-reality."[5]

---

reason for the abandonment of the term *being* seems to be his concern to avoid any semblance of "propositional metaphysics," which he thought had pejorative connotations. I address this matter in greater detail in Chapter 4.

2. Voegelin, *Israel and Revelation,* 3.

3. Eric Voegelin, *Conversations with Eric Voegelin,* 55; *Israel and Revelation,* 1.

4. Eric Voegelin, *Anamnesis,* trans. and ed. Gerhart Niemeyer, 63.

5. *Order and History,* vol. 5, *In Search of Order,* 16; "The Meditative Origin of the Philosophical Knowledge of Order," 49.

As all participation is perspectival, it effectively limits the human experience of reality: "The community with its quaternarian structure is, and is not, a datum of human experience. It is a datum of experience in so far as it is known to man by virtue of his participation in the mystery of its being. It is not a datum of experience in so far as it is not given in the manner of an object of the external world but is knowable only from the perspective of participation in it." Humans find themselves in the midst of an encompassing whole about which they can and do wonder, but which they can never completely know. The reason for this is that there is no vantage point apart from the reality of participation from which human beings can apprehend reality as they do objects in the external world.[6] We are always already "in." The reality that encompasses human beings activates but never completely satisfies our wonder; as we plumb the depth, the horizon recedes before us.

Yet even though the human perspective can never completely grasp reality as a whole, our "ultimate, essential ignorance is not complete ignorance."[7] Questions can help to specify and bring into focus the "known unknown" within which we find ourselves. Our questions function heuristically; when we give full rein to our capacity for wonder, the structure of the reality in which we participate begins to take shape. It is not a matter of human beings adding or giving structure to a previously amorphous reality; rather, the ever-present structure of reality emerges more clearly in consciousness as we attempt to orient ourselves by raising and answering questions about our place and role within the whole. In doing so, important dimensions of our experience of reality begin to stand out with greater clarity. Thus it is that we orient ourselves within reality by speaking of God and man, world and society. It must be emphasized that these terms do not refer to objects that are "out there" waiting to be discovered by the human seeker. Nor do the partners in the community of being occupy neatly compartmentalized areas of reality. Instead, they represent the tensions of existence reflected in the questions we raise about our experience of participation. Such experiences of reality are eventually articulated as the divine and human, the cosmic and earthly poles "within" the wider whole. This is what is

6. Voegelin, *Israel and Revelation*, 1; *Anamnesis*, 163.
7. *Israel and Revelation*, 2.

meant when we speak of the partners in the community of being. As we shall examine in greater detail in Chapter 2, the articulation of participatory experience will entail a development from a more compact account of experience in which the consubstantiality of the partners is emphasized, to a more differentiated perspective in which God and man, world and society are more clearly distinguished.

When we begin to ask about the relationship between reality as the encompassing whole and the reality of the "things" *(ta onta)* encompassed, we come to the question of the "ground." For Voegelin one of the most important symbols arising from the human quest to make sense of reality was the symbol of the "ground." The search for the ground is a constant in all civilizations and all societies, because in all ages human beings have wondered about the origins of the gods, the cosmos, their communities, and themselves. To speak of the ground is to become aware of that dimension of the encompassing whole that is specified by the questions "Why is there something rather than nothing?" and "Why is that something as it is?" The ground can be neither directly known nor given in intuition; yet it can be deduced from our experience of participation and from our experiences of other beings. Voegelin explains:

> That being which is the ground of all experienceable particular being is an ontological hypothesis without which the experienced reality of the ontic nexus in human existence remains incomprehensible, but it is nowhere a datum in human existence rather it is always strictly transcendence that we can approach only through meditation. It cannot be drawn from that Beyond of finiteness into finiteness itself. Our human finiteness is always within being.[8]

Although the ground cannot be known, our experience of participation and of other entities in the world leads us to posit a ground of all beings as an ontological hypothesis. We witness birth and death, lasting and passing. Where have we come from? What awaits us? From where do "things" emerge into existence and to where do they return? The ground symbolizes our experience of reality as the creative origin of all things. Whatever is not the creative ground belongs to the "things." As such the "things" include those objects in the external world that we observe coming to be and perishing, but the "things" also encompass the gods, humans, the cosmos, and society.

8. *Anamnesis*, 32; *Conversations*, 2.

To reflect upon the ground of these partners in the primordial community of being is to engage in theogony, anthropogony, cosmogony, and historiogenesis, respectively. Although the ground may be approached from each of these directions, it is important to bear in mind that reflection on the origins of any area of reality is always traceable back to the one ground. The ground and the "things" are not to be separated from one another; they are not independently existing realities. In the following passage Voegelin employs the Aristotelian term *apeiron* to discuss the ground and its relationship to the emergent "things": "The Apeiron and the things are not two different realities in a static relationship one toward the other; they are experienced as modes of being, or as poles of a tension within the one, comprehensive reality."[9]

Both the ground and the things are real. As real, they are to be understood not as separate entities standing apart from one another but as tensional poles within reality as a whole. It is, of course, necessary to distinguish the mode of being of the ground from that of the things. If participation is to be equated with existence, then the ground of participation cannot be said to "exist" in the same fashion as the participatory "things." One is faced, then, with the paradox of a "nonexistent" ground that sustains the existence and order of all areas of reality even though it does not itself belong as an existent thing to any one of these areas.[10] Further distinctions can be made among the "being things" themselves; for example, the being of divine things is very different from that of physical objects, yet both are considered to be among the things that emerge from the ground.

Reality, then, is experienced by the human participant as an encompassing whole whose structure reveals itself through a process in which the ground and the things are increasingly distinguished from one another. In addition to experiencing reality as comprehensive and as structured, participants also experience reality as dynamic. In the following passage, Voegelin emphasizes this dimension of participation: "Reality in this comprehensive sense is experienced as engaged in a movement of transcending itself in the direction of eminent reality. . . . Reality is not a static order of things given to a

9. *Order and History,* vol. 4, *The Ecumenic Age,* 59–60, 216–17.
10. Voegelin, *Conversations,* 51; *Ecumenic Age,* 72, 77–78.

human observer once for all; it is moving, indeed, in the direction of emergent truth."[11]

How are we to make sense of the notion that the comprehensive (It-) reality is itself engaged in a movement toward eminent reality? Would not, then, the emerging eminent reality be the more comprehensive reality? Would the newly designated comprehensive reality also, then, be engaged in movement toward a more eminent reality? Could we ever articulate the structure and movement of reality in a way that would avoid this infinite expansion of ever-more-encompassing wholes? How can reality move toward a greater degree of reality? Voegelin was aware of the paradox of a "recognizably structured process that is recognizably moving beyond its structure."[12] Yet while he might have sympathized with the questioner, he would also, I believe, have found such questions somewhat misguided. In such questioning there is already a tendency (which Voegelin saw as almost unavoidable given the limitations of the predominantly "thingly" mode of human language) to try to imagine the modes and the tensional poles of being. The problem then becomes one of hypostatization and reification of the tensions within reality. To think of reality in such a way is to imagine the less comprehensive areas of being in relation to the encompassing whole as "things within things." The movement of reality then becomes a case of one "thing" changing into another rather than as mystery in process. In order to avoid such an error, one must return again to the very concrete experiences of participation shared by human beings in all cultures and at all times.

As noted earlier, people are aware of things both human and nonhuman as lasting and passing, as emerging into existence and returning to the ground of being, and as situated somewhere between the poles of mortality and immortality, imperfection and perfection. It is this universal experience that is captured in the symbols of the Apeiron, the ground, the depth of the psyche, and in Voegelin's final writings, as the Beginning.[13]

11. *Ecumenic Age*, 216–17.
12. Ibid., 227.
13. See Voegelin's works "Immortality: Experience and Symbol"; "The Gospel and Culture," 176; *Israel and Revelation*, 2–5; "Equivalences," 119–20; "The Beginning and the Beyond: A Meditation on Truth," 174; *Ecumenic Age*, 17; and "Equivalences," 126.

A further question arises, however. Is the temporal flux of reality, experienced as the lasting and passing of *ta onta,* a self-enclosed process, or can we speak of an atemporal reality out of which the cosmic flux itself emerges and toward which it is drawn? Voegelin thought that it was appropriate to speak of a dimension of reality as "out of time." He refers to reality in this mode as the "Beyond."[14] He also thought there was reason to postulate such a mode of being. Voegelin maintained that the crucial epoch-making events of history are in fact instances of this reality beyond time entering into the temporal process; indeed, it is the human response to such events that propels history. In such experiences, those addressed find themselves drawn in the direction of the Beyond. At the same time, the parousia of the Beyond creates in the recipients an awareness of reality as engaged in movement beyond itself in the direction of the Beyond. What is the relationship of the symbols "Beginning and Beyond" to the symbol of the ground? It would seem as if the "Beginning and the Beyond" represent a further stage in the development of reflection upon the ground. The ground that hitherto had been experienced primarily as the origin of all things in space and time, the "Beginning," comes to be recognized as being itself beyond the cosmic process, the "Beyond" of space and time. The ground then becomes the "divine" ground. This is also the origin of the language of transcendence and immanence. The words *immanent* and *transcendent* "cannot be used as absolute adjectives to anything, but only as correlatives designating two poles of the existential tension." The consequence of this understanding of transcendence and immanence is that "God is then realized to be *the* God who is the divine ground of everything (as against the world with its spatio-temporal contents). . . . There is no world without the god, and no god without the world. There is an immanent world only in relation to a transcendent ground." For Voegelin, the symbols of Beginning and Beyond were "the unsurpassably exact expression" of the directions in which reality is experienced.[15] As later chapters will consider, the degree to which human beings are able to strike a balance between the pulls of the Beginning and of the Beyond will have tremendous consequences for social and political life.

14. *Ecumenic Age,* 9; *In Search of Order,* 30.
15. *Ecumenic Age,* 228; *Conversations,* 52–53; *Ecumenic Age,* 9.

Having distinguished between reality in its dimensions of Beginning and Beyond, we are in a better position to answer our earlier
question as to how it is that reality can move in the direction of
eminent reality, and to situate these symbols in relationship to the
encompassing It-reality. To speak of Beginning and Beyond is not to
speak of two "areas" within It-reality, nor is it, in the case of the
Beyond, to envisage a realm of being beyond It-reality. It-reality is the
ultimate symbol; the symbols of Beginning and Beyond do not represent additional "things" that have been discovered, but are a way of
accounting for our experience of reality as structured, as in flux,
and as engaged in movement toward ultimate transfiguration. As
such they are to be understood as tensional poles or modes of being
within the dynamically structured It-reality. There is no reality beyond the It-reality; there is only a developing awareness of its structure and its movement. In one of his last works, Voegelin expresses
this view of reality in a way that captures both its intelligible structure
and its essential openness to mystery:

> The comprehending It-reality moves formatively through the thing-
> reality from a Beginning that does not begin in things to an End that
> does not end in things. The Beginning and the End of the story are
> experienced as a Beyond of the formative, tensional process of reality.
> The meditative wandering through the constants in the tensional pro-
> cess thus becomes luminous for a reality beyond the tensions that can-
> not be attained within tensional existence. The super-constant above
> the constants is not a principle of order whose proper application will
> dissolve the disorder of Cosmic order, but the experience of the para-
> doxic tension in formative reality, of the tension between the divine
> reality experienced as formatively present at the ordering pole of the
> tensions and the divine reality experienced as a Beyond of its concrete
> manifestations in the process, between the God who reveals himself in
> his presence in time and the God who remains the experienced but
> unknown reality beyond time.[16]

CONSCIOUSNESS

In discussing the structure and movement of reality, I have used the
terms *participation, experience, symbol,* and so forth, without clearly
indicating what they mean in the context of Voegelin's thought. However, more precision is called for at this stage in answer to further

16. *In Search of Order,* 106–7.

questions. Human beings have been described as having experiences of participation in an encompassing structure and process. But what is meant by "experience"? What does it mean to be "conscious" of our participation in being? To raise such questions is to ask about the point of intersection between the human and the divine. It is to raise the question of consciousness. Why not begin, then, with consciousness, if it turns out that it is in consciousness that reality is known? Admittedly, this could be done, but I prefer to begin as Voegelin does at the start of *Order and History,* with the fact that humans find themselves already "within" being. Whether one begins from the perspective of consciousness or of reality, the crucial point is that the two concepts be understood in their integral relationship.

The importance of a theory of consciousness is evident in Voegelin's assertion "The problems of human order in society and history originate in the order of consciousness. Hence the philosophy of consciousness is the centerpiece of a philosophy of politics."[17] Voegelin's theory of consciousness is perhaps the most unusual feature of his thought. An account of consciousness is something more likely to be found in the writings of a psychologist or a cognitional theorist; we are generally not inclined to expect such an analysis from a political philosopher.[18] Yet one of the strengths of Voegelin's philosophy is his insistence on recovering those primordial experiences of reality that find expression in culture, society, and polity. He is not content to ask, "What are the meanings that inform our social and political institutions?"; he pushes further to wonder, "What are the experiences of reality that emerge into consciousness and give rise to such meanings?" To investigate a question of this nature, one needs to have an understanding of reality and of the consciousness in which it becomes lucid. It is only then that we will be able to make sense of Voegelin's assertion that consciousness "is the luminous center radiating the concrete order of human existence into society and history."[19]

What, then, can be said about this "luminous center"? Again we

17. "Consciousness and Order: Foreword to *Anamnesis* (1966)," 35; *Anamnesis,* 3.

18. Or perhaps we should say from *contemporary* political philosophers; certainly Plato in Book IV of the *Republic* (427a–445c) was very much concerned with the relationship between psyche and society. See *Great Dialogues of Plato,* trans. W. H. D. Rouse (New York: New American Library, Mentor, 1956), 224–46.

19. Voegelin, "Consciousness and Order," 36.

return to the notion of participation. Up to this point the discussion has focused on the reality that is illuminated in participation. To raise the issue of consciousness is to speak of the same reality from the perspective of the awareness that constitutes the "within." In other words, there is participation only because we are aware of ourselves as participating. Consciousness does not merely accompany participation; it is participation. The structure and movement of reality become the objects of meditation because there is a "place" (an unavoidable spatial metaphor) within reality where reflection arises. Consciousness is the "site" and the "sensorium of human participation." As Voegelin presents it in *Anamnesis:* "A reality, called man, relates itself, within an encompassing reality, through the reality of participation—called consciousness—to the terms of participation as reality."[20]

In his *Autobiographical Reflections* Voegelin acknowledges the debt his theory of consciousness owed to William James's notion of "pure experience." James rejected the notion of consciousness as an entity or as "a special stuff or way of being." He also called into doubt the primordiality of the subject/object distinction, and maintained that consciousness as intentional was founded on a prior, "pure" experience, an irreducible immediacy. "The instant field of the present," he wrote, "is at all times what I call the 'pure' experience. It is only virtually or potentially either object or subject as yet. For the time being, it is plain, unqualified actuality, or existence, a simple *that.*" Voegelin speaks approvingly of James's approach: "In developing his concept of pure experience, James put his finger on the reality of the consciousness of participation, inasmuch as what he calls pure experience is the something that can be put into the context either of the subject's stream of consciousness or of objects in the external world. This fundamental insight of James identifies the something that lies between the subject and object of participation as the experience."[21] Before one can speak of a conscious subject and its relationship to an object, there is the prior reality of which consciousness and what it is "consciousness of" are but dimensions. Antecedent to the language of subject and object is the immediate, undifferentiated experience

20. Sandoz, *Voegelinian Revolution,* 179; Voegelin, "Immortality," 90; *Anamnesis,* 163.
21. Voegelin, *Autobiographical Reflections,* 72; William James, *Writings, 1902–1910,* 1151; Voegelin, *Autobiographical Reflections,* 72.

that becomes luminous to itself at the "place" we name "consciousness." Consciousness is inseparable from the reality that it illumines; there is no consciousness that "looks at" reality.

It would be dangerously misleading, though, to move from the inseparability of consciousness and reality in the originating or "pure" experience to the conclusion that reality must then be constituted by consciousness. Voegelin is insistent that such is not the case. Consciousness illuminates only that area of reality in which it occurs; "processes transcending consciousness are not experienceable from within." Reality is unlimited, but consciousness is not. Far from being constituted by consciousness, the reverse is true: consciousness arises only within the reality that it illumines. Voegelin employs the term *psyche* in an attempt to capture both the limited nature and the openness to the unfathomable depth that characterizes consciousness. *Psyche* is a heuristic term expressing the fact that while the area enlightened by consciousness is limited, consciousness simultaneously points toward the reality that lies beyond its borders, that is, the "known unknown." Consciousness can plumb the depth without ever being able to encompass it: "We experience psyche as consciousness that can descend into the depth of its own reality, and the depth of the psyche as reality that can rise to consciousness, but we do not experience a content of the depth other than the content that has entered consciousness."[22]

That which moves consciousness in its exploration of reality is its inherent questioning unrest. Consciousness is dynamic. The border between consciousness and the encompassing whole is not a wall, but rather a site of wonder and questioning. The depth, the ground that eludes the grasp of consciousness also serves to attract and move consciousness by the very fact of its unknowability. Humans exist in tension toward the ground: a tension experienced as a drawing from the divine pole and as a seeking questioning from the perspective of mortals.[23] In his later writings Voegelin paid increasing attention to that attraction from the Beyond that moves the questioner to transcend even the tension toward the ground.

Having identified consciousness as the site of questioning unrest within reality, we are now in a better position to give an account of

22. *Anamnesis,* 21; "Equivalences," 126.
23. *Anamnesis,* 92–95, 149.

what Voegelin means by "experience." As I have already noted, his own view of consciousness has much in common with James's notion of "pure experience." James viewed experience as located neither in subject nor in object but in the immediacy embracing both. Such radical empiricism includes but is not limited to sense impressions; that is, "the relations that connect experiences must themselves be experienced relations, and any kind of relation experienced must be accounted as 'real' as anything else in the system." In Voegelinian language this means that the tensional poles of existence are neither imaginative nor conceptual constructs imposed upon reality, but rather the very structure of reality achieving clarity as it emerges in consciousness. To raise questions as to whether one's images, concepts, or thoughts correspond correctly to their objects is to already fragment the pure experience into a hypostatized subject and object rather than to see them as "terms" (Voegelin would say "poles") within the immediately given experience. This point is crucial in understanding Voegelin. He definitely viewed his philosophy as being empirically grounded in experience, but experience was not to be conceived in a crude or naively empirical fashion that would limit its meaning to an intentionalist account in which either sense objects or thought objects stood apart from a conscious subject. As we shall see, Voegelin did acknowledge the role of intentionality in knowing. It is, however, a strictly subordinate role. This is because experience has to do primarily with the mysterious point of intersection and tension where consciousness and reality meet, not with either of the poles constituted by and grounded in that tension.[24] Experience, then, is not a newly discovered area to be added to the foregoing account; it is but another perspective on the meditative complex. If the discussion of reality emphasized the whole that is illumined, and the discussion of consciousness that by which it is illumined, discussions of the notion of experience in Voegelin's work make clear that reality and consciousness are inseparable and that any analysis must begin at the place of their contact.

While Voegelin's conception of experience owed a great deal to the radical empiricism of William James, his appreciation of the dynamic movement and tension toward the divine ground at the heart of experience was from his study of Plato and Aristotle. Experi-

---

24. James, *Writings*, 1160; Voegelin, *Autobiographical Reflections*, 72–73.

ence is essentially "metaleptic," an overlapping of divine appeal and human questing. It is the simultaneous presence of divine and human reality. Experience, then, is constituted by the consciousness of participation in the "in-between." The term *in-between,* or *metaxy,* is borrowed from Plato, and it occupies a prominent place in Voegelin's thought. Human existence is always existence in the metaxy; experience is always "in-between":

> Man experiences himself as tending beyond his human imperfection toward the perfection of the divine ground that moves him. The spiritual man, the *daimonios aner,* as he is moved in his quest for the ground, moves somewhere between knowledge and ignorance *(metaxy sophias kai amathias).* "The whole realm of the spiritual *(daimonion)* is halfway indeed between *(metaxy)* god and man" *(Symp.* 202a). Thus the in-between—the *metaxy*—is not an empty space between the poles of the tension, but the "realm of the spiritual"; it is the reality of "man's converse with the gods" (202–203), the mutual participation *(methexis, metalepsis)* of human in divine, and divine in human, reality.[25]

Every human society bears testimony to its preoccupation with existence in the metaxy through the language of "life and death, immortality and mortality, perfection and imperfection, time and timelessness; between order and disorder, truth and untruth; between *amor Dei* and *amor sui.*"[26] In coming to understand and live within this tension, that is, in seeking and implementing order, humans give shape to history, society, and polity.

If experience is essentially metaleptic, and consciousness is the site of this experience, then the question arises as to the status of individual human consciousness within reality. Consistent with his analysis of consciousness and experience, Voegelin preferred not to speak of human consciousness as an individual "I" or as an intentionally oriented subject, although, as we shall see, he admitted that there is a dimension to human existence where such language is justified. In fact, in his 1943 essay "On the Theory of Consciousness," he explicitly calls into question whether there is any "I" given in consciousness at all.[27] In Voegelin's work, the human being is to be

---

25. Voegelin, *Autobiographical Reflections,* 73; "The Beginning and the Beyond," 173; *Anamnesis,* 103.
26. Voegelin, "Equivalences," 119.
27. "There seems, then, to be no need to look for the constitution of a flow of consciousness. Furthermore it seems to me that there is no I that would be the

primarily understood as that place within the community of being where reality becomes luminous to itself in consciousness. He asserts: "There is no such thing as a 'man' who participates in 'being' as if it were an enterprise that he could as well leave alone; there is, rather, a 'something,' a part of being, capable of experiencing itself as such, and furthermore capable of using language and calling this experiencing consciousness by the name of 'man.'" Human consciousness can also be described as the immanent pole within the tensional metaxy.[28] To avoid confusion, we must constantly recall that "immanent" and "transcendent" are indices assigned to areas of the primary experience; they do not refer to entities or things in relationship to one another as subject and object. Thus understood, human consciousness becomes the site of wonder and questioning unrest in tension toward the divine ground. The result of such language can be seen in Voegelin's reference to the great Greek philosopher as "the part of reality that goes by the name of Plato."[29]

A number of questions arise that the preceding discussion has done little to clarify. Are "human being" and "human consciousness" the same? Is human consciousness simply an emanation of a single, universal consciousness manifesting itself in individuals in the manner of a Fichtean Ego? Toward the very beginning of this chapter it was affirmed that human existence is participation. Later it was stated that participation is consciousness. Are we then to conclude that human existence is to be equated with consciousness? Voegelin must have been aware that his terminology could be open to misinterpretation, and he sought to avoid this danger:

> Human consciousness is not a free-floating something but always the concrete consciousness of concrete persons. The consciousness of the existential tension toward the ground, therefore, while constituting the specific human nature that distinguishes man from other beings,

---

agent of the constitution. It is doubtful whether consciousness has the form of the I, or whether the I is not rather a phenomenon in consciousness. . . . The 'I' seems to me to be no given at all but rather a highly complex symbol for certain perspectives in consciousness" (*Anamnesis*, 19). Voegelin's concern here seems to be to preserve his insights into consciousness as constituted by metaleptic participation in reality, rather than to have consciousness be understood as somehow constructed by an individual constituting agent. What is given are experiences of participation, not a "self" that somehow structures the "flow" of consciousness.

28. Voegelin, *Israel and Revelation*, 2; *Anamnesis*, 176.
29. Eric Voegelin, "Wisdom and the Magic of the Extreme: A Meditation," 343.

is not the whole of his nature, for consciousness is always concretely founded on man's bodily existence, through which he belongs to all levels of being, from the anorganic to the animalic. . . . Any construction of history as the unfolding of *the* consciousness—whether it be a consciousness of humanity, God's consciousness, history's consciousness, or an absolute mind—is incompatible with the discrete reality of consciousness.

While human *nature* is characterized by conscious tension toward the ground, humans also share in other levels of being with their bodies. For purposes of later discussion it is important to note that this bodily existence will serve as the basis for social existence.[30] Human consciousness, while the most essential level of being, is not the totality of human existence. As human, consciousness is individual; it is always located in a body.

This relationship between body and consciousness presented problems for Voegelin. In the early essay "On the Theory of Consciousness," he notes that since consciousness is experienced only as consciousness, "the substantive unity of human existence, which must be accepted as ontological hypothesis for the understanding of consciousness's basis in body and matter, is objectively inexperiencable. That does not mean, however, that there is no such thing." This difficulty did not disappear. Nearly forty years after he wrote this essay, Voegelin attributed the tension between the interpretation of reality in terms of a meditative complex and the interpretation of it in terms of an intentionalist account in terms of subject/object in part to "the fact that human consciousness is corporeally localized."[31] It is ironic that someone like Voegelin, whose theory of consciousness is so anti-Cartesian in tone, should experience a dilemma similar to that faced by Descartes in trying to account for the unity of body and consciousness. It is a dilemma that I believe returned to haunt him as he grappled with problems of social and political reality, the very places where body and spirit meet.

To be human, then, is to partake of both consciousness and concrete, bodily existence. Voegelin's final formulation of the relationship between reality and consciousness reflects this distinction and its paradoxical nature. Because consciousness is located in a body, "reality assumes the position of an object intended." As a result,

30. *Anamnesis,* 180, 201.
31. *Anamnesis,* 31; "Meditative Origin," 49.

"reality acquires a metaphorical touch of external thingness," "an aura of externality." "In relation to our corporeal localization, everything of which one has consciousness, this 'something' is co-experienced as an 'outside' of this corporeal existence." Understood in this fashion, consciousness has the structure of intentionality, while the corresponding reality is conceived of as being present in the mode of "thing-reality" or "thingness."[32] Intentionality for Voegelin was, at least in this regard, analogous to the sense perception of objects outside ourselves. (The reason for my qualification here is that, as I hope to illustrate shortly, there is within Voegelin's thought a notion of intentionality that does not seem to presuppose this subject/object, inner/outer split.) That being the case, it is important to bear in mind that the structure of consciousness as intentional, while similar to the perception of sensible objects, is not limited to such perception. What Voegelin had in mind is what we mean when we speak of consciousness as "being conscious of something," "being aware of something," "thinking of something," and so forth. Because of the intentional structure of consciousness, even the "non-objective" areas of reality, for example, God, are recast in "objective" form, where "objective" has connotations of externality:

> While they (the phenomena pertaining to the non-objective area of participation) do not belong to the things of the spatio-temporal world, they are related to that world because they are experienced by men in spatio-temporal existence. The peculiar "objective" quality of the phenomena . . . stems from the fact that consciousness is not *intellectus unus,* i.e., not a single cosmic, divine, or human consciousness, but the discrete consciousness of concrete men.[33]

The result of the application of intentionality to non-objective reality is that the "objectifying intention of consciousness is therefore always in conflict with the consciousness of non-objects."[34] The dilemma of intentional consciousness, then, would seem to be that a reality such as God, which can never be an object, that is, something with an aura of externality, tends to be rendered that way by humans because of the embodied and spatially located character of human consciousness.

Voegelin, however, recognized another mode of consciousness,

32. *In Search of Order,* 15; "Meditative Origin," 49.
33. *Anamnesis,* 179.
34. Letter to D. Walsh, quoted in Joseph McCarroll, "Some Growth Areas in Voegelin's Analysis," 293.

which he described as "luminosity." Consciousness as luminous arises from the fact that both bodily located consciousness and the "things" of which it is conscious belong to a larger reality, the encompassing "It-reality." To speak of the "It-reality" is to advert to the reality "in which consciousness occurs as an event of participation between partners in the community of being." In such an experience, "reality moves from the position of an intended object to that of a subject, while the consciousness of the human subject intending objects moves to the position of a predicative event in the subject 'reality' as it becomes luminous for its truth."[35] The encompassing whole, of which consciousness in the mode of intentionality forms but a part, is illuminated from within by consciousness in the mode of luminosity. *Intentional* consciousness is always a "consciousness of something"; consciousness as *luminous* "lights up" the reality of which human consciousness and the other "things" are but a part. It is existence in the metaxy and not any particular "thing" that enters consciousness in the mode of luminosity. Consequently, Voegelin maintains that it is legitimate to speak of the "It-reality" as a "subject" of consciousness: "The subject of this luminosity, in which this occurrence, 'consciousness', happens predicatively, is not the human 'I', but the 'It-reality'." Voegelin's account of consciousness as luminosity is consistent with his analysis of experience; just as experience cannot be broken up into its constituent poles, the consciousness that arises in experience has the same "in-between" character. Luminous consciousness lies "somewhere 'between' human consciousness in bodily existence and reality intended in its mode of thingness."[36]

In articulating the structure of consciousness as intentional and luminous, the danger of reification is always present; for to articulate is to delimit and, in a sense, to "objectify" a reality such as consciousness in a way that can never do justice to its elusive, metaleptic character. To avoid reification, Voegelin makes it clear that his analysis refers to "modes" of consciousness. Intentionality and luminosity should not and cannot be separated from one another as if they were distinct faculties. Nor can we attribute a separate, supra-individual consciousness to the "It-reality" which then somehow communicates with the bodily situated consciousness of individual human beings.

35. "Meditative Origin," 49; *In Search of Order,* 15.
36. "Meditative Origin," 49; *In Search of Order,* 16.

Consciousness is always bound to the human perspective within the community of being (which is the only perspective we have). As such it is always simultaneously located both bodily and within the metaxy. One way of addressing this ambiguity is to distinguish between consciousness as site and as sensorium:

> As far as consciousness is the site of participation, its reality partakes of both the divine and the human without being wholly the one or the other; as far as it is the sensorium of participation, it is definitely man's own, located in his body in spatio-temporal existence. Consciousness, thus, is both the time pole of the tension (sensorium) and the whole tension including its pole of the timeless (site). Our participation in the divine remains bound to the perspective of man.[37]

Despite the admittedly paradoxical character of the complex that comprises reality and consciousness, it is possible to summarize concisely the results of Voegelin's analysis. We can speak of consciousness as possessing an intentional and a luminous mode. Correlative to these modes there is reality with its corresponding structure as thing-reality and It-reality. Consciousness as subject intends reality; as object it is itself part of a comprehending reality. In similar fashion, reality as intended has the character of an object, while as the reality of the divine/human metaxy "it is the subject of which consciousness is to be predicated."[38]

LANGUAGE, SYMBOLS, AND REFLECTIVE DISTANCE

Our analysis would be incomplete if it did not address the status of language within the meditative complex, since it is by means of language that we are able to elucidate our experience of participation. As one might expect, language shares in the paradox of the relationship between reality and consciousness. Just as there is no vantage point beyond reality from which an observer can gaze upon its structure, there is no language existing independently, ready to be applied to the structures of reality and consciousness. Language participates in the reality to which it refers as much as any of the partners within the community of being share in the encompassing whole.[39] The structure of language mirrors the structure of the complex from

37. Voegelin, "Immortality," 90.
38. *In Search of Order,* 16.
39. Ibid., 17.

which it emerges. Expressions deriving from the intentional aspect of consciousness are "concepts," while those emerging from conscious-ness as luminous are described as "symbols."[40] In accord with his emphasis on luminosity, Voegelin's discussion of language focuses on symbols rather than concepts.

Symbols are "the language phenomena engendered by the pro-cess of participatory experience."[41] Humans not only participate in reality, they express their experience of that participation in symbols. The symbol does not "correspond" to something "discovered" in the metaxy. The process of participation itself gives rise to symbols as reality becomes increasingly luminous to itself. In the following chap-ter I will discuss in more detail the differentiating process in which symbols emerge; for now, though, it will suffice to call attention to some of the implications of understanding symbols in this fashion.

First of all, a symbol is neither a "human conventional sign signi-fying a reality outside consciousness" nor "a word of God conve-niently transmitted in the language that the recipient can under-stand." The symbol participates in both human and divine reality; hence, the symbol in some sense makes present the divine reality it symbolizes.[42] Second, since the reality that becomes luminous in consciousness is itself in flux, the engendered symbols are always open to refinement; they never represent a final possession of truth.

In making use of language to describe symbols, we come to an issue that has been present in the background throughout this dis-cussion and in Voegelin's own writings. The problem is evident in the frequent use of quotation marks around words used in the exegesis of the meditative complex and in those instances where words such as *subject, object, site, pole,* and so forth are employed despite the realization that they are inadequate to capture the truth of the reality to which they refer. This can be due either to their spatio-temporal orientation or to the connotations they have acquired in the history of philosophy. Can a language saturated with concepts deriving from the fact that humans are embodied creatures ever be adequate for analyzing existence in the metaxy? What is the status of the terms *It-reality, thing-reality, intentionality,* and *luminosity?* Have we simply gen-

40. "Meditative Origin," 50.
41. *Autobiographical Reflections,* 74.
42. Ibid.

erated more concepts, or are they indeed symbols? In raising such questions we come to that dimension of consciousness that Voegelin labels "reflective distance." With the symbol of reflective distance, the analysis undertaken in this chapter has come full circle. We began our discussion by focusing upon the fact that people are aware of themselves as participating in a reality greater than themselves. That awareness, that experience of participation, is constituted by consciousness as intentional and as luminous. Yet there is a further dimension to consciousness that has to do with the fact that consciousness is reflexively present to itself. This reflective distance is present in consciousness before any explicit acts of conceptualization or meditative exegesis. In other words, not only is consciousness paradoxically structured, but it can become aware of itself as such. This is precisely what Voegelin has attempted to do in his work. In answer, then, to the question of whether such reflection is a matter of intentional consciousness or of consciousness in the mode of luminosity, he gives the following reply:

> I would say that we are doing neither the one nor the other; but we are reflecting on the complex of consciousness. We are having to do with a reflective attitude which emerges whenever one has to speak about such things. . . . In reflective distance the entire problem of luminosity and intentionality is now transposed into a language of reflection, in which this problem is spoken about as if there were a reality independent of reflection. Naturally, we could not talk about it if reflection were not already present as a component of consciousness, for only so can one differentiate it.[43]

The loss of reflective distance can be the source of grave deformations of reality. When that occurs, the constructions that emerge from reflection can become confused with the existence of participatory consciousness in the metaxy, resulting in a loss of openness to the ground and its replacement by the reflective constructions of the particular thinker.

Voegelin recognizes that even when reflective distance has been taken into account it is still difficult to avoid speaking of intentionality and luminosity as if they were objects, and it is equally difficult to refrain from discussing the meditative complex "as if there were a reality independent of reflection." It would seem as if

43. *In Search of Order,* 40–44; "Meditative Origin," 50.

the intentional structure of consciousness is inescapable. Given Voegelin's understanding of intentionality and objectivity, this can present a problem for him as he practices the method of meditative exegesis. Correctly, I believe, Voegelin wishes to avoid the danger of allowing experience to become hypostatized or reified. The reduction of the originating experiences to propositional truth was, for Voegelin, no merely academic issue; propositional truth is too easily manipulated in the service of competing ideologies that are not content to remain within the academy, but erupt violently into the political realm.[44] At the same time, while we can appreciate Voegelin's concerns, what are we to make of his own claims concerning the structure of reality and consciousness? Voegelin is certainly not hesitant in making judgments concerning the proper way in which to speak about reality, even if such judgments are meant to inculcate a spirit of humility in those making ontological/epistemological claims and to affirm the essentially mysterious nature of the encompassing whole. What he is led to do is to remind his readers over and over again that while his language may easily lend itself to reification due to human language's inherent limitations, he is in no way referring to objects in the mode of thing-reality. As noted earlier, Voegelin accepts this situation as the inevitable result of the paradox that consciousness is both luminous and intentional. Even his most sympathetic critics,[45] though, have raised the question of whether this paradox might not be somewhat lessened if the structure of consciousness were to be interpreted in another way.

Some have suggested that a broader view of intentionality is what is needed in Voegelin's account. A revision in the understanding of intentionality would of course entail a corresponding revision in the notion of objectivity. Recall that in Voegelin's thought, intentional consciousness, due to its location in a body, is modeled on a subject/object paradigm in which the subject is an "inside" while objects are "outside." Intentional knowing becomes a matter of "taking a look," which is then contrasted with knowing as luminous participation. If intentional knowing means taking a look, objects become the things

---

44. *Anamnesis*, 183–99.
45. Fred Lawrence, "On 'The Meditative Origin of the Philosophical Knowledge of Order,'" in Fred Lawrence, ed., *The Beginning and the Beyond: Papers from the Gadamer and Voegelin Conferences*, 59–64; McCarroll, "Some Growth Areas," 291–97.

looked at, "already out there" in the world. It comes as no surprise, then, that Voegelin finds the intentional model inadequate in speaking of God and the soul, because these realities are not encountered in the same fashion as objects in the external world.

It is at this point that the need for a richer understanding of intentionality becomes apparent. I would suggest that Voegelin did indeed possess a broader notion of intentionality, but that this dimension of his thought was never fully developed because of his continued use of language in which intentional consciousness is likened to a mental looking in which objects are somehow "out there" to be seen. Yet the resources for a more nuanced view of intentionality are certainly to be found in Voegelin's writings. In particular, the symbol of the "Question" is a rich source for a notion of intentionality that need not be understood by analogy to sight.

The symbol of the Question is Voegelin's thematization of the "questioning unrest" that characterizes the human being as wonderer.[46] In speaking of the Question, Voegelin seems to have in mind that primordial wonder operative in all societies at all times. It is the Question that moves us to reflect upon such basic concerns as why there is something rather than nothing, to contemplate our lasting and passing as well as that of the other "things," and to respond to the drawing of the divine Beyond. In any given age, the Question as wonder may be more or less reflectively conscious of itself as operative; but whatever the level of reflective consciousness in a given society, this dynamic and primordial desire to know is always present, whether articulating itself in terms of myth, science, religious experience, philosophy, or art.

Voegelin is also quite clear that the Question is not just any question but the quest concerning the mysterious ground of all Being. The Question intends reality, and as such it is "not a question concerning this or that object in the external world, but a structure inherent to the experience of reality. . . . The Question as a structure in experience is part of, and pertains to, the In-Between stratum of reality, the Metaxy. There is no answer to the Question other than the Mystery as it becomes luminous in the acts of questioning."[47]

---

46. *Ecumenic Age*, 316–35. See also Voegelin, "Gospel and Culture," 174–79; and "Reason: The Classic Experience," 268–70.

47. *Ecumenic Age*, 319–20, 317, 330.

The Question, then, is broader than any particular question. It is the underlying dynamism of wonder, the pure desire to know and to orient ourselves authentically within reality, that underlies and animates every particular question and investigation. Through our "acts of questioning" we are oriented toward the Mystery that is reality in all its fullness. It is through these same acts of questioning that the Mystery in which we participate becomes luminous.

It would seem evident, then, that in the Question we have a notion of intentionality that has nothing in common with ocular vision. It is the Question that moves us toward understanding, that does not allow us to be satisfied with partial answers, that challenges us to authenticity by pressing us to bring our lives into conformity with the truth of reality apprehended in consciousness. It is nothing less than a radical intending moving us from ignorance to knowledge, and from knowledge to responsible behavior, until our understanding and living come to reflect more and more the divine Beyond toward which we are, by nature, oriented. It is through this intending, through our *questions*, that we are related to reality—an intending and questioning that have to do with the unfolding of wonder, not with "taking a look." The questioning unrest, the faith, hope, and love that intend the ground do not come up for inspection, they are not there to be "seen"; rather, they are manifestations of the Question inherent to the experience of reality. My point here is that with the symbol of the Question and its various modes, for example, seeking, wondering, questioning, as well as *cognitiones fidei, amoris, et spei,* Voegelin has provided his readers with an account of intentionality which does not render the subject and object in terms of inner and outer, and which does not reduce objects to external "things." Surely Voegelin believes that by our questions we do indeed "intend" the divine ground, not as an external object, but as the Mystery to which we are all oriented as wonderers.

What this indicates is that there can be found in Voegelin's work an idea of intentionality/objectivity in which "object" is not to be conceived in terms of externality, but rather as a heuristic notion referring to that which is intended by questioning. For certainly Voegelin speaks of reality, the divine ground, God, and the Beyond as the ultimate sources and referents of the Question; as mysteries, which, while never exhausted by our questions, are nevertheless specified, by means of our questions, as the transcendent pole within reality. He would insist, for example, that the divine ground comes to be known in the very process of questioning, and that it must never be conceived as being in any sense spatially distant from the questioner.[48] Intentionality, then, need not be understood as implying a subject/object split, in which "object" has connotations of externality.

We are left in a peculiar situation with regard to Voegelin's ideas concerning intentionality. On one hand, there is Voegelin's explicit account of intentionality as oriented toward objects having an aura of externality. But there is also present in his thought (perhaps less explicitly but in many ways more profoundly) a notion of intentionality emerging from the thematization of the Question as that which intends reality. Voegelin had, I believe, a tendency to recognize only the former as intentionality, and as a result he found himself confronted with the paradox that the "objectifying intention of consciousness is always in conflict with the consciousness of non-objects."[49] It would seem, though, as if there is implicit in Voegelin's thought a way in which to discuss "consciousness of non-objects" in terms of intentionality more broadly understood. The problem for his interpreters becomes one of trying to understand his aversion to speaking about the human orientation toward mystery as "intentionality," and his rejection of the term *object* when applied to transcendent realities.

The following suggestion may offer a possible explanation. Might it not be the case that while Voegelin recognized that intentionality as he understood it is not applicable to the meditative exegesis of experience, he also *assumed that the "subject/object split" model of intentionality is correct?* While rejecting the positivist claim that knowing is only valid when modeled on the method of the natural sciences, did he not tacitly accept the positivist account of what it is that constitutes knowing in the natural sciences? Did he not presuppose, at least at some level, that knowing things in the external world is a confrontation like perception or looking?[50] In doing so, Voegelin was led to argue as follows: (1) Intentionality is modeled on the experience of objects in the external world. (2) However, existence in the metaxy is not describable in terms of the experience of objects in the external

48. *Anamnesis,* 95.
49. McCarroll, "Some Growth Areas," 295.
50. Ibid.

world. (3) Thus, existence in the metaxy cannot be approached from the perspective of intentionality. As a result of this narrow understanding of intentionality, consciousness as intentional is contrasted with consciousness as luminous, and it is knowing as luminosity that comes to the fore as the preferred way of rendering the experience of participation.

As a way of avoiding this predicament, might we not conceive of intentionality in a manner other than "looking"? Must all intentional acts be imagined as being analogous to sense perception? One possible path out of this impasse is, as suggested earlier, to specify intentionality in terms of the questioning unrest that is integral to conscious participation in the metaxy.[51] To do so would obviate the paradox of consciousness in which the objectifying, intentional mode of consciousness is always in conflict with the luminous consciousness of non-objects. Intentionality so conceived need not be juxtaposed with meditative exegesis but can be understood as constituting its dynamic core. When wonder replaces the analogy of sense perception as the core of intentionality, the danger of knowing being misconstrued as a subject/object confrontation is significantly lessened, because our potential for wonder and for raising questions ranges far beyond the confines of sensible, observable experience. Indeed, the intention of our questioning is unrestricted. Likewise the correlative notion of "object" is transformed from an "already out there" to whatever is intended in questioning. Of course this would include all finite objects previously construed as being merely "external" to the subject, but it is equally important to note that in this regard transcendent being can also be considered an object, since it is always possible to ask questions concerning the divine ground of existence.

The luminous dimension of consciousness could also be interpreted from the perspective of questioning. Here the emphasis would fall on the mysterious primordiality of wonder rather than on its unfolding in particular intentional acts of raising and answering questions. Humans are aware of themselves as sites of wonder, with horizons limited only by the range of their questions. As Voegelin has noted, our wonder emerges from the depth of the ground. Consciousness as luminous is another way of accounting for the fact that

51. Lawrence, "On 'The Meditative Origin,'" 59–64.

before we ask any particular questions we are oriented by and in wonder, a wonder that is boundless. To speak of luminosity is to acknowledge the *nous* that Aristotle discovered as underlying our spontaneous desire to know, or to recognize with Aquinas that the notion of being propelling our questioning is a "created participation of uncreated light."[52] It is also to take seriously Voegelin's symbol of the "psyche," which can descend in wonder into its own encompassing reality and articulate its structure, without ever exhausting its depth. Luminosity, understood in such a fashion, is certainly not alien to either the spirit or the letter of Voegelin's thought. At the same time, it avoids the unnecessary contrast between consciousness as luminous and consciousness as intentional.

Obviously these critical reflections are not meant to be exhaustive; nor are they meant to call into question the tremendous strengths of Voegelin's approach. His refusal to reify the divine and human poles of existence, his attention to the originating experiences that give rise to the symbols that inform human existence, and his insistence that a philosophy of politics must be grounded in a theory of consciousness represent an important attempt to both recover and reinvigorate political philosophy. In particular, it must be emphasized just how insightful Voegelin is when discussing the structure of knowing. He is correct in pointing out the differences between knowing a thing in the world of sense and knowing transcendent reality; certainly the reduction of God to a "thing" is a trivialization and reification of an ultimately mysterious reality. The divine pole of reality can never be likened to external objects. In this regard I find myself in complete agreement with Voegelin.

If certain questions have been raised concerning the tensions in Voegelin's theory of consciousness, this has been done in an effort to deal seriously with his assertion that consciousness "is the luminous center radiating the concrete order of human existence into society and history."[53] If, as Voegelin maintained, the order of consciousness is intimately related to the order of society, then any tensions present in a theory of consciousness are likely to have implications in the social and political realm. The strengths and weaknesses of the theorist's philosophy of consciousness will make their presence felt in his

52. Ibid., 61–63.
53. Voegelin, "Consciousness and Order," 35.

political theory. Eventually this issue will have to be addressed; but before that can be done, some account of the major developments of consciousness must be provided. This analysis so far has concentrated on the structure of consciousness and its relationship to the structure of reality. Much has been made of the structure of reality becoming luminous to itself in consciousness. We now turn our attention to the unfolding of consciousness and the significant forms it has taken in history.

TWO

DIFFERENTIATIONS OF CONSCIOUSNESS

COMPACTNESS AND DIFFERENTIATION

The primordial community of being is initially experienced in the mode of compactness. The partners within this community (God, man, world, and society) are distinguished, but greater emphasis lies on their consubstantiality than on their separateness. All the "things" encountered in this compact experience are considered to be "real" and "true"; "all of them are themselves and at the same time consubstantial, so they can be related to each other through genesis, which in its turn is expressed in the mythical narrative of their generation."[1] At this stage no language or symbolization has yet emerged with which to clarify the modes of being characteristic of the various partners in the primordial community.

What *does* impress itself strongly in the compact mode of the primary experience is the awareness of reality as a "whole." This is not to say that the whole is known. As emphasized in the preceding chapter, participation is always perspectival; there is no vantage point outside reality from which the whole enters our horizon as would an object in the external world. Yet despite the fragmentary nature of our insights into reality, Voegelin maintains that humans preserve a trust *(pistis)* "in the underlying oneness of reality, its coherence, lastingness, constancy of structure, order, and intelligibility," a trust that is sufficient to give rise to the symbol "Cosmos." This is the cosmos of the primary experience; it is not yet the differentiated world of nature and natural phenomena, nor the world created by the transcen-

1. *Israel and Revelation*, 3; *Anamnesis,* 160.

35

dent God of the Hebrew and Christian scriptures. "Rather, it is the whole, *to pan,* of an earth below and a heaven above—of celestial bodies and their movements; of seasonal changes; of fertility rhythms in plant and animal life; of human life, birth and death; and above all, as Thales still knew, it is a cosmos full of gods."[2] To speak, then, of the primary experience of reality in the mode of compactness is to describe reality as "cosmos" and its form as "cosmological."

What is the relationship of the cosmos to the partners within the community of being? As noted above, the whole is not an object of knowledge but of trust. It was also noted that in the primary experience the partners easily blend into one another and have their genesis from one another. In doing so they serve as analogues that attempt to render intelligible the cosmic whole that cannot be fully known. Voegelin offers the example of two symbolisms of kingship. The first symbolism depicts the king in the style of a ruler over the four quarters of the world. His rule is analogous to the rule of the god over the cosmos. The source of the analogy is not, however, the primary experience of the cosmos, but the experience of the physical universe and the movements of the planets. In the second symbolism, the king is symbolized as either divine himself, as a son of god, or as a divine-human mediator. Here the analogy springs from a sense of the presence of the gods within the cosmic whole. In the first instance the cosmos has blended with the "world" as phenomenal universe; in the second it has combined with the gods. Voegelin's point is that these symbolisms only "work" because there is already present a trust in the consubstantiality of the partners within a cosmos that is not to be identified with any particular partner. At the same time, on the level of compactness, the analogies provided by the partners in the community of being are the best means available by which to symbolize the mystery of the whole. This is only possible, though, because of the experience of an "underlying, intangible embracingness" that provides the ground for the consubstantiality of the areas of reality.[3]

It is the experience of a nonexistent, underlying embracingness that accounts for the essential instability of the cosmological form and that leads to its eventual differentiation. The "something" that

2. "Equivalences," 127; *Ecumenic Age,* 68.
3. *Ecumenic Age,* 72.

supplies existence while being itself nonexistent comes to be recognized as being somehow different from the other partners within the compact cosmic experience. The source of this recognition, Voegelin explains, is the experience of lasting and passing that is characteristic of human reflection on existence:

> Consubstantiality notwithstanding, there is the experience of separate existence in the stream of being, and the various existences are distinguished by their degree of durability. One man lasts while the others pass away, and he passes away while the others last on. All human beings are outlasted by the society of which they are members, and societies pass while the world lasts. And the world not only is outlasted by the gods, but is perhaps even created by them. Under this aspect, being exhibits the lineaments of a hierarchy of existence, from the ephemeral lowliness of man to the everlastingness of the gods.[4]

Once a hierarchy of existence emerges, it is accompanied by an awareness that the more lasting existences are the more comprehensive and that they are somehow the source of existence for the lower "things" within the hierarchy. At this stage, though, we remain firmly within the cosmological form; the nonexistent ground has been apprehended but not yet differentiated, and consciousness, while operative, has not been thematized. What is experienced amid the lasting and passing of the partners within the community of being is the tension of existence out of nonexistence; indeed, it is this very tension that accounts for the hierarchical ordering of beings. In humans the tension takes the form of a questioning unrest concerning the where-from and the where-to, from which will radiate the crucial differentiations of consciousness.[5]

The emergence of a hierarchy of being within the cosmological style of truth due to the experienced tension of existence out of nonexistence points to the fundamental instability of this symbolic form. As we have seen, within the compact form of symbolization the partners within the community of being can serve as analogues for the cosmic whole. This is only possible because the "things" are in the cosmos and the cosmos is in the "things." What happens, though, to the "equality" of the partners when the tension of existence makes itself felt, when, as Voegelin observes, "this claim to equal represen-

---

4. *Israel and Revelation*, 3–4.
5. *Ecumenic Age*, 73, 77; *Anamnesis*, 92, 175; Sandoz, *Voegelinian Revolution*, 197.

tativeness is superseded by distinctions of representative rank in which the apprehended but not differentiated tension in reality imposes itself on the compactly symbolized areas of intracosmic reality"? When this occurs, the fracturing of the cosmological form is prevented by according some of the partners a higher degree of representativeness within the cosmos. The universe and the gods, for example, fulfill the role of the nonexistent ground because "they are more cosmic than man and society." This is the peculiarly cosmological manner of dealing with the tension of existence; in this fashion the cosmos becomes tensionally closed.[6]

Eventually, the cosmological style of truth begins to crack because of the tensional pressure inherent in metaxic existence. Even the hierarchically arranged analogies of being provided by the symbols "god," "man," "world," and "society" are found lacking in their ability to render the reality experienced. A symbolization in terms of a hierarchy of being no longer suffices to render adequately the experience of participation; "the compression of the tension into the In-Between of cosmic reality becomes critically untenable when the astrophysical universe must be recognized as too much existent to function as the non-existent ground of reality, and the gods are discovered as too little existent to form a realm of intracosmic things."[7]

When this point is reached, the stage is set for differentiation. New insights into the experience of participation result in a need for a more adequate set of symbols to express the experience. Nor is the creation of new symbols simply a fine tuning or refinement of previous ones; what is at stake is proper attunement to the order of being. To realize "the discovery of imperfect participation, of a mismanagement of existence through lack of proper attunement to the order of being, of the danger of a fall from being, is a horror indeed, compelling a radical reorientation of existence." Such a radical reorientation is nothing less than a "leap in being."[8] The leap in being is an "epochal event that breaks the compactness of the early cosmological myth and establishes the order of man in his immediacy under God." A leap in being is a breakthrough; like all significant

6. *Ecumenic Age,* 76–77.
7. Ibid., 77.
8. *Israel and Revelation,* 9–11.

insights it cannot be planned. The conditions for its occurrence may be present due to the experienced inadequacies of the cosmological style of symbolization, yet it remains a gracious in-breaking. "Questioning unrest" arising from the tension of existence may set the conditions, but the differentiation of the compact experience is always in response to the movement of the nonexistent ground.[9]

The effect of the leap in being is to engender a consciousness of a before and an after. Prior symbolizations and their respective societies are consigned to a past, while the leap constitutes the time of the participant as a historical present radiating meaning over prior ages and events. In the leap, there has occurred an insight into the truth of order and the possibility of attunement to that order. Such an insight is not a "subjective" reading of otherwise meaningless events; it is in fact "the entering of the soul into divine reality through the entering of divine reality into the soul."[10] The leap is not an interpretation, but an event. It is both an insight into the structure of reality, that is, the truth of order, and an occurrence within that reality.

A question that arises with regard to the leap in being is how and to what extent the leap affects the reality within which it occurs. In other words, does the leap in being constitute a change within the encompassing reality? Voegelin does not give a univocal answer to this question. Because he does not, we will consider one Voegelinian passage in which it appears as if a leap in being is indeed a change within reality, and some other writings in which it seems equally clear that the structure of reality remains unchanged after a differentiating leap has occurred.

Perhaps the clearest expression of the point of view that a leap in being results in a change within reality is to be found in the introduction to *Israel and Revelation*, where Voegelin, speaking of the leap in being and the simultaneous "turning around" in the participant, writes:

> And this turning around, this conversion, results in more than an increase of knowledge concerning the order of being; it is a change in the order itself. For the participation in being changes its structure when it becomes emphatically a partnership with God, while participa-

---

9. Voegelin, *Order and History*, vol. 2, *The World of the Polis*, 1; *Israel and Revelation*, 10; *Anamnesis*, 95.

10. *Israel and Revelation*, 130–31.

tion in mundane being recedes to second rank. The more perfect attunement to being through conversion is not an increase on the same scale but a qualitative leap. . . . Thus a change in being has actually occurred, with consequences for the order of existence.[11]

On one level Voegelin is calling attention to something that is rather obvious. When a leap in being happens it is quite clear that reality has been altered in some way. Up until that point there has been no leap; after that point, there has. Therefore something has happened, there has been a change. In some cases a person has gone from a state of ignorance in relation to the structure of reality to a state of illumination as to the role of consciousness within reality; such was the experience of the Hellenic philosophers. In other cases, an individual or a people become strikingly aware of transcendent reality in a way previously unknown; such was the case with Moses and Israel. In both cases, though, reality has "changed" due to the differentiating leap, because in both cases the leap has taken place "within" reality. To recall a point made in Chapter 1, there is no perspective outside reality in which differentiating events occur; they are always already "within" reality. In other words, an insight into reality constitutes a change in reality. In the strict sense of the word, then, a "change" does indeed take place in reality whenever a leap in being breaks with a former state of compactness.

The question could be raised, though, with regard to the passage from *Israel and Revelation* quoted in the preceding paragraph, whether or not Voegelin is speaking of a "change in being" in a way that goes beyond this strict sense of the word *change*. More seems to be implied in this passage than an awareness of a before and an after. Indeed, he is careful to point out that such a change is "more than an increase of knowledge"; it is a change in the order of being itself. Now Voegelin would certainly have been conscious of the fact that, strictly speaking, an "increase of knowledge" would constitute a change in the order of being by the criteria mentioned in the previous paragraph. A change of knowledge is still a change within reality, because reality is all encompassing. However, Voegelin seems to have had something else in mind in this case. For he emphasizes that "participation in being changes its structure when it becomes emphatically a partnership with God." Perhaps most intriguing is the claim that the change

11. Ibid., 10–11.

in being has "consequences for the order of existence." It would seem that Voegelin, in this instance, had more in mind than an increased degree of illumination concerning the structure of reality. The structure of human participation has been altered, and that participation includes both a mundane and a transcendent pole. To say that participation has changed is to say nothing less than that human existence has changed; it has become an existence encompassing both concrete bodily social existence and openness toward the transcendent divine ground. The question then becomes "How will existence be affected by the leap in being? If the structure of participation has changed, what will its effects be on social/political reality, that place of intersection between the mundane and the transcendent?" At this stage in his analysis, Voegelin had merely raised a central question that his later work would explore.

If it is not exactly clear what the consequence of a change in being is for the order of existence, Voegelin states flatly what it is not: "Nevertheless, the leap upward in being is not a leap out of existence. The emphatic partnership with God does not abolish partnership in the community of being at large, which includes being in mundane existence. Man and society, if they want to retain their foothold in being that makes the leap into emphatic partnership possible, must remain adjusted to the order of mundane existence."[12] To some degree the leap in being may diminish the importance of life in the world for those who have had such an experience, but such persons still remain firmly within the confines of "the order of mundane existence." Yet the question arises as to what it means to be bound by the order of mundane existence. What is the order of mundane existence? To what extent can or does the leap in being affect this order? The first three volumes of *Order and History* are an extended attempt to wrestle with this issue. At the start of *Israel and Revelation,* however, all we know is that some kind of change in being has occurred and that it does not put an end to the concerns of mundane existence. Later writings would more carefully specify the area affected by this leap in being.

Having examined an instance where it appears as if the leap in being effects a change in the structure of being and our participation in it, we now turn to passages in which the point is made that the

12. Ibid., 11.

structure of reality remains unchanged after the leap. In discussing the consequences of the movement from a more compact, mythical symbolization to a more philosophically differentiated one, Voegelin clarifies:

> As we contrast the philosophical image of being to the mythical one of reality, we obviously do not wish to say that it is reality that has changed but rather only our image of reality. In the context of this statement, "reality" becomes a kind of constant given, the structure of which is seen better by the philosopher than by the philomyther. This idea has a solid core, inasmuch as there is indeed a difference of truth between the compact-cosmic and the noetically differentiating experience, in relation to which difference reality appears as a constant. Reality is constant in relation to the differential of truths in consciousness.[13]

While previously the emphasis had been placed on the leap as "more than an increase of knowledge," here it is clear that reality is constant and that what has changed is our image of that reality. The change that is acknowledged here is of a "difference of truth" between a compact and a more differentiated symbolism. However, this passage is followed almost immediately in the text by an acknowledgment that "consciousness . . . is a reality of human participation, and this reality is characterized by a presence of experience that puts phases of lower grades of truth behind itself, as the past. Reality, then, is not constant." In this case, however, the statement that reality is not constant pertains not to a change in being, as it does in *Israel and Revelation,* but rather to a changed insight into the structure of being that consigns previous conceptions to the past. What is notable here is that change has begun to be specified in terms of the order of *consciousness,* something absent from the first volume of *Order and History.* With the introduction of the reality of consciousness we have an indication as to why the term *leap in being* would eventually give way to the symbol "differentiation of consciousness." Admittedly, a change in consciousness is still a type of change. My point, though, is to focus on what I perceive to be a shift in emphasis from *Israel and Revelation* to *Anamnesis* concerning the consequences of the leap in being.

If there was any question as to the area of reality affected by

---

13. *Anamnesis,* 165.

differentiations of consciousness, or leaps in being, it is likely to be dispelled by the following passage from *The Ecumenic Age:*

> The truth of existence discovered by the prophets of Israel and the philosophers of Hellas, though it appears later in time than the truth of the cosmos, cannot simply replace it, because the new insights, while indirectly affecting the image of reality as a whole, pertain directly only to man's consciousness of his existential tension. . . . I have circumscribed the structure of the event as strictly as possible, in order to make it clear how narrowly confined the area of the resulting insights actually is: The new truth pertains to man's consciousness of his humanity in participatory tension toward the divine ground, and to no reality beyond this restricted area.[14]

The leap in being described in *Israel and Revelation,* with its radical consequences for the order of existence, has become a differentiation of consciousness that illuminates human existence in the metaxy. Also, the results of the differentiation are specified even more precisely in *The Ecumenic Age* than in *Anamnesis.* There it was stated that the differentiation had affected the image of reality; in *The Ecumenic Age* it is further noted that the image of reality is only indirectly affected—it is the consciousness of human existence as tension toward the divine ground that emerges through differentiation. It is perhaps this shift in emphasis that can help to explain why *leap in being* comes to be replaced with *differentiation of consciousness* as the most appropriate term with which to describe the break with cosmological form. For it seems as if the break turns out to have been less radical than Voegelin had previously thought. The cosmos has been illuminated, not altered in its structure; only consciousness has changed. This is not to minimize the importance of the differentiation of consciousness. It is simply to follow Voegelin in clearly delimiting what it is that has changed in the movement from compactness to differentiation.

One might well ask whether there is any way to reconcile those passages in which Voegelin indicates that the leap in being results in a change in the structure of reality with those places where he seems to move away from his earlier position. Commentators have suggested various solutions. Ellis Sandoz, an important interpreter of Voegelin's thought, is aware of the difficulty posed by this question.

---

14. *Ecumenic Age,* 8.

In his analysis he comes down strongly on the side of maintaining that, despite Voegelin's references in *Israel and Revelation* to a change in being, "being is being: the nature of being does not change." Sandoz also believes that Voegelin was alert to this problem and eventually resolved it. For John W. Corrington, Voegelin's delimitation of the areas affected by the movement from compactness to differentiation represents a "considerable departure" from the approach of the first three volumes of *Order and History:*

> In the earlier volumes there is no sharp distinction between the pneumatic or noetic insights and the context in which they appear. The manifold of existential reality was taken to be invaded from the divine ground by the new insights. . . . In some certain sense, the cosmos itself becomes a new thing by virtue of the entrance into the truth of the Prophet or philosopher. . . . What was not present in the previous volumes was the kind of language that required the reader to understand that the subject of *Order and History* was, indeed, the history of order as it emerged in human consciousness—and nothing else.[15]

In his review of *The Ecumenic Age,* Bruce Douglass finds ambiguity in Voegelin's claim that volume 4 marks a break with the first three volumes. Admittedly, the boundaries between cosmological and noncosmological forms have been blurred, and we can no longer neatly separate cosmological from historical epochs. Yet, at the same time, "the principal claims presented in the earlier volumes are repeated, with only minor modification in *The Ecumenic Age.*" Nonetheless, there has been a break. Voegelin's "theory of the structure of existence comes to the forefront of the analysis," "the emphasis is much more on the permanent or recurring features of human experience," there is a "Platonic stress on permanence," and finally, "the tendency is for the philosophy of history to be absorbed into ontology."[16] Douglass, then, while rejecting the notion of a radical break, underlines the fact that a shift has taken place—a shift in which the emphasis is placed upon the *unchanging* dimensions of reality.

There is something to be said in favor of each of these views. Sandoz has framed the issue effectively and acknowledged frankly that it is a source of tension in Voegelin's thought. Corrington's focus on the is-

15. Sandoz, *Voegelinian Revolution,* 121; Corrington, "Order and Consciousness/Consciousness and History: The New Program of Voegelin," in Stephen A. McKnight, ed., *Eric Voegelin's Search for Order in History.*
16. Douglass, "The Break in Voegelin's Program," 4.

sue of consciousness faithfully reflects Voegelin's concerns and is consistent with the development of his thought from *Anamnesis* onward. Douglass does not pay much attention to the theory of consciousness as it is formulated in *The Ecumenic Age,* concentrating instead on the structure of reality. The strength of his position lies in his insight into the underlying continuity in Voegelin's development, while at the same time he describes the shift in approach that has taken place.

In my view, Voegelin's understanding of the consequences of the leap in being/differentiation of consciousness changed from the time of the writing of *Israel and Revelation* to the publication of *The Ecumenic Age.* In *The Ecumenic Age,* the area affected by the leap in being has been circumscribed far more carefully and narrowly than would seem to be indicated by the language of the introduction to *Israel and Revelation.* This can be attributed largely to the development of Voegelin's theory of consciousness. As both the range and the limitations of consciousness became clear to him, so did the area encompassed by the differentiation. That development led to a continual refinement of language that eventually resulted in the replacement of "leap in being" with "differentiation of consciousness." And this development is not a radical break; it is closer to an evolution. It is, I believe, part of a gradual process in which Voegelin clarified and made explicit the theory of consciousness with which he had been concerned for some time. Indeed, he viewed a philosophy of consciousness as the key to the renovation of political science as long ago as the 1920s.[17] In response, then, to the question as to whether or not it is possible to reconcile Voegelin's earlier statements concerning the possibility of a change in being with his later work, my answer would be that while there is a significant difference between earlier and later statements, the differences represent a notable shift in emphasis rather than a rejection or abandonment of previous views. Above all this shift testifies to the increasing importance and continuing development of Voegelin's theory of consciousness throughout his work.

THE NOETIC DIFFERENTIATION OF CONSCIOUSNESS

The compactness of the primary experience of the cosmos eventually gives way as the partners in the primordial community of being come

17. Voegelin, "Consciousness and Order," 35.

to be understood as limited in their ability to fully symbolize the experience of participation within the hierarchy of being. What is needed, then, is a differentiation of consciousness that more clearly articulates the experience. This section will investigate what it is that is articulated in the movement from compactness to differentiation, what are the boundaries of such a differentiation, and what are the specifically "noetic" symbols that have emerged in the movement.

In the broadest sense, what is illuminated in differentiation is reality and human participation in it. The divine and the earthly, previously undifferentiated by cosmic symbolism, are now understood in terms of immanent and transcendent poles within the one reality:

> The insight of the noetic experience dissolves reality's image of the cosmic primary experience. The place of a cosmos full of gods is taken up by a dedivinized world, and, correlative to it, the divine is concentrated into the transcending ground of being. Immanent and transcendent are spatio-metaphorical indices attributed, in the postnoetic dispensation, to the areas of reality that have become, respectively, the world of things in space and time, and the divine being of the ground beyond space and time.[18]

With the differentiation of the divine and worldly poles of existence there also emerges an awareness of human nature as existence in the metaxy. When the divine ground has been differentiated, human existence is clarified as being constituted by tension toward the ground. Humanity is found to lie somewhere between the divine and the mundane. To be conscious of existence in the metaxy as such is to become more explicitly aware of the structure of participation. In other words, what happens in the differentiation is that participation in reality attains self-consciousness. Consciousness becomes explicit to itself. Differentiated, then, are (1) the structural poles of reality, and (2) consciousness as the reality of human participation through which the structures of both reality and participation are made explicit.[19]

This is not all that is distinguished. Eventually there is also differentiated the Beyond of the metaxy.[20] This entire process by which reality and human participation as consciousness become articulate to themselves is what Voegelin means by the term *noetic differentiation*.

18. *Anamnesis,* 159; *Conversations,* 12–13, 53.
19. *Conversations,* 61–62; *Anamnesis,* 148, 173.
20. Voegelin, "Gospel and Culture," 188.

At times Voegelin also employs the term in a more specific way, that is, in order to specify the self-clarification of the structure of consciousness. It is important to bear in mind, though, that what we are dealing with here when speaking of "reality," "consciousness," and so forth, are not isolated structures that are discovered and then related to one another, but rather dimensions of a whole that are defined by their relationships to one another. Because of this, any light shed on the structure of consciousness will also serve in some fashion to illuminate reality as a whole. Thus it is justifiable, when speaking of the noetic differentiation, to make use of the term to describe both the process in which compactness yields to greater clarity and the self-interpretation of the consciousness through which that clarity is achieved.

Before specifying the effects of the noetic differentiation more closely it is important to understand how carefully its range is circumscribed. Voegelin is emphatic in asserting that the differentiation does not eliminate the tension of existence: "The symbolization of participating existence, it is true, evolves historically from the more compact form of the cosmological myth to the more differentiated forms of philosophy, prophecy and the gospel, but the differentiating insight, far from abolishing the *metaxy* of existence, brings it to fully articulate knowledge." This is of course consistent with those passages noted in the preceding section of this chapter, in which Voegelin maintains that the structure of reality does not change in the movement from compactness to differentiation. Noetic differentiation may enhance and clarify participation, but it must not be conceived of as a stance that is somehow apart from the participation it articulates. The differentiation does not free the person in whom it has taken place from the tensions and burdens of life in this world. There is no undisturbed Archimedean point from which the differentiated consciousness gazes down with sympathy upon its struggling brothers and sisters: "Existence in the in-between of divine and human, of perfection and imperfection, of reason and passions, of knowledge and ignorance, of immortality and mortality is not abolished when it becomes luminous to itself. What did change through the differentiation of reason was the level of critical consciousness concerning the order of existence."[21]

21. Ibid.; *Anamnesis,* 112.

Once these limits of the noetic differentiation are understood, it is easier to make sense of Voegelin's claim that such differentiation does not dispel or eliminate the primary experience of the cosmos; "the new truth can affect the belief in intra-cosmic divinities as the most adequate symbolization of cosmic-divine reality, but it cannot affect the experience of divine reality as the creative and ordering force in the cosmos." Indeed, one of the "breakthroughs" of *The Ecumenic Age* was Voegelin's realization that the primary experience of the cosmos and its attendant cosmological symbolism were remarkably tenacious. Concern about the cosmos and its origins is a constant; every culture employs symbols through which it gives expression to its experience of the Beginning. The only thing that changes, due to the increased luminosity of consciousness, is the *manner* of symbolization. The *cosmological form* of symbolization may be superseded in clarity by the differentiations of consciousness, but it persists long after they have occurred. Voegelin has gone so far as to say that, with reference to noetic consciousness, "it is a differentiating correction of the compact preknowledge, but it does not replace the latter. Our knowledge of order remains primarily mythical even after noetic experience has differentiated the realm of consciousness and noetic exegesis has made its logos explicit."[22] Although a differentiation of consciousness may have taken place, Voegelin wished to underline the fact that the stability and order of the cosmos continue to impose themselves forcefully upon those who experience the differentiation. It is our consciousness of tension toward the ground that has altered; the structure of reality remains the same.

The noetic differentiation does not do away with either the cosmos or the tension of existence. A further, related question is whether consciousness only emerges when differentiation has taken place. Does consciousness come to be only when it is differentiated? In other words, although the differentiation of consciousness does not abolish any of the tensions and structures of reality, does its emergence constitute a new "area" within reality? Consistent with his position that reality remains unchanged by the differentiation, Voegelin maintains that "human consciousness—let us definitely state this point—has reality in the form of participation and the material

---

22. *Ecumenic Age*, 7–9, 175; *Anamnesis*, 150.

structure of *ratio* even when the existential tension is low and the reality realized by consciousness correspondingly small." In another place he states: "Consciousness is reality, but it is not one of the realities that the cosmic primary experience discerned in the encompassing reality. Consciousness is the experience of participation, participation of man in his ground of being."[23] Consciousness, then, is always present in human experience. In the compact primary experience it has not yet been made explicit. Consciousness is performative before it becomes thematized. Given Voegelin's understanding of participation, this comes as no surprise. As he notes repeatedly, there is no time when humans are not involved in participation, nor is there any perspective apart from participation in reality. If participation is a given of human experience, then consciousness is as well, because for humans, participation is conscious. Before participation and consciousness are distinguished as structures within reality, they are already operative. Persons living within the cosmic primary experience are certainly *aware* of themselves as participating in a reality; that is, they are *conscious* of the presence of the other partners in the community of being. Symbolizations are the creations of conscious beings, not somnambulists. What the differentiation does is to make explicit the function and structure of consciousness; it illumines from within that by which humans experience and articulate their participation in reality.

The noetic differentiation neither abolishes nor augments reality. Our task now is to more carefully specify what it is that takes place when consciousness differentiates noetically. We begin by observing that the noetic differentiation was the epochal achievement of the classical Hellenic philosophers, especially Plato and Aristotle.[24] This Hellenic advance possesses a threefold significance. First there is the insight into the mystery and structure of reality. Further penetration of the experience underlying the insight leads to the discovery of consciousness as the sensorium of the process, that is, that by which human beings participate in reality. Finally there is the recognition of consciousness as the site where reality becomes luminous to itself.[25]

The process of differentiation generates language symbols that

23. *Anamnesis*, 168–69, 175.
24. Voegelin, *The New Science of Politics: An Introduction*, 66–78; *Anamnesis*, 89–91.
25. *Ecumenic Age*, 177.

render the experience of participation more clearly. One of the most important symbols to arise from the quest of the Hellenic thinkers is "psyche." With this symbol the classical philosophers were able to give voice to that dimension of themselves that they experienced as the site of openness toward the divine ground and as the sensorium of order. Upon its discovery, the psyche "is found as a new center in man at which he experiences himself as open toward transcendental reality." When that happens, "the true order of the soul can become the standard for measuring both human types and types of social order because it represents the truth about human existence on the border of transcendence." The breakthrough into the truth that "the polis is man writ large" is a consequence of the differentiation of the psyche. The human psyche can become the basis for social critique only because its differentiation entails the discovery of the transcendental truth that "God is the Measure."[26]

In his later, post-*Anamnesis* writings, Voegelin would speak about the Hellenic differentiation of the psyche in a way that would reflect the development of his theory of consciousness. No longer would the psyche be described as "a center in man," since such language could easily be misconstrued as indicating a structure in the form of subject/object intentionality. Instead, Voegelin would find that the Greek philosophers had discovered psyche as "the symbol for a site or matrix of experience that surrounds and comprehends the area of conscious experience." Hence psyche and consciousness are related in the following fashion: "There is psyche deeper than consciousness, and there is reality deeper than reality experienced, but there is no consciousness deeper than consciousness."[27] If psyche is likened to an iceberg, then consciousness is the tip extending out of the depth. Psyche is the link between consciousness and the depth, the continuum along which consciousness can descend and ascend as it plumbs and illuminates the inexhaustible riches of the ground.

The Hellenic thinkers recognized the place of the psyche and its relationship to consciousness and to the ground. Beyond this, they further differentiated the psyche in terms of its own structure. In doing so they developed the symbol "nous," a symbol that would

26. *Anamnesis*, 95; *New Science of Politics*, 67–68; *Order and History*, vol. 3, *Plato and Aristotle*, 86.
27. Voegelin, "Equivalences," 126.

eventually lend its name to the process from compactness to differentiation.

The discovery and articulation of "nous" was in response to social disarray. Voegelin explains:

> I shall not deal with the "idea" or a nominalist "definition" of reason but with the process in reality in which concrete human beings, the "lovers of wisdom," the philosophers as they styled themselves, were engaged in an act of resistance against the personal and social disorder of their age. From this act there emerged the *nous* as the cognitively luminous force that inspired the philosophers to resist and, at the same time, enabled them to recognize the phenomena of disorder in the light of a humanity ordered by the *nous*. Thus, reason in the noetic sense was discovered as both the force and the criterion of order.

It is nous that structures the psyche and enables it to resist disorder, because it is through nous that the psyche as the sensorium of order becomes "cognitively luminous" to itself. Nous is that "area" of the psyche that can articulate its attunement to divine order as the criterion for both personal and social order. If psyche symbolizes the human as being constituted by openness toward the divine ground, then nous is that openness raised to consciousness. This is precisely what constitutes differentiation as "noetic": "Noetic interpretations arise when consciousness, on whatever occasion, seeks to become explicit to itself. The endeavor of consciousness to interpret its own logos shall be called noetic exegesis."[28]

If the experience of social disorder is the proximate reason for the emergence of nous, that is only because within the soul of the philosopher there is already an inchoate apprehension of the order of the ground that enables the philosopher to resist the surrounding disorder. Disorder is experienced as such because in the soul of the philosopher there is already a pre-articulate apprehension of the divine ground as the source of order. In the philosopher's psyche this tension toward the ground is experienced as a state of questioning unrest:

> From the experience of his life in precarious existence within the limits of birth and death there rather rises the wondering question about the ultimate ground, the *aitia* or *prote arche*, of all reality and

28. *Anamnesis*, 89, 148.

specifically his own. The question is inherent in the experience from which it rises; the *zoon noun echon* that experiences itself as a living being is at the same time conscious of the questionable character attaching to this status. Man, when he experiences himself as existent, discovers his specific humanity as that of the questioner for the where-from and the where-to, for the ground and the sense of his existence.[29]

Questioning, then, is at the heart of noetic differentiation, and it is the thematization of this questioning that marks the differentiation as peculiarly "noetic." The classical philosophers, in particular Socrates, Plato, and Aristotle, are credited with having developed a vocabulary in which to speak about the various directional pulls and movements that constitute questioning. Among the symbols that have emerged from the experience of the Hellenic thinkers are: wondering *(thaumazein);* seeking and search *(zetein, zetesis);* and questioning *(aporein).* These philosophers were also sensitive enough to their own experience to realize that wondering, seeking, and questioning are propelled by a primordial desire to know. We are conscious of our ignorance and desire to move beyond it. Voegelin, following Aristotle, insists that there would be no questioning unrest unless we were moved by the ground that is our goal: "Without the *kinesis* of being attracted by the ground, there would be no desire for it; without the desire, no questioning in confusion, no awareness of ignorance. There could be no ignorant anxiety, from which rises the question about the ground, if the anxiety itself were not already man's knowledge of his existence from a ground of being that is not man himself." Prompted by this movement of attraction *(kinetai),* our questions have direction. The ensuing directional movement of nous is therefore not blind; we are in search of a known unknown, the divine ground of being. Voegelin refers to the movement as "knowing questioning" or "questioning knowledge." Aristotle referred to both the directional factor of consciousness and the ground that elicits the knowing questioning as "nous"; to avoid confusion Voegelin uses the term *ratio* when speaking of nous as the intentional "directional" structure of consciousness.[30]

Aristotle's dual understanding of nous was not due to any lack of philosophical perspicacity, but was rather the means by which he

29. Ibid., 92–93.
30. Ibid., 148, 149, 154.

indicated the merging of questioner and questioned. The consciousness that is in search of and drawn by the ground is also the consciousness that becomes aware of itself as the site where both its own structure and that of the ground become luminous to themselves. In the noetic differentiation, consciousness articulates itself as both intentional and luminous:

> The man who asks questions, and the divine ground about which questions are asked, will merge in the experience of questioning as a divine-human encounter and reemerge as the participants in the encounter that has the luminosity and structure of consciousness. The ground is not a spatially distant thing but a divine presence that becomes manifest in the experience of unrest and the desire to know. The wondering and questioning is sensed as the beginning of a theophanic event that can become fully luminous to itself if it finds the proper response in the psyche of concrete human beings—as it does in the classic philosophers.

According to Voegelin, noetic exegesis entails a threefold result. First, consciousness, as rooted in concrete human beings, discovers its material structure to be the direction-giving "ratio." Second, consciousness finds itself to be the "luminosity of knowledge about the tension toward the ground." Third, it comes to understand itself as a questing process in which earlier, less luminous symbolizations are designated as the "past."[31] The first two results of the noetic differentiation have already been discussed; the third result must await a discussion of history. We turn now to the other epochal differentiation of consciousness, the pneumatic differentiation.

PNEUMATIC DIFFERENTIATION

The pneumatic differentiation is part of the same movement from compactness to differentiation that generates the noetic differentiation. It arises, as does the noetic, from the realization that symbolizations based upon analogues taken from cosmic, social, and human order are inadequate in reflecting the being of the "divine partner on whom the community of being and its order depend."[32] In the case of the pneumatic differentiation, though, the focus is on the divine pole of experience, rather than on human questing, as is manifest in the noetic movement. It is because of this emphasis on

---

31. Ibid., 95–96, 154.
32. *Israel and Revelation*, 9.

the divine pole and its effect on human existence that Voegelin employs the term *pneumatic* (from the Greek *pneuma*, i.e., spirit) when analyzing this differentiation of consciousness.

In the earlier volumes of *Order and History*, Voegelin locates the emergence of the pneumatic differentiation within the experience of ancient Israel. In Israel "the world-transcendent God reveals himself as the original and ultimate source of order in world and man, society and history, that is, in all world-immanent being." Later formulations of the pneumatic experience will refer to the differentiation of "absolute Being"; and eventually the "Beyond" will come to be recognized as the most fitting symbolization of the divine pole.[33]

As noted earlier, one of the effects of the noetic differentiation is to illuminate the divine ground along with the articulation of consciousness as both site and sensorium of the ground. What, then, is peculiar to the pneumatic experience of the ground? Generally speaking, the pneumatic differentiation emphasizes the movement of the divine Beyond toward the human rather than the human tension toward the divine ground, as manifested in questioning unrest. Certainly in *Israel and Revelation* the focus is on the dramatic breakthrough of God into the lives of a particular group of people: "The conversion is experienced, not as the result of human action, but as a passion, as a response to a revelation of divine being, to an act of grace, to a selection for emphatic partnership with God. The community, as in the case of Israel, will be a chosen people, a peculiar people, a people of God."[34] As we shall see shortly, the notion of God constituting a people by an act of grace will eventually be transformed into the "parousia of the Beyond" in the soul of a philosopher. In both instances, though, what marks these experiences as pneumatic is the presence of the divine pole as mover, whether it be by forming a community through the bestowing of the divine *ruach* (spirit) or in the differentiation of the divine Beyond in the soul of the individual.

---

33. Ibid., xi; Sandoz, *Voegelinian Revolution*, 152; Voegelin, *Ecumenic Age*, 16; *In Search of Order*, 29–37, 96–97; "The Beginning and the Beyond," 173–232.

34. *Israel and Revelation*, 10. One might well point out that, for Voegelin, the Platonic analogy of the Cave also relates an experience of passion and grace; a *periagoge*, or "turning around." See, in particular, Voegelin, "Meditative Origin," 43–45; and "Gospel and Culture," 184–86. However, Voegelin also continued to maintain that in the pneumatic differentiation the Beyond was experienced with an intensity and power that not even Plato was able to achieve. See *Ecumenic Age*, 12–13, 249–51.

At the core of the Israelite experience is an awareness of the immediacy of divine presence. Unlike the Hellenes, the Hebrews did not approach the divine Beyond by means of speculation. As human, they no doubt wondered about their experience, but their wonder was not prompted by questions concerning the structure of the cosmos. Israel's experience of God was not at first mediated by questions concerning order and disorder. We can scarcely imagine Moses moving about the Israelite camp asking "What is justice?" Questioning in the Hebrew context arose from the fact that the divine had broken into their existence in a forceful way. It was the intensity of divine presence that characterized the Israelite experience of order.[35] It created the Hebrews as a people existing in a "present under God." With this form of pneumatic differentiation in Israel, history emerges as a process constituted by human response to the divine Beyond.

According to Voegelin, the pneumatic differentiation, as it took shape in Christianity, represented both continuity with the experience of Israel and a significant advance. The sovereign and transcendent God of Israel who was revealed as Creator, Lord of Justice, and Savior was also the God worshiped by Christians. The intensity and immediacy of Israel's encounter with the divine remained at the heart of the Christian tradition. At the same time, the Christian differentiation moved beyond that of Israel in two important ways. First of all, the universalism implicit in Israel's experience, but never fully articulated because of its ties to the land of Canaan, is made explicit in the Christian Gospel's summons to both Jew and Gentile. Secondly, in the Christian orbit the individual soul was able to disengage itself from collective existence, something that had never occurred in Israel.[36] Christianity, benefiting from the Hellenic differentiation of the psyche in the fifth and fourth centuries B.C., was able to preserve the intensity of the Israelite experience while at the same time understanding the revelation of the divine Beyond as addressed to the soul of every human being.[37] The insights of the noetic differentiation were thus incorporated into the Christian experience of God.

This fusion of Hebrew and Hellenic experiences gives Christian-

35. *Ecumenic Age,* 97.
36. *Israel and Revelation,* 139; *World of the Polis,* 10; *Israel and Revelation,* 240.
37. *Ecumenic Age,* 14; *World of the Polis,* 203; Voegelin, "History and Gnosis," 83.

ity its distinctive character as a religion of divine/human mutuality. Voegelin describes the truth thus revealed as "soteriological truth," which is seen as an advance beyond the "anthropological truth," that is, the noetic differentiation of the Hellenic philosophers:

> The impossibility of philia between God and man may be considered typical for the whole range of anthropological truth. The experiences that were explicated into a theory of man by the mystic philosophers had in common the accent on the human side of the orientation of the soul toward divinity. The soul orients itself toward a God who rests in his immovable transcendence; it reaches out toward divine reality, but it does not meet an answering movement from beyond. The Christian bending of God in grace toward the soul does not come within the range of these experiences—though, to be sure, in reading Plato one has the feeling of moving continuously on the verge of a breakthrough into this new dimension. The experience of mutuality in the relation with God, of the *amicitia* in the Thomistic sense, of the grace which imposes a supernatural form on the nature of man, is the specific differentiation of Christian truth.[38]

It is in the person of Jesus Christ that the closeness between God and humanity is seen most clearly. At the heart of the Christian experience there is what Voegelin refers to as the "epiphany of Christ." With the appearance of Christ "the formation of humanity has become transparent for its meaning as the process of transformation." In Christ, the formative movement of the Beyond in the soul of every person is realized with maximum clarity. The truth of existence in the metaxy as the human response to the pull of the Unknown God, whose presence reaches into any receptive soul, is embodied most clearly in the person of Jesus. Hence "Incarnation" means "the reality of divine presence in Jesus as experienced by the men who were his disciples and expressed their experience by the symbol 'Son of God' and its equivalents." The Incarnation expresses "the experience, with a date in history, of God reaching into man and revealing him as the Presence that is the flow of presence from the beginning of the world to its end. History is Christ written large." While the presence of the divine Beyond in Christ represents the apex of differ-

---

38. Voegelin, *New Science of Politics,* 77–78. Voegelin would later abandon the term *soteriological truth.* I will suggest some possible reasons for this change shortly, when I discuss the relationship between the pneumatic and noetic differentiations.

entiation, it remains an episode, albeit an important one, in the wider dynamic of the movement of Reality beyond its own structure: "Transfiguring incarnation does not begin with Christ, as Paul assumed, but becomes conscious through Christ and Paul's vision as the eschatological *telos* of the transfiguring process that goes on in history before and after Christ and constitutes its meaning."[39] The question as to whether Voegelin's Christology can be reconciled with that of orthodox Christian belief is a complicated one, beyond the scope of this work.[40] Voegelin's interpretation of the Christ event is mentioned here because, as we shall soon see, there is a connection between the epiphany of Christ and some of the excesses to which the pneumatic differentiation is prone.

If in the incarnation of Jesus Christ the divine Beyond is experienced in its presence in the human soul, it would seem as if in the Pauline vision of the Resurrected the emphasis is placed on the eschatological direction of reality moving beyond its structure toward its ultimate telos:

> Hence, Paul does not concentrate on the structure of reality that becomes luminous through the noetic theophany, as the philosophers do, but on the divine irruption which constitutes the new existential consciousness, without drawing too clear a line between the visionary center of the irruption and the translation of the experience into structural insight. . . . The theophanic event, one may say, has for Paul its center of luminosity at the point of pneumatic irruption; and the direction in which he prefers to look from this center is toward transfigured reality rather than toward existence in the cosmos.[41]

In his vision of the risen Christ, Paul became convinced that the same glorious destiny awaited all those who opened themselves to the

---

39. *Ecumenic Age,* 17; "Gospel and Culture," 198, 201, 207; *Ecumenic Age,* 244; Eugene Webb, *Eric Voegelin: Philosopher of History,* 233; Voegelin, "Immortality," 78; *Ecumenic Age,* 270.

40. For more on this matter, see William M. Thompson, "Voegelin and Jesus Christ," in John Kirby and William M. Thompson, eds., *Voegelin and the Theologian: Ten Studies in Interpretation;* Eugene Webb, "Eric Voegelin's Theory of Revelation," in Ellis Sandoz, ed., *Eric Voegelin's Thought: A Critical Appraisal;* Bruce Douglass, "A Diminished Gospel: A Critique of Voegelin's Interpretation of Christianity," in Stephen A. McKnight, ed., *Eric Voegelin's Search for Order in History;* Gerhart Niemeyer, "Eric Voegelin's Philosophy and the Drama of Mankind," 28–39; Frederick D. Wilhelmsen, "Professor Voegelin and the Christian Tradition."

41. *Ecumenic Age,* 246.

divine presence as Jesus had done. So overwhelmed was he by his experience that he was led to proclaim Jesus as the Son of God. Paul's vision was one of such intensity that he came to appreciate it as more than a theophanic event breaking into the metaxy. For Paul, the vision was the beginning of transfiguration itself. What links the Pauline vision with the other occasions of pneumatic differentiation is the emphasis on the intensity of divine irruption and a relative indifference toward questions having to do with the structure of the cosmos. This is also what distinguishes Paul's vision from the noetic quest of Plato and Aristotle:

> The Pauline analysis of existential order closely parallels the Platonic-Aristotelian. That is to be expected, since both the saint and the philosophers articulate the order constituted by man's response to a theophany. The accent, however, has decisively shifted from the divinely noetic order incarnate in the world to the divinely pneumatic salvation from its disorder, from the paradox of reality to the abolition of the paradox, from the experience of the directional movement to its consummation. The critical difference is the treatment of *phthora*, perishing. In the noetic theophany of the philosophers, the *athanatizein* of the psyche is kept in balance with the rhythm of *genesis* and *phthora* in the cosmos; in the pneumatic theophany of Paul, the *athanasia* of man is not to be separated from the abolition of *phthora* in the cosmos.

According to Voegelin, Paul has understood correctly that the core of any theophanic experience is its pneumatic center.[42] It is from this core that noetic analysis radiates outward. What becomes problematic in the case of pneumatic differentiation is not the theophanic experience itself, but, as we shall examine shortly, the tendency toward imbalance implicit in the very intensity of the experience.

THE RELATIONSHIP BETWEEN NOETIC AND PNEUMATIC DIFFERENTIATIONS

Having described the character and scope of the pneumatic differentiation, it is now possible to discuss the relationship between the pneumatic and the noetic differentiations. I shall proceed by offering a brief sketch of the development of Voegelin's thought on this

42. Ibid., 242, 248, 241, 244.

issue, followed by an analysis of the differences between the two differentiations and the peculiar liabilities to which each is subject.

In his early work, that is, *The New Science of Politics* and the first three volumes of *Order and History,* Voegelin acknowledges a distinction between reason (or philosophy) and revelation. The two symbols represent two important sources of Order and Truth.[43] Philosophy is aware of the unseen Measure as the source of true order, but it is only in the revelatory realm of Hebrew and Christian experience that the Measure reveals itself as the gracious God beyond the cosmos.

Voegelin eventually abandoned this distinction, insisting strongly that it is unnecessary once it is understood that both philosophy and revelation are theophanic symbols:

> In Christian theology there is the encrusted conception that revelation is revelation and that classic philosophy is the natural reason of mankind unaided by revelation. That is simply not true empirically. Plato was perfectly clear that what he is doing in the form of a myth is a revelation. He does not invent it by natural reason; the God speaks. The God speaks, just as in the prophet or in Jesus. So the whole conception which is still prevalent today, not only in theological thinking but penetrating our civilization: "on the one hand we have natural reason and on the other hand revelation," is empirically nonsense. It just isn't so.

In a later work, the reason/revelation distinction is likewise rejected and attributed to ethnic differences between Hellenic and Israelite cultures. These ethnic factors result in a difference in emphasis or accent between the noetic and pneumatic orbits. Both are theophanic, both are aware of the divine; what distinguishes them is that the noetic thinkers emerge in a society that is culturally predisposed toward expressing its experience of the divine in terms of the search, the *zetesis,* while prophets and saints occur in an imperial context in which the quest is not thematized, resulting in a strong emphasis on *ruach,* or *pneuma,* as the most adequate symbol by which to express the divine presence underpinning the search for truth.[44]

---

43. Voegelin, *New Science of Politics,* 76–78; *World of the Polis,* 1, 204, 218–19.

44. Voegelin, *Conversations,* 104–5; "Meditative Origin," 45–47. See also Voegelin, "Response to Professor Altizer's *A New History and a New but Ancient God,*" in *Collected Works,* vol. 12, 293; *Ecumenic Age,* 48, 229, 244; "Gospel and Culture," 188–89; "Meditative Origin," 44; Sandoz, *Voegelinian Revolution,* 212; and Thompson, "Voegelin and Jesus Christ," 199.

If it is true that both noetic and pneumatic differentiations emerge in response to theophanies, it was equally clear to Voegelin that the two share a common noetic core. At least this is certainly true of the Christian variation of the pneumatic differentiation.[45] He notes: "The noetic core is the same in both classic philosophy and the gospel movement. There is the same field of pull and counterpull, the same sense of gaining life through following the pull of the golden cord, the same consciousness of existence in an In-Between of human-divine participation, and the same experience of divine reality as the center of action in the movement from question to answer."[46]

The rejection of the distinction between reason and revelation and the assertion of the simultaneity of theophany and noetic core should come as no surprise given the development of Voegelin's thought on the nature of reality and consciousness. The language of natural reason/revelation does not fit well into a schema in which reality is understood as an encompassing whole where the divine and human are linguistic indices of the tensional poles within this wider reality. In Voegelin's account, theophanic presence and noetic response tend to merge, for indeed they do not represent separate realities, but rather a thematization of the one process in which Reality becomes increasingly luminous to itself.

Now, while it may be true that Voegelin rejects the distinction between reason and revelation, this does not mean that there is little or no difference between noetic and pneumatic differentiations. On the contrary, the illumination of the structure and movement of Reality through conscious participation admits of varying degrees of clarity, intensity, and balance. At the risk of simplification, I would say Voegelin believed that the noetic differentiation is superior in clarity and balance with respect to the structure of the participating psyche within the metaxy, while in the pneumatic differentiation the divine Beyond is experienced with unrivaled immediacy and inten-

45. In his later writings, Voegelin's attention to the pneumatic differentiation is focused on Christianity, which, as we have already seen, he believes to be superior to the earlier Israelite differentiation. References to the Israelite differentiation become increasingly scarce in his final work, and when it is mentioned it is usually in a negative way, as contributing to the metastatic derailments of our time. See Voegelin, *In Search of Order,* 33–37.

46. Voegelin, "Gospel and Culture," 192.

sity. In what sense this is the case will occupy us presently as we examine the strengths and weaknesses of these differentiations.

The strength of the pneumatic differentiation lies in the intensity of its experience of the divine Beyond, its emphasis on the eschatological movement of reality, and its insistence that the most important truth about human existence is that humanity is constituted by its relationship to this Unknown God beyond the metaxy who reaches into the human soul and moves the soul through loving attraction. As we have noted, Voegelin believes this truth to have been embodied most perfectly in the Incarnation of Jesus Christ and to have been experienced and articulated most intensely by Paul. What is particularly striking about the Christian form of differentiation is that the Unknown God is revealed as being present in the individual human soul. In Christianity, the eschatological existence of each individual person has been articulated with a forcefulness not achieved by philosophy. This final step was never taken by Plato, who remained bound to a certain degree (or, as Voegelin suggests, chose to remain bound) by the myth of the cosmos:

> *Having* the knowledge of the unknown God just as much as Jesus, does not lead Plato to a differentiation of God in man. He says: if there is that presence of such an unknown God, he is a God about whom we can say nothing; we know only that there *is* one. The known gods, the son of God, the *monogenes theos*, the First-born, remains the cosmos, in Plato. The same words appear in the Gospel of St. John to designate Christ; but *the* great difference is that a man is the *monogenes theos* and not the cosmos.[47]

The peculiarly Christian differentiation differs from the Israelite form in that the relationship to the Beyond is articulated in terms of the *individual* respondent. In relationship to the noetic differentiation as described by the classical philosophers, the difference lies in the degree of intensity with which the *Beyond* is revealed as present in the individual. Thus, the Christian differentiation has inherited the strengths of preceding differentiations. At the same time, this unique combination also contains within itself the potential for dangerous distortion.

The greatest strengths of the pneumatic differentiation are also

---

47. Voegelin, *Conversations*, 82. See also "History and Gnosis," 82–85; *Ecumenic Age*, 28, 250–51, 303–4; and "Gospel and Culture," 208.

closely linked to its greatest defects. Voegelin adverts to these possibilities in "The Gospel and Culture":

> The movement that engendered the saving tale of divine incarnation, death, and resurrection as the answer to the question of life and death is considerably more complex than classic philosophy; it is richer by the missionary fervor of its spiritual universalism, poorer by its neglect of noetic control; broader by its appeal to the inarticulate humanity of the common man; more restricted by its bias against the articulate wisdom of the wise; more imposing through its imperial tone of divine authority; more imbalanced through its apocalyptic ferocity, which leads to conflicts with the conditions of man's existence in society; more compact through its generous absorption of earlier strata of mythical imagination, especially through the reception of Israelite historiogenesis and the exuberance of miracle working; more differentiated through the intensely articulate experience of loving-divine action in the illumination of existence with truth.[48]

The main lines of Voegelin's critique of the pneumatic differentiation are present in this passage. Positively, the realization that each person can respond with openness to the divine Beyond gives to Christianity a universality and fervor that is not present in the writings of the classical philosophers; after all, the kingdom of God is accessible to all who will accept it. The power of this message is largely responsible, according to Voegelin, for the "imperial tone of divine authority" that characterizes the Christian Gospel, since once this truth has been revealed in Christ there can be no thought of compromise with paganism.

However, these positive characteristics are accompanied by equally dangerous temptations. The pneumatic experience may be so overwhelming that the recipient is in danger of losing his balance vis-à-vis the structure of participation in reality. The theophany is of such intensity that the balance between Beginning and Beyond, between the structure of reality and its eschatological goal may be lost, resulting in a "neglect of noetic control" and a tendency toward "apocalyptic ferocity." This temptation presents itself along the entire range of pneumatic differentiation, from Israelite prophetism to Pauline vision. When indulged, it results in a disturbance of consciousness in which the tension of existence in the metaxy is ignored. The pneumatic visionary may seek to escape from or to abolish the tension of

---

48. "Gospel and Culture," 189.

existence by various means. As we shall see shortly, the means chosen usually fall into two broad categories: on the one hand there is the tendency to denigrate existence in the world as the result of the theophany, and on the other there is the expectation that a faithful response to theophany will bring an immediate transfiguration of the believer's present situation. In general, Voegelin saw evidence of the first tendency in the development and historical role of Christianity, while the second tendency is more characteristic of Israelite prophetism and apocalyptic.[49]

The major forms of pneumatic deformation are metastasis, apocalyptic, and gnosis. Metastasis arises when the experience of pneumatic differentiation is so powerful that it "gives birth to the vision of a world that will change its nature without ceasing to be the world in which we live concretely." The breakthrough of divine reality so overwhelms the recipient that:

> The new image of the world resulting from the experience can be understood as a new world; and the process of change itself can turn into a structural datum of reality that can be extrapolated into the future. As that changeability that is experienced in participation mutates into images of a changeable reality comprising the poles of participation, we have the roots of the phenomena of metastatic beliefs: The gradualistic idea of infinite progress in the time of the world, the apocalyptic visions of the catastrophe of an old world and its *metastasis* into a new one resulting from divine intervention; the revolutionary ideas of a *metastasis* manipulated by human action; and so on.

Under the category of metastasis Voegelin would include much of Isaiah's prophetic imagery, as well as its modern Marxist variants. The imagery of the Isaian messianic oracles, with its evocations of a day when the wolf will lie down with the lamb and swords will be hammered into plowshares, as well as the Marxist dream of a world freed of exploitation and greed through the ascendancy of the proletariat, are examples of metastatic vision.[50] What is peculiarly metastatic in these instances is that the images evoked are drawn from the

49. Voegelin, "World Empire and the Unity of Mankind," 185–86; *New Science of Politics,* 118–19; *Ecumenic Age,* 20–27; *Conversations,* 28; *Anamnesis,* 166; *Israel and Revelation,* 431–88; Voegelin, "On Christianity," 451.

50. *Israel and Revelation,* 452; *Anamnesis,* 166; Voegelin, *Science, Politics, and Gnosticism,* 88–92; Voegelin, *From Enlightenment to Revolution,* 273–302; *Israel and Revelation,* xiii, 454, 478–81; *Conversations,* 26–29.

world in which we live, but that world becomes one in which the tensions of existence have disappeared. In metastasis, the limitations inherent in the human condition are to be rejected and overcome *within the world.* The world in which we live is to be perfected, either through the power of God or of human beings.[51]

Metastasis, then, would seem to derive from a dissatisfaction and impatience with present reality stemming from an intense experience of the world-transcendent God. Through an act of faith or through sheer force of will, the metastatic thinker attempts to manipulate reality and to bring about a change in the structure of being itself. It is this manipulative dimension of the metastatic attitude that leads Voegelin to label it as a sophisticated form of magic. The problem, of course, is that, as discussed earlier, there can be no change in the structure of being; the differentiations simply illuminate its structure, they do not eliminate it. The vision of eschatological transfiguration does not abolish life in the metaxy, because humans still live in searching tension toward the ground, however true it may be that our final destiny lies beyond that tension. Even though someone like Paul was gifted with the vision of ultimate human destiny beyond the vicissitudes of metaxic existence, a vision superior even to that of Plato, the greatness of his insight was undercut by his metastatic tendency to bring history to an end by pulling the final telos of reality into the present through his fervent belief in the imminent Parousia of the Lord.[52]

The inevitable disappointment engendered by metastatic expectations leads to the next stage of pneumatic deformation—apocalyptic. Voegelin does not always carefully distinguish between apocalyptic and metastatic phenomena; it appears from his writings that apocalyptic is the form metastasis assumes under the pressure of an intransigent reality. That is to say, when the metastasis of reality does not occur, the metastatic dreamer anticipates a time of unparalleled catastrophe that will be brought to an end by dramatic divine intervention. The reason for this is that the impact of theophany is so intense that when it fails to eliminate the evils in the recipient's present situation, that situation is judged to be devoid of meaning,

51. In Chapter 7 I will consider more fully what these limitations inherent in the human condition might be, and why I believe Voegelin's position on this issue suffers from a certain degree of ambiguity.

52. Voegelin, *Autobiographical Reflections,* 68; *Ecumenic Age,* 250–70.

and salvation is sought in the imminent restoration of divine order by means of God's cataclysmic judgment.[53]

The fervor of apocalyptic expectation in no way increases the probability that its vision will become reality; like the metastatic prophet, the apocalyptic visionary is doomed to disappointment. After these first two stages of pneumatic deformation, the stage is set for the third, the gnostic drama. Gnosticism is a topic that interested Voegelin throughout his career. Its centrality, however, as the key to explaining contemporary disorder, seemed to decrease in later years.[54] Nonetheless it is important to give some attention to this phenomenon as a variant of the pneumatic deformation that Voegelin associates with social and political disorder.

When the anticipated divine intervention does not occur, apocalyptic vision may give way to an even more pessimistic view of reality in which there is no longer any hope that the present world can be redeemed. The time is then ripe for a gnostic speculation which "construes the genesis of the cosmos with its catastrophes of ecumenic-imperial domination as the consequence of a psychodramatic fall in the Beyond, now to be reversed by the gnostics' action on the basis of their pneumatic understanding (gnosis) of the drama. The Beginning was a mistake to begin with and the end of the gnostic story will bring it to its End."[55]

The combination of theophanic intensity and pragmatic disillusionment creates a situation in which the world and its history are viewed as a reality to be abolished and replaced with a perfect world, or they are understood as the realm of the evil god who has imprisoned spirit in matter, a world from which escape is possible only by means of knowledge (gnosis). Order is no longer to be found in

---

53. *Israel and Revelation,* 454; *Ecumenic Age,* 26; *Conversations,* 28; *In Search of Order,* 33; "Equivalences," 129; "World Empire," 184–86; *Ecumenic Age,* 26; *In Search of Order,* 33.

54. Compare the importance Voegelin places on gnosticism in *Science, Politics, and Gnosticism* with its place in later writings, where it is seen as one of several contributors to the creation of modernity. See *Autobiographical Reflections,* 66–67. Also to be noted is the fluidity with which Voegelin employs terms that refer to "pneumopathological consciousness." *Metastasis, apocalyptic,* and *gnosis,* while distinguished, are sometimes used interchangeably, or they are employed as if synonymous with disordered consciousness in general. For an excellent treatment of these issues, see Michael Franz, *Eric Voegelin and the Politics of Spiritual Revolt,* 1–38.

55. *In Search of Order,* 33.

the world; it has contracted into the psyche of the gnostic. At the heart of gnosticism, then, is "the enterprise of returning the pneuma in man from its state of alienation in the cosmos to the divine pneuma of the Beyond through action based on knowledge." As in metastasis and apocalyptic, the tension of existence is simply ignored or bypassed; the uncertainty of life in the metaxy is too much to bear.[56]

The conditions for the emergence of gnosticism are set by the pneumatic differentiation:

> The intensely experienced presence of the Beyond brings the problem of the beginning to intense attention. When the formerly unknown god of the Beyond reveals himself as the goal of the eschatological movement in the soul, the existence of the cosmos becomes an ever more disturbing mystery. Why should a cosmos exist at all, if man can do no better than live in it as if he were not of it, in order to make his escape from the prison through death?

Voegelin saw basically two paths open to the gnostics—they can live in the world as if freed from the burdens of temporality, or they can act as if eternal perfection can somehow be brought into this world. The first approach was characteristic of ancient gnosticism, while the second is the chosen method of their modern confreres. In both cases gnostics act in order to free the world from its present travails and usher in a state of perfection, whether earthly or heavenly.[57] Both options are dangerous; a devaluation of life in the world by those overwhelmed by the presence of the divine Beyond can create a vacuum in which political life is ceded to those who are not attuned to the structure and movement of reality. Even more deadly, in Voegelin's view, is the tendency in modern gnostic movements toward an immanentization of the Beyond. From their unhappiness with the world as it is and the uncertainty of a life lived in tension within the metaxy, modern gnostics cannot return to the comfort of the compact "world full of gods," since the differentiations of consciousness have made that impossible. At the same time, the dogmatization of religious experience and the doctrinalization of metaphysics have contributed heavily to the modern "climate of opinion" where the originating experiences of transcendence have been lost.[58] Rejecting the transcendent God, dissat-

---

56. *Ecumenic Age,* 20; *New Science of Politics,* 122–26; *Ecumenic Age,* 17–27; "Gospel and Culture," 210–11.

57. *Ecumenic Age,* 19; Voegelin, "What Is History?," 51.

58. *Anamnesis,* 183–213; *Ecumenic Age,* 36–58.

isfied with the present, the modern gnostic looks toward the establishment of a new world, a realm of perfection, by human means. In this fashion the Beyond is brought to earth even if the gnostic himself has no belief in the Beyond. With his own superior knowledge and insight into the meaning of history, the gnostic possesses the key to future perfection. All that remains to be done is to make a resistant reality conform to his vision by whatever means necessary.

Given the fact that gnosticism is primarily a deformation of the pneumatic differentiation, a word must be said about its relationship to both the Hebrew/Jewish and Christian forms of this differentiation. Voegelin acknowledges that not all gnosticism is tied to the pneumatic differentiation; gnostic speculation can be found in cosmological societies as well.[59] However, the Israelite and Christian orbits are particularly congenial to the development of gnosticism. It is not difficult to understand why this is the case because, as we have seen, the Israelite and Christian focus on the Unknown God is easily susceptible to imbalance. The language of pneumatic experience is readily appropriated by gnostic thinkers, as seen in the struggle between gnostics and the Church Fathers. The cultural milieu that gives rise to metastasis and apocalyptic also provides the conditions for the growth of gnosticism. Christianity is particularly liable to gnostic perversion, Voegelin believed, owing to its superior differentiation of the eschatological movement of reality and its recognition of the presence of the divine Beyond in the individual soul. And yet it is precisely the qualities that constitute the excellence of the Christian differentiation that are open to the greatest distortion. This explains why Voegelin, while acknowledging the advance represented by Christianity, qualifies his praise with a warning as to its potential dangers: "Considering the history of Gnosticism, with the great bulk of its manifestations belonging to, or deriving from, the Christian orbit, I am inclined to recognize in the epiphany of Christ the great catalyst that made eschatological consciousness an historical force, both in forming and deforming humanity."[60]

59. Voegelin, "On Gnosticism," in Peter J. Opitz and Gregor Sebba, eds., *The Philosophy of Order: Essays on History, Consciousness, and Politics*, 460; *Ecumenic Age*, 23.

60. *Ecumenic Age*, 27, 20. See also Voegelin, "Gospel and Culture," 210–11; Voegelin, "World Empire," 170–88; and Bruce Douglass, "The Gospel and Political Order: Eric Voegelin on the Political Role of Christianity" and "Diminished Gospel," 139–54.

Despite the superiority of the pneumatic differentiation in symbolizing the presence of the divine Beyond in history and in the human soul, Voegelin maintained an ambivalent attitude toward it, primarily because of its unfortunate propensity to imbalance. In this regard it is the noetic differentiation that is superior to the pneumatic. The balance found in the work of the noetic thinkers is the necessary restraint on pneumatic excess:

> The epochal consciousness of the classic philosophers did not derail into apocalyptic expectations of a final realm to come. Both Plato and Aristotle preserved their balance of consciousness. They recognized the noetic outburst for the irreversible event in history that it was, but they also knew that reason had been the constituent of humanity before the philosophers differentiated the structure of the *psyche*, and that its presence in human nature had not prevented the order of society from falling into the disorder which they resisted. To assume that the differentiation of reason would stop the rise and fall of societies would have been absurd.

The tendency of the prophets to derail into metastasis can be understood as "the consequence of pneumatic differentiation in a tribal society, wanting in noetic differentiation and conceptual distinctions."[61]

The antidote to pneumatic imbalance is to take seriously the "postulate of balance" exemplified in the work of Plato.[62] The need to recall this postulate is rooted in the paradox of reality as "a recognizably structured process that is recognizably moving beyond its structure." It is incumbent upon the philosopher to hold this tension in balance, overemphasizing neither the lastingness nor the eschatological character of reality. Indeed, the philosopher must remind his peers that the paradox is "the very structure of existence itself." Voegelin goes so far as to suggest that the uncertainties concerning the adequate symbolization of the Beyond found in Plato's later dialogues were introduced deliberately because Plato was afraid that "the elaboration might disturb the balance of consciousness."[63] Plato saw clearly that differentiations of consciousness did not abolish life

---

61. *Anamnesis*, 90; *Ecumenic Age*, 27.
62. *Ecumenic Age*, 228.
63. Ibid., 232. It would seem as if this view is a step away from Voegelin's earlier position, in *The New Science of Politics*, where Plato is understood as having come close to a pneumatic breakthrough but as having been unable to do so. See *New Science of Politics*, 77–78.

in the cosmos, that the structure of being was not affected by the newly gained insights. By insisting on balance Plato attempted to guard against "the flooding of consciousness with imaginations of transfigured reality that will devalue existence in the cosmos under the conditions of its structure." While recognizing that we are oriented toward a reality that extends beyond the nous, Plato reminds us that our pursuit of immortality takes place in the metaxy, with its "apeirontic burden of mortality."[64]

A final point to be made with regard to the relationship between pneumatic and noetic differentiation concerns the type of language to be used in analyzing the structure and movement of reality. Here the priority of noetic language is clear. Indeed, the noetic differentiation is constituted by the discovery of the structure and movement of reality in the consciousness of the classic philosophers. According to Voegelin, the symbols created by these noetic thinkers remain the basis for any analysis of reality; they may be augmented as historical circumstances warrant, but they will not be surpassed in clarity and precision.[65] The language of noesis is *the* language with which to talk about these matters. Pneumatic symbols, with the possible exception of "eschatology," are assigned a minor role in analysis because of their lack of clarity and their susceptibility to derailment.

Now that I have described the major differentiations of consciousness and delineated their relationship to one another, it is possible to offer some critical observations. As noted above, Voegelin considered both noetic and pneumatic differentiations to be theophanic events. The recovery of this theophanic dimension in the Hellenic philosophers is, I believe, one of the great strengths of Voegelin's position. His understanding of philosophy as "the love of being through love of divine Being as the source of its order" makes it clear that philosophy and theology, far from addressing themselves to the analysis of separate realms of being, are engaged in a common exploration of reality. Both are animated by the insight that to be human is to be oriented toward transcendence. Finally, if the sign of an excellent interpretation is its ability to make sense of all the relevant data in an intelligible way, then Voegelin's is clearly a superior account.

64. *Ecumenic Age,* 234, 237.
65. See *Anamnesis,* 89–115; *Ecumenic Age,* 212–38; *New Science of Politics,* 27–51; *Conversations,* 62–70, 101; and *Science, Politics, and Gnosticism,* 15–22.

For example, where other interpreters stumble or are puzzled by Aristotle's seemingly "odd" decision to end the *Nicomachean Ethics* with a discussion of contemplation, Voegelin is able to deal with the issue far more effectively, without being led to conclude that the discussion of happiness in Book 10, chapters 6 through 8, is somehow discontinuous with the overall argument of the *Ethics*.[66] He can do so because it is clear to him that the nous as it exists in the human being shares in some fashion in the divine Nous.[67] Similar instances could be drawn from his interpretation of Plato. It is not a matter of Voegelin's doing violence to these philosophical texts in order to make them fit a preconceived schema; it is rather the result of his having an insight into the originating experiences that gave rise to philosophy. When such experiences are understood in terms of the search for and tension toward the divine ground, there is revealed in the data an intelligibility that is more difficult to discover when one operates from a perspective in which "reason" is immanent and discontinuous with transcendence.

If it is clear that both noetic and pneumatic differentiations are theophanic in character, it is also clear that, from Voegelin's point of view, it is the noetic differentiation that takes precedence as the criterion for judging the truth of order. The pneumatic experience goes beyond the noetic in terms of differentiating the eschatological movement of reality and the loving presence of the Unknown God in the individual soul. At the same time, because of the pneumatic potential for imbalance, Voegelin tended to view pneumatic phenomena with a certain degree of wariness, and to insist upon noetic restraint as the counterbalance to this tendency. Of course there *are* instances when pneumatic excesses are in need of noetic control, but in his efforts to guard against such pneumatic distortions, did Voegelin perhaps run the risk of subjecting pneumatic experiences to noetic criteria? And in so doing, did he downplay that which is peculiarly pneumatic? It is a danger that he did not always manage to avoid.[68]

66. For example, see Martha C. Nussbaum, *The Fragility of Goodness: Luck and Ethics in Greek Tragedy and Philosophy*, 373–77. For Voegelin's interpretation, see *Plato and Aristotle*, 304–14.

67. *Anamnesis*, 89–97; *Ecumenic Age*, 232, 237.

68. For similar observations see Douglass, "Diminished Gospel," 139–54; Niemeyer, "Drama of Mankind," 28–39; and Pheme Perkins, "Gnosis and the

While one can applaud Voegelin's sensitivity to the divine appeal and responsive movement common to both noetic and pneumatic cultures, it remains possible to question whether his own criticism in regard to the pneumatic differentiation keeps him from appreciating its distinctiveness in relation to the noetic differentiation. In reacting against pneumatic excess, has he perhaps downplayed the very strength of the pneumatic movement?

The critical priority given to noetic analysis is evident in Voegelin's treatment of pneumatic experience. In his treatment of the gospel movement, Voegelin notes that while the Gospel, with its differentiation of the Beyond in the individual soul, represents an advance over the noetic differentiation, that advance is essentially a better focusing of the common noetic experience.[69]

Certainly Voegelin's insight concerning the common ground shared by the Gospel and philosophy is a sound one. In particular, *The Gospel according to John* is filled with the symbolism of divine-human drawing and seeking. But the problem lies not so much in what Voegelin says as in what he does not say. In his treatment of the Gospel the emphasis is almost solely on its function as a differentiation of consciousness in the metaxy. We find little or nothing about the public teaching, the public actions, and the miracles of Jesus as signs pointing to an eschatological reversal of fortune and an eschatological transvaluation of values that is to begin in the present.[70] When such themes are acknowledged they are either attributed to an apocalyptic fantasizing that mars the gospel movement or dismissed as unrealizable ideals for social life.[71]

The observation has been made that in interpreting Christianity as he did, Voegelin lost the sense of the Gospel as salvation *in the specifically Christian sense*. As already noted, the use of the term *soteriological principle* disappears in his later writings, although it must be admitted that Voegelin continues to stress the divine bending in love as an important element in Christianity. What we do not find in either early or later works is any serious attention to the problem of sin. In this regard Bruce Douglass notes:

Life of the Spirit: The Price of Pneumatic Order," in Kirby and Thompson, eds., *Voegelin and the Theologian.*

69. Voegelin, "Gospel and Culture," 192.

70. See Ben F. Meyer, *The Aims of Jesus,* 129–73.

71. *Plato and Aristotle,* 226; "Gospel and Culture," 209–10; "World Empire," 184–88.

It is true that Voegelin uses soteriological language occasionally: he speaks, for example, of the Gospel as a "saving tale." The salvation in question, however, would appear to have a somewhat different character from that of the New Testament. It is more the attainment of meaning than the restoration of a broken relationship with God or the creation of a "new man." Rather than transcending what Voegelin calls the "tension of existence," it simply reflects it. Especially in his more recent writings Voegelin seems to be taking great pains to minimize or even deny the possibility of any kind of fundamental change in the human condition as a result of revelation.[72]

In making this point, Douglass has hinted at, if not made fully explicit, what it is about Voegelin's treatment of the pneumatic differentiation that is disturbing. In later chapters I will return to this point, but for the present it will suffice to mention briefly a partial source of the problem. Voegelin praises Plato and Aristotle for the admirable balance of consciousness found in their work. In both cases the "Anaximandrian experience of the Apeiron extends its balancing effect into the symbolization even of the God behind the Olympian gods," and both philosophers, while acknowledging the process of immortalization, conceive it only within the confines of an "apeirontic burden of mortality."[73] The balance of consciousness to be found in these philosophers would seem to consist in a recognition of the divine Beyond accompanied by a sensitivity to an Anaximandrian process of becoming and perishing that governs the cosmos. The Beyond may be differentiated in consciousness, but the world in which the recipients of this differentiation live remains under the constraints of the mundane laws that govern existence.[74] Undoubtedly, this balance does prevent some of the excesses Voegelin notes in his criticism of the pneumatic differentiation, for when one acknowledges cosmic necessity there is little danger of metastasis becoming a problem. I would argue, though, that at the heart of authentic pneumatic experience there is a profound sense that it is this very Anaximandrian fatalism that has been or will be overcome, and that the grip of cosmic necessity has been broken. The prophetic vision and Christian hope spring from a sometimes inarticulate and

72. Douglass, "Diminished Gospel," 139–54 (quotation on p. 146); Niemeyer, "Drama of Mankind," 28–39; Douglass, "Diminished Gospel," 146.

73. *Anamnesis*, 90; *Ecumenic Age*, 227–38 (quotations on pp. 236–37).

74. In Chapter 7, I will return to this point because I believe it is an area of Voegelin's thought that he never adequately clarified.

inchoate but always powerfully experienced awareness of the God who is more powerful than cosmic Ananke. The God encountered in pneumatic differentiation is not only the Beyond who is articulated both in communal and individual terms, but the one who breaks the bonds of sin and death. Voegelin rightly observed that this anticipation and hope have been the source of tremendous disorder, but in criticizing the pneumatic figures from the perspective of Platonic/Aristotelian "balance," had he perhaps lost sight of what is at the very core of the pneumatic experience? Was he careful enough in distinguishing a pneumatic vision that derails into unrealistic expectations of perfection from a pneumatic vision that serves as a catalyst in moving beyond resignation toward a balanced approach to personal and social transformation? In other words, is there in Voegelin's criticism of pneumatic differentiation a hesitancy to come to terms with what it is that Christians mean when they speak of grace, that is, a supernatural movement disproportionate to our "natural" capacities, capable of effecting a higher integration of human consciousness and human activity?[75]

Pneumatic excess has indeed been at the center of some destabilizing social and political tendencies, but one could also make the case that pneumatic experience can be an even more effective preserver of balance than the noetic. Might it not be the case that the problem of immanentization and an overestimation of the powers of reason are more likely to occur under conditions where human reason has gained a certain autonomy in its role as the sensorium of reality's structure, and where the God beyond the metaxy is experienced *less* intensely than in the pneumatic experience? On the other hand, could not the "balance" between differentiated consciousness and cosmic necessity lead to resignation and fatalism in the face of social disorder? Far from acting as an agent of imbalance, might not the God encountered in pneumatic experience act as a necessary balancing presence, insuring that the "ratio" differentiated in consciousness does not claim for itself an omniscience and omnipotence that it does not possess, while at the same time empowering and inspiring human beings confronted with political disorder and social

75. This is a difficult question, and answering it would require a full study on Voegelin's theory of revelation. But it does seem to be the case that Voegelin's rejection of the natural/supernatural distinction contributes to this problem.

malaise? One could argue plausibly that such an insight is at the heart of the Hebrew and Christian traditions. Voegelin was aware of this:

> Philosophy and Christianity have endowed man with the stature that enables him, with historical effectiveness, to play the role of rational contemplator and pragmatic master of a nature which has lost its demonic terrors. With equal historical effectiveness, however, limits were placed on human grandeur; for Christianity has concentrated demonism into the permanent danger of a fall from the spirit—that is man's only by the grace of God—into the autonomy of his own self, from the *amor Dei* into the *amor sui*. The insight that man in his mere humanity, without the *fides caritate formata,* is demonic nothingness has been brought by Christianity to the ultimate border of clarity which by tradition is called revelation.[76]

One may raise the question as to whether Voegelin, in his later writings, allowed this insight to be overshadowed by his concern to avoid the dangers to which he felt the pneumatic differentiation was liable.

The problem to which I have been alluding may very well be implicit in Voegelin's understanding of reality and consciousness. If the advances of which Voegelin speaks pertain to the differentiation of *consciousness* only (and it would appear that they do),[77] in the increasing illumination of the structure and movement of reality, then the pneumatic differentiation is simply a further illumination of the one process of reality becoming increasingly luminous to itself. Certainly the development of Voegelin's theory of consciousness and reality moved in this direction. In this context, the noetic and pneumatic differentiations become ethnic variants within the wider process, with the noetic differentiation possessing a superior degree of balance. The form in which the differentiation of consciousness is expressed has more to do with the particular culture in which it emerges than with any substantive difference as to what is articulated. What *is* articulated is the one process of the Whole—reality— as it becomes increasingly luminous for its structure and movement.[78]

76. *New Science of Politics,* 78–79.
77. *Ecumenic Age,* 8.
78. Voegelin, "Meditative Origin," 43–51. I think it is a valid question as to whether or not this represents a shift in understanding on Voegelin's part. It seems to me that he more clearly emphasized the uniqueness of the pneumatic differentiation in his earlier works, e.g., *The New Science of Politics* and *Israel and Revelation,* than in his later writings, where the emphasis seems to be on its role as a dimension of the one process of the It-Reality becoming luminous.

When Voegelin speaks of "equivalences" of experience and symbolization, it seems that this is exactly what he has in mind: that, cutting across cultures and historical epochs, one can discern structural constants that are reflected in the various human attempts to articulate the experience of participation.[79]

While Voegelin can be praised for his effort to penetrate to a level of reality beyond symbols—indeed beyond the experiences themselves, to the depth out of which experiences emerge[80]—the theory of equivalences is not without its own ambiguous implications. For if Hellenic and Israelite differentiations are equivalent variations within the one process of reality becoming luminous, then what becomes of the nature of an "advance"? It would appear to be limited to the increasing illumination of the structures and tensions of reality. In this regard, we recall from the preceding chapter Voegelin's insistence that reality does not change. It is at this point that his own interpretation of the pneumatic differentiation may enter into a tension with that expressed by the pneumatic visionaries themselves, for whom, as we noted earlier, the divine/human encounter would seem to imply more than an illumination of the process of the Whole. For Voegelin, to the extent that the pneumatic visionaries articulate those dimensions of reality underemphasized by their noetic counterparts and thereby contribute to reality's further illumination, the pneumatic contribution constitutes an advance in differentiation; but, as we shall see more clearly in later chapters, Voegelin views with deep suspicion any implication that these insights are to be extended to altering or changing the structure of reality in any of its dimensions other than consciousness, such as social and political change.

Another potential danger in a theory of equivalences is that the equivalent nature of experiences or symbolizations may come to overshadow the differences between them. When this happens, a continuity may be posited between distinct phenomena that may not take into account other equally notable differences. In Voegelin's case, this temptation can sometimes be seen in his linking of ancient and modern pneumopathologies. In doing this, Voegelin may have grasped profound affinities that have escaped other interpreters, but

---

79. "Equivalences," 115–33.
80. Ibid., 123–33.

as we shall note in later chapters, there are times when he may overstate his case, and such overstatement may be at least in part attributable to an uncritical application of the notion of equivalence.

In this regard one could consult Pheme Perkins's appreciative yet critical approach to Voegelin's analysis of gnosticism. Contra Voegelin, she maintains that the pneumatic differentiation in its Christian form was primarily directed toward the community, not the individual, and that the gnostics of the early Christian era did not conceive of themselves as in any way possessing the Spirit to which they responded. If Perkins is correct and the ancient gnostics did not hold such individualistic attitudes or engage in "radical perversions of the spirit," which Voegelin associates with the modern philosophical and ideological movements that he also labels as "gnostic," then what can be said about the continuity between ancient gnosticism and modern ideologies? While not ruling out the possibility of some affinity between the two, we must not read into such similarity any direct continuity; indeed, Voegelin himself has admitted that the phenomena of modern ideologies is more complex than he had initially imagined. The problems of modernity cannot simply be attributed to gnostic derailment.[81]

Obviously, these observations are scarcely exhaustive. My purpose has been to suggest some possible implications stemming from Voegelin's theory of consciousness and differentiation. Later chapters will attempt to draw out some of these implications more explicitly. But at this stage it is worthwhile to call to mind that the way in which one conceives of consciousness and its relationship to reality will have important consequences for one's notion of society and social change. For the consciousness of which we speak is *human* consciousness, and it is human beings who are largely responsible for the shape of their societies. What might the relationship be between these differentiations of consciousness and the societies in which they arise? How might they condition or influence one another? These are important questions, but before we address them we must turn our attention to Voegelin's analysis of society.

---

81. Perkins, "Gnosis and the Life of the Spirit," in Kirby and Thompson, eds., *Voegelin and the Theologian*.

THREE

SOCIAL REALITY

THE CONCRETE CONSCIOUSNESS AND SOCIETY

Now that we have discussed the broader contours of Voegelin's philosophical horizon, it is possible to situate social reality within the context of reality as a whole. As was the case with the preceding chapters, we begin with the human experience of participation. Concerning participation, we recall Voegelin's observation that it is always the participation of a concrete consciousness:

> Human consciousness is not a free-floating something but always the concrete consciousness of concrete persons. The consciousness of the existential tension toward the ground, therefore, while constituting the specific human nature that distinguishes man from other beings, is not the whole of his nature, for consciousness is always concretely founded on man's bodily existence, through which he belongs to all levels of being, from the anorganic to the animalic.

The consciousness of tension toward the ground is based upon and rooted in physical, chemical, and biological levels of being. The human being incorporates the various levels in what Voegelin, following Aristotle, refers to as the "synthetic" nature of man. Each person is a microcosm of the cosmos itself. The levels within the hierarchy of being are related to one another in such a way that the higher, conscious levels are materially dependent upon the lower, while the lower levels are organized by the higher. In other words, lower strata condition but do not determine the possibilities for action and thought in higher strata.[1]

---

1. *Anamnesis,* 200, 208; *Ecumenic Age,* 334. See also *Anamnesis,* 33, 147; and *Ecumenic Age,* 333.

In answer to the question as to just how the various tiers are linked and synthesized by the human being, Voegelin explains:

> Speaking ontologically, consciousness finds in the order of being of the world no level which it does not also experience as its own foundation. In the "basis-experience" of consciousness man presents himself as an epitome of the cosmos, as a microcosm. Now we do not know in what this basis "really" consists; all our finite experience is experience of levels of being in their differentiation; the nature of the cosmos is inexperienceable, whether the nexus of basis be the foundation of the vegetative on the inorganic, of the animalic on the vegetative, or of human consciousness on the animal body. There is no doubt, however, that this basis exists. Even though the levels of being are clearly distinguishable in their respective structures, there must be something common which makes possible the continuum of all of them in human existence.[2]

Humans clearly differentiate between the various realms of being; we distinguish human life from that occurring on the inorganic, vegetative, and animalic levels. At the same time we experience ourselves as participating in and being founded upon all these levels. Human consciousness does not experience itself as separate from the body; consciousness is always aware of itself as incarnate. What is the basis for this experience? This "basis," this "something common" is none other than the ground of being that permeates and gives rise to all levels of existence while remaining unknowable in itself. It is, as noted in the first chapter, the "ontological hypothesis without which the experienced reality of the ontic nexus in human existence remains incomprehensible." The ground is the common substance from which arise the "things" that constitute the various ranks of being. The structure and movement of the ground provide the continuity between these ranks of being. It is this continuity that comprises the unity of the human person; indeed, it is precisely in the presence and unfolding of the ground that human existence is constituted. A person does not exist "in" the metaxy; the human is that "site" where the process of reality, as it unfolds through the hierarchy of being, becomes illuminated from within.[3]

The unity of the human person, then, is rooted in the ground that

2. *Anamnesis*, 28.
3. *Anamnesis*, 32; *Ecumenic Age*, 334–35.

serves as the continuum between all the levels of being that constitute human life, from bodily existence to consciousness of eschatological destiny. No more than the ground itself, though, is this unity
"objectively" experienceable in Voegelin's terms; our consciousness
of the relationship between the various levels of being is conditioned
by a bodily existence that tends to cast the "things" into a subject/
object mode where "object" has connotations of externality. Thus
"our finite experience is experience of levels of being in their differentiation." The continuity between the levels of being, which has its
source in the depth of the ground, remains ultimately beyond the
grasp of human knowing, since "we do not experience a content of
the depth other than the content that has entered consciousness."[4]
This applies as well to the relationship between body and consciousness; the substantive unity of human existence, like the ground itself,
becomes an ontological hypothesis deduced from the human experience of participation in all levels of being. This is not to question the
existence of this substantial unity; on the contrary, Voegelin would
maintain that our awareness of ourselves as participating in reality in
its various levels through both body and consciousness points toward
just such a unity.

The ground that provides the continuity for the synthetic nature
of the human person also serves as the "horizontal" source of unity.
Consciousness is always concrete, that is, found only in individual
human beings. There is no single embracing collective consciousness
of which individuals are but phenomenal manifestations. At the same
time, consciousness is not private: "In order to avoid misunderstandings, it should be noted that consciousness is real discretely but that
the field of history does not for that reason dissolve into a field of
persons of whom every one has a private consciousness for himself,
in the classical sense of *idiotes*. For consciousness is the existential
tension toward the ground, and the ground is for all men the one
and only divine ground of being."[5]

To be human is to exist in tension toward the ground. If that is the
case, then human consciousness, while founded in the bodies of
individuals, shares a common nature by virtue of its constitutive
orientation to the one divine ground. This is the experience of the

4. *Anamnesis,* 179; "Meditative Origin," 49; "Equivalences," 126.
5. *Anamnesis,* 179.

ground articulated in the Heraclitean symbol of *xynon,* the "common." To speak of *xynon* is to recognize the Logos permeating reality as the source of order making possible human understanding and community. Refusal to acknowledge *xynon* is to imagine that one's consciousness is private, and by so blocking off reality, one becomes an *idiotes.*[6]

From the concrete consciousness encompassing both bodily existence and consciousness toward the ground, we expand the analysis to social reality. Like concrete consciousness, the structure of social reality will be found to consist in both a bodily dimension and a transcendent orientation toward the ground of being.

It is the bodily dimension of concrete consciousness that serves as the basis for social existence. Human beings have bodies, "and through their bodies participate in the organic and inorganic externality of the world." This "external" existence is part of the ontological structure of human life. Because consciousness is concrete, there arise the practical tasks of securing food and shelter, raising and educating children, and so forth. The social order emerges from the response of concrete consciousness to the necessities imposed by life in the world: "This [social existence] may grow quantitatively from the family, to the labor-dividing small society, to that size in which ordering consciousness finds the material basis for the unfolding of the *eu zen,* the good life, Aristotle's criterion of the *eunomia,* the good social order."[7]

The growth of society is not merely the banding together of isolated individuals to form a social contract; Voegelin points out that human beings are inherently social: "Existence in society, by force of birth and nurture within a family, is ontologically, not by choice, the manner of human existence. The alternative to existence in one concrete society—short of not being born at all or of committing suicide—is not solitary existence but existence in another concrete society. Human existence is social, and there is no clear line that would separate personal from social order."[8]

To meet common human needs intelligently and to provide for their own safety, people attempt to devise a social order that will

6. *World of the Polis,* 231–33; *New Science of Politics,* 27–28.
7. *Anamnesis,* 200; *New Science of Politics,* 31, 33; *Anamnesis,* 200.
8. Voegelin, "The Nature of the Law," 49, 56–57.

accomplish these goals. Essential to this undertaking is the creation of some form of organization in terms of representative rulership:

> No matter how well ordered society may be, its corporeality, compelling it to provide material care and the control of the passions, requires an existence in the form of organized rulership. The organization of society through representatives charged with care for the social order within and for defense against external dangers is the *conditio sine qua non* of society to such an extent that the investigation and description of the various pragmatic organizations is a main part of political science. A theory of politics cannot stop there, however, since this part deals only with that aspect of political reality that is founded in man's corporeality.

The need to satisfy material requirements and control the passions compels the creation of some sort of organized authority. When this occurs, *society* can truly be said to have come into being. In Voegelin's work, then, a society comes into existence when a group of people establish an order that enables them to continue in existence and to act in the world. It is just such a society, "organized for action to maintain itself in existence," that forms the primary field of order for human beings.[9]

Voegelin refers to this process by which human beings form themselves into societies in order to act effectively in the world as social "articulation." The purpose of articulation is the establishment of a representative with the authority to act on behalf of the society as a whole; indeed, as noted above, without such a representative it is difficult to speak of a group of people as a society at all: "A multitude of men exists as an ordered society inasmuch as it is articulated into rulers and ruled. A society comes into existence through social articulation that results in the creation and acceptance of a representative, and it remains in existence as long as it has accepted representatives. Organization for action, both internal and external, through a representative, is the manner in which a society exists." The type of representative will vary from society to society, as does the degree to which the political role of the members of any given society is articulated. The articulation of the representative can range in scope from a monarchy to a radically

9. *Anamnesis*, 200; *New Science of Politics*, 36–37; *World of the Polis*, 1.

democratic evocation, such as Lincoln's government "of the people, by the people, for the people."[10]

The representative of a society will be accepted only as long as he serves to realize the "idea" of the society, that is, to preserve the society's existence while providing a setting for the unfolding of the good life. As an illustration of what is meant by the "idea" of a people articulating itself, Voegelin refers back to the *intencio populi* recognized by Fortescue:

> The *intencio populi* is located neither in the royal representative nor in the people as a multitude of subjects but is the intangible living center of the realm as a whole. The word "people" in this formula does not signify an external multitude of human beings but the mystical substance erupting in articulation; and the word "intention" signifies the urge or drive of this substance to erupt and to maintain itself in articulate existence as an entity which, by means of its articulation, can provide for its well-being.[11]

The language of "mystical substance" notwithstanding, the "idea" of a society would seem to be the shared set of understandings and judgments that inform the process of social articulation. In articulating itself in terms of a representative, a society must possess some prior notion of what it is that is to be articulated. Just what this "mystical substance" is and what it is that the "idea" of a society attempts to articulate will be discussed in the second part of this chapter.

The authority of the representative is a function of his or her ability to realize the idea of the society through institutional embodiment, "and the power of a ruler has authority in so far as he is able to make his factual power representative of the idea." Power is essential for effective rule, but at the same time, power divorced from the goal of securing the order of society and realizing its idea will possess no authority. In this regard, authority always precedes the legal or constitutional order; "in so far as a power has representative authority, it can make positive law."[12]

---

10. *New Science of Politics,* 37, 41; "The Nature of the Law," 59; *New Science of Politics,* 40.

11. *New Science of Politics,* 44.

12. Ibid., 48, 49. On this question of the particular institutional "set-up" as being subordinate to the "idea" seeking to be articulated, note Voegelin's reflections on the origins of the American constitution, in which he concludes: "The

It is this distinction between the idea and its taking shape in the authoritative institutional structures of each particular society that leads Voegelin to differentiate between elemental and existential representation. The elemental aspect of society refers to its "external" dimension, that is, the type of institutions and representatives it has, the procedures for electing or appointing representatives, and the legal system; in other words, the "set-up" by means of which a society operates in the world.[13] The notion of elemental representation applies to any society in which there exists an authority claiming to act on behalf of its citizens. However, such representation is not limited to those societies with "representative" institutions, such as the United States and other Western democracies. Voegelin offered the example of the Soviet Union as an instance where, despite the absence of popular elections, the Soviet government was still to be considered representative in that it acted for its people on the world stage and commanded obedience at home.[14]

To understand the meaning of existential representation we return to Voegelin's insight that the genuine authority of the representative power precedes its translation into institutional form. We recall likewise that authority rests in the ability of the representative to realize the "idea" of the society. To the extent that a representative is able to accomplish this, it can be said to be existentially representative. When a representative in the elemental sense ceases to be representative in an existential sense through its inability or unwillingness to serve the "idea" of its society, then its hold on authority becomes precarious:

> In order to be representative, it is not enough for a government to be representative in the constitutional sense (our elemental type of representative institutions); it must also be representative in the existen-

---

genesis of the American Constitution in the events between 1776 and 1789 furnishes perhaps the finest object-lesson for the growth of authoritative power in a new society, accompanied as it was by superb craftsmanship in devising legal forms for the stable structure. The case is of special importance for our analysis, because the protraction of the social process and the manner in which the questions of legality and constitutionality are subordinated to the questions of creating and ordering the nation leave no doubt whatsoever on which side the weight of the complex phenomenon of law lies" ("The Nature of the Law," 36–37).

13. "The Nature of the Law," 31, 33, 49–50. See also Sandoz, *Voegelinian Revolution*, 98–99.

14. "The Nature of the Law," 36.

tial sense of realizing the idea of the institution. And the implied warning may be explicated in the thesis: If a government is nothing but representative in the constitutional sense, a representative ruler in the existential sense will sooner or later make an end of it; and quite possibly the new existential ruler will not be too representative in the constitutional sense.[15]

What Voegelin seems to have in mind here is the not uncommon situation in which the presently ruling authority (whether "representative" in a constitutional sense or not) ceases to act effectively on behalf of its citizens, that is, it no longer acts in a way as to foster the "good life" for the people. In its failure, the de facto "elemental" representative has failed to realize the "idea" of that society, and is thereby in danger of being replaced by another authority that will more effectively embody the "idea" and thus represent the people not only elementally, but "existentially" as well, where *existentially* means precisely the ability of leadership to act effectively in realizing the "idea" of a society. Voegelin's point seems to be that when the elemental structure of society is no longer reflective of those underlying meanings that constitute the "idea" of a society, a tension will arise between the present "set-up" and the "idea" that was to be articulated in that institutional arrangement. As we shall see, this sort of tension was a topic at the very heart of Voegelin's enterprise.

Problems arise when elemental and existential representation do not coincide. In the works that followed *The New Science of Politics* (in particular the first three volumes of *Order and History*), Voegelin turned his attention to just these problems. The language of elemental and existential representation would disappear, however, as he began to probe more deeply into the source of all representation— human participation in the divine ground.

Until now the analysis has focused on the external dimension of society as it develops out of concrete consciousness. We have alluded thus far only to the fact that the "idea" of a given society emerges from a commonly shared understanding informing the process of social articulation. We have prescinded from questions as to the content of what is to be articulated in society. It is to such questions that we now turn.

15. Ibid., 49.

SOCIETY AND THE TRUTH OF ORDER

By reason of our concrete consciousness, every society is founded in bodily existence. Still, Voegelin would maintain that this external dimension of society does not completely explain social reality. Although it may be true that "the organization of society through representatives charged with care for the social order within and for defense against external dangers is the *conditio sine qua non* of society," at the same time "a theory of politics cannot stop there, since this part deals only with that aspect of political reality that is founded in man's corporeality. . . . A theory of politics must cover the problem of the order of man's entire existence." Indeed, it is this insight that seems to have provided Voegelin with the impetus to propose a "new" science of politics. While acknowledging that "the investigation and description of the various pragmatic organizations is a main part of political science," he also insisted that such an approach is incomplete.[16]

The reason that political science as an inventory of institutions and their practices is inadequate is that it limits itself to a description of phenomena in the external world, to "things" given in intentional consciousness. Just as a limitation of reality to the "externally" rendered thing-reality given in intentional consciousness overlooks the participation in the encompassing whole apprehended in consciousness as luminous, in similar fashion a narrow focus on the institutional structure of society, its "externality," bypasses the question of its ultimate ground and meaning.

Even though he had not yet elaborated his theory of consciousness, this insight was evident to Voegelin when he wrote *The New Science of Politics:*

> Human society is not merely a fact, or an event, in the external world to be studied by an observer like a natural phenomenon. Though it has externality as one of its important components, it is as a whole a little world, a cosmion, illuminated with meaning from within by the human beings who continuously create and bear it as the mode and condition of their self-realization. It is illuminated through an elaborate symbolism, in various degrees of compactness and differentiation—from rite, through myth, to theory—and this symbolism illuminates it with meaning in so far as the symbols make the internal

16. *Anamnesis,* 200; *New Science of Politics,* 1, 27, 35, 49–50.

structure of such a cosmion, the relations between its members and groups of members, as well as its existence as a whole, transparent for the mystery of human existence. The self-illumination of society through symbols is an integral part of social reality, and one may even say its essential part, for through such symbolization the members of a society experience it as more than an accident or convenience; they experience it as of their human essence. And inversely, the symbols express the experience that man is fully man by virtue of his partici-pation in a whole which transcends his particular existence, by virtue of his participation in the *xynon,* the common.[17]

Society is not simply a series of pragmatic responses to the needs for shelter, food, and so forth; the particular forms that these responses assume are in an even more important sense an expression of how human beings view themselves, their shared life, and the universe they inhabit.

Behind every social structure there are meanings that inform that structure. To know those meanings one must look at the symbols produced by each society in order to grasp how its people under-stand their place in reality: "Since a society expresses its experience of order by corresponding symbols, every study of order must con-centrate on the acts of self-understanding and then pursue from this center the ramifications into the order of collective existence—in other words, into the government and administration, the economy, the social hierarchy, the educational system, and so on." Symbols reveal how a group of people has oriented itself in the cosmos; to understand the meaning of a society's institutions one could do no better than to begin with an examination of its symbols. A symbol is not merely a visual or literary artifact produced by a society; a group of people does not suddenly decide to "create some symbols" after having mastered the demands of pragmatic existence. Symbolic ex-pression and its institutional embodiment are intimately intertwined. Symbols are *constitutive* of society in that they both express and shape the horizon of its members.[18]

When we attempt to get "behind" the symbols that constitute a society's self-understanding, we are once again brought face to face with the human experience of participation, for symbols are at-tempts to render that experience. Social existence is one of the four

17. *New Science of Politics,* 27–28.
18. *Anamnesis,* 205, 144.

fundamental "areas" articulated in the experience of participation. The proximate horizon of human participation is society, for human existence is always social. Like all experiences of participation, social existence involves an awareness of lasting and passing. One person dies, another lives; eventually I too will die, but the society to which I belong will not come to an end with my demise. The very regularities which we observe and in which we share while we live and which will continue after we die, the recurring schemes of social life, such as marriage, family life, birth, education, the ongoing procurement of food and shelter: all point to the lastingness of order beyond personal existence. In creating and maintaining societies, human beings attempt to perpetuate and secure this experienced lastingness, because it is the social sphere that is the primary field of order and it is in society that order is experienced with the greatest intensity and immediacy.[19]

The experienced lasting of society does not, however, exhaust the human quest for meaning. The continuation of society beyond one's personal existence prompts further questions as to the nature of the broader reality in which society itself is situated. After all, society may outlast me, but will it last forever? Societies come into existence and decline, while the world remains. And finally there are the immortal gods, whose lastingness exceeds even that of the world. The cosmos, of which society is but a part, consists of a hierarchy of being distinguished by varying degrees of lastingness. The meanings that inform a given society and the embodiment of these meanings in societal structures and symbols reflect this awareness, in the sense that our desire for "attunement" extends beyond the boundaries of the particular societies of which we are a part to the encompassing whole that includes not only every concrete society, but the gods and cosmos as well.[20]

No more than participation itself is this adjustment to the order of being a matter of indifference or choice. Although it may be the role of philosophers and prophets to elucidate this responsibility, the burden of attunement falls upon every man and woman. Far more is at stake than the continuation of biological existence; of even greater concern is "the profounder horror of losing, with the passing of

---

19. "The Nature of the Law," 41; *World of the Polis*, 1.
20. *Israel and Revelation*, 4.

existence, the slender foothold in the partnership of being that we experience as ours while existence lasts."[21]

It is this experienced need for attunement to the order of being that is expressed compactly through terms referring to a substance pervading that order: "Such terms are the Egyptian *maat,* the Chinese *tao,* the Greek *nomos,* and the Latin *lex [ius?].*" In more differentiated language this same experience will be rendered in terms of the relationship to the ground. The aforementioned mysterious "substance," the "idea" in need of social articulation is the expression of human participation in the ground. There exists a "common good," an "intencio populi," because all human beings share a common nature constituted by their relationship to the ground. What is articulated in the order of a society is a people's relationship to the ground in varying degrees of differentiation. At times this relationship will be expressed with compactness, as in the Egyptian notion of *maat,* while in other instances it will appear more completely differentiated in the respective Platonic and Israelite insights that the substance of society is psyche and that social life is to be ordered in the light of transcendence. In any case, what is common to all such formulations is the attempt to order social life in terms of the true order of reality apprehended in participation: "Every society is burdened with the task, under its concrete conditions, of creating an order that will endow the fact of its existence with meaning in terms of ends divine and human."[22]

Indeed, it is this orientation toward the ground that helps to distinguish a society as "political." For the most part Voegelin does not insist upon a careful distinction between *society* and *political society;* he often uses the two terms interchangeably.[23] But when he does differentiate the two, in order for a society to be a political one, two conditions must be met: (1) People must have articulated themselves as a society and produced a representative. (2) The society must seek to order its life in accordance with the truth discovered in tension toward the ground.[24] Where this acknowledg-

21. Ibid., 5.

22. "The Nature of the Law," 24; *Israel and Revelation,* ix.

23. In *The New Science of Politics* Voegelin tends to speak of "political society" (1, 31, 49). In the essay "What Is Political Reality?" from *Anamnesis,* the term *society* is used.

24. *New Science of Politics,* 27, 49; Sebba, "Prelude and Variations," in Sandoz, ed., *Eric Voegelin's Thought,* 21.

ment of the ground is lacking, we can speak of "masses" but not of political society.[25] Like the Greek philosophers whom he admired, Voegelin believed that authentic human life is always social, and that genuine social existence is always political. Like Plato and Aristotle, Voegelin viewed society as the context in which the good life, that is, life lived in accordance with the truth of order, is made possible; and that good life is only possible in a political society in which there are institutions in place to provide the security and material means for its emergence.

Whether experienced compactly, as life in accordance with *maat*, or more differentiatedly, as existence in relationship to the ground, the process of attunement is marked by a certain degree of tension. This tension stems from the fact that people experience the possibility of a fall from being as somehow tied in with their own response to the truth of order revealed in participation. Human beings experience an obligation to attune the order of their existence to the order of being: "Within the range of society, the realization of the order of being is experienced as the burden of man. When we refer to the 'tension' in social order, we envisage this class of experiences."[26] In addition, then, to satisfying the pragmatic needs for food, shelter, and so forth, which stem from the externality of society, there is also the tension resulting from the need to order social existence in the light of the divine ground. Every society is confronted with two tasks: to insure its continued existence in the world, and to order itself in accordance with the true order of reality as it emerges in participation. The tension that characterizes social life arises from this attempt to satisfy the exigencies of pragmatic existence while simultaneously embodying the truth of order in social form.[27] The experience of order imposes an obligation on the participants to realize this order in the social sphere. This experienced pressure to bring social order into conformity with divine order is a permanent feature of human life; the tension can never be abolished.[28]

25. Voegelin, "The German University and the Order of German Society: A Reconsideration of the Nazi Era," 26–27.

26. "The Nature of the Law," 43–44.

27. In "The Nature of the Law," Voegelin refers to this tension between empirical and divine order as the "Ought in the ontological sense" (p. 44). The term seems not to have occurred in his later work.

28. Ibid., 59–60, 61.

Within this tension, social life unfolds. Human reason mediates between participation in the ground of being and the social embodiment of this experience. Every society represents an attempt at attunement to the truth of order. In every case it is a matter of trial and error; the truth of order is never discovered as a social blueprint or as a set of eternal and immutable "natural laws" to be applied to concrete situations.[29] For this reason there always exists the possibility that human beings may miss the mark in their struggle to attune social order to the divine ground. The goodness of a society depends on the actions of its citizens; human beings are free and responsible for the existence and continued survival of their societies. The good society does not come about by following an easily instituted plan or blueprint; what is needed is imagination, experimentation, and the flexibility to embody the truth of order in light of existing exigencies. This is a struggle in that there will always be a tension "between standard and achievement, between achievement and the potentiality of falling short of it, between a groping for knowledge of order and the crystallization of that knowledge in articulate rules, between the order as projected and the order as realized, between what ought to be and what is."[30]

The tension is always in relationship to the mysterious ground of being whose presence then needs to be translated into social life by means of human insight and ingenuity. The key, then, to the successful incarnation of order in society is not the discovery of universal and necessary ethical laws, but rather the openness of humans to the divine ground, or, in other words, the permeability of human existence to the movement of being. This openness is, in Voegelin's work,

> the almost forgotten knowledge of the philosopher, that ethics is not a matter of moral principles, nor a retreat from the complexities of the world, nor a contraction of existence into eschatological expectation or readiness, but a matter of the truth of existence in the reality of action in concrete situations. What matters is not correct principles about what is right by nature in an immutable generality, nor the acute consciousness of the tension between the immutable truth and its mutable application (possibly even with tragic overtones), but the changeability, the *kineton* itself, and the methods to lift it to the reality

29. In particular, see Voegelin's treatment of "right by nature" in Aristotle (*Anamnesis*, 60–61).
30. "The Nature of the Law," 43.

of truth. The truth of existence is attained where it becomes concrete, i.e., in action.[31]

Were people to always act with the intelligence that stems from living in attunement toward the ground, the possibility would be greater of realizing a social order that reflects the truth of order. Unfortunately and all too often, such disturbing human tendencies as pride, inertia, cowardice, complacency, ignorance, and folly interfere with this achievement. The passions, then, are every bit as much a part of the human person as is *nous*. Because of this, the degree to which people allow themselves to be permeated by the ground of being will vary widely. Although what is distinctive about human nature may be our potential responsiveness to reason, when confronted with a concrete situation there is no guarantee that reason will always prevail.[32] Some will allow themselves to be controlled by their passions and lusts, thus disturbing and hindering the realization of order in society.

What is to be the response of society to the presence of such disorderly and destabilizing passions? We recall that the necessity for an organized rulership arose not only from the exigencies of providing for the material needs of the populace but also in order to restrain the passions. It is also the case that a society can be recognized as such only to the degree that it insures its own lastingness in time. Selfish passions undermine the cooperation required to sustain social life. If passions, then, were to be given full rein, society as a lasting order would cease to exist. To prevent this from happening, allowance must be made for the use of force.[33]

The primary reason for employing force is that people do not always act intelligently, and consequently they may need to be compelled to act in accordance with the truth of order. Another reason is that there are often several equally sensible ways in which to solve concrete problems concerning the common good, but they cannot all be chosen. A particular approach must be selected, and once that is done those who may have opposed such a solution must cooperate in the implementation of the chosen plan for the good of society as a whole. If they refuse to do so or in any way attempt to sabotage the

31. *Anamnesis,* 63.
32. "The Nature of the Law," 63; *Anamnesis,* 64–65; Voegelin, "On Readiness to Rational Discussion," 270.
33. *Anamnesis,* 200; "The Nature of the Law," 61–64.

adopted approach, then compulsion may be required. Finally, a resort to force may be required because of the inevitable "calculus of
error" involved in every attempted realization of order in social
terms. All people, including those representatives and leaders
charged with the implementation of order, are liable to the sometimes disordering effects of the passions. As a result, the tension
between true order and empirical order can never be permanently
abolished. When the members of a society, with the truth of order as
their criterion, become dissatisfied with the imperfection of their
representatives, it may be necessary to use force in order to counter
such unrealizable demands for perfection: "We have only to imagine
what would happen if taxpayers could refuse payment until the ex-
penditures of the government stand rational scrutiny in the light of
true order. If the existence of society is to be preserved, the debate
cannot be permitted to degenerate into individual decision and
resistance."[34]

Before deposing or replacing a society's organized rulership in
the name of the truth of order, that society's members must balance
the potentially disruptive results of the desired change against the
need for the stability and lastingness that make society possible at all:

> The tension between true order and empirical order, we conclude,
> never can be abolished, though the discrepancy can be held, by var-
> ious devices, to a minimum that will not motivate the people to revolt.
> Even a not-so-good representative may be preferable to a violent up-
> heaval, given the inevitable and incalculable disorganization of life
> that accompanies a revolution and the not-at-all-certain prospect that
> the next representative will be any better than his predecessor. The
> undisturbed order of society enters as a good in its own right into the
> normativity of legal rules. In every society, the lawmaking process
> rests for its validity on the understanding that a considerable margin
> of error must be allowed with regard to the truth of order in the on-
> tological sense. Although there are limits to the proportions that the
> error may assume, existence in an imperfectly ordered society, with
> numerous and even gross injustices in single cases, is preferable to dis-
> order and violence.[35]

Confronted with the possibility of social chaos stemming from an
overly zealous attempt to bring social order into conformity with the

34. "The Nature of the Law," 61–62.
35. Ibid.

order of being, it is wise to remember that imperfect attunement is better than disorder.[36]

It seems, then, that as long as there is tension between the truth of order and the empirical order of society, the use of force will remain a permanent means of balancing the demands of true order with those of pragmatic survival. In his review of a volume dealing with the relationship between law and the international order, Voegelin writes:

> There seems to be a connection between the idea of order and the existence of a power to maintain it. While Professor Scott is certainly justified in asserting frequently that might does not make right, it is unfortunately equally true that it makes an order, and that without it an order can be neither created nor maintained. Because the possession of power does not grant the righteousness of the order maintained by it, power and the application of force frequently are found to be immoral in themselves. It seems to be one of the most difficult things for a political thinker to separate clearly the problem of the contents of an order from the problems of enforcing it. The question of right enters into the principles on which an order is built; the maintenance of an order will have always, human nature being what it is, to rely on the instrument of force.[37]

The creation of social order is a difficult task. The truth of order apprehended in participatory consciousness is not easily translated into institutional form. The problem stems from the constitution of the human person, who, on the basis of consciousness, is oriented toward the life of reason, that is, existence as an unfolding of the response toward the ground of being, but who, on the basis of corporeality, must provide for material needs and rightly order the passions. The resulting tension characterizes social life as people seek to strike a balance between the embodiment of the truth of order and the demands of pragmatic existence in the world. Their efforts to do so, "while imperfect, do not form a senseless series of failures."[38] What such efforts do manifest is a series of responses to differentiations of consciousness.

36. *Israel and Revelation,* 11.
37. "Right and Might," in *Collected Works,* vol. 27, 86.
38. *Israel and Revelation,* ix.

SOCIAL ORDER AND DIFFERENTIATIONS OF CONSCIOUSNESS

Differentiations of consciousness always occur within a society. It is in the consciousness of concrete men and women that order is experienced, and it is there that the differentiations arise. When the tension of existence between the truth of order apprehended in participation and the imperfect, passing social order in which one lives becomes too great to be encompassed by the present symbolization of order, then the stage is set for differentiation. The particular institutional and cultural order of the society may set the conditions for the occurrence of differentiation, but cannot be said to determine or cause it.[39] Not every social and cultural setting is equally conducive to differentiation: "The great noetic and pneumatic differentiations do not occur among paleolithic hunters and fishers, but in ages of cities and empires; some social and cultural situations appear to be more favorable to differentiating responses than others. The structure of man's earthly existence in society, thus, is somehow involved in the process of differentiating consciousness." From Voegelin's perspective, no definitive answer can be given as to why differentiations happen when they do;[40] we can only observe that certain social settings and conditions seem to favor their emergence.

Often it is social disorder that creates a situation ripe for differentiation. In such cases the surrounding social corruption prompts the philosopher or prophet to seek knowledge of that order by which one can call the present social order to account, whether the criterion discovered be divine Nous or the word of God. And yet even where it is the experience of disorder that evokes the pursuit of true order, the resultant differentiation is never solely a reaction to social chaos, but has also been prepared in some sense by the previous development of the society in which it takes place. In the preceding paragraph we noted how certain levels of social development seemed to be better suited for the emergence of differentiations than others. The level of knowledge of the ground achieved within a particular society and the degree to which this knowledge has been translated into its institutions is also of crucial importance in creating a climate

---

39. *Anamnesis*, 200; *Plato and Aristotle*, 247, 323; *Ecumenic Age*, 306; "History and Gnosis," 85; "What Is History?," 36; "The Nature of the Law," 67.

40. *Ecumenic Age*, 306, 316–18.

for differentiation. In this regard Voegelin notes how the work of Plato and Aristotle would have appeared as "odd fancies" to their contemporaries had not the stage for such a project been set by the historical precedent of the Athens of Marathon and the public cult of tragedy. Likewise, the revelation to Moses of the God beyond the gods, while certainly a decisive break with cosmological form, arose in a context where movements in the direction of monotheism were already developing. In other words, while social disorder may be a catalyst in the process of differentiation, it remains only one of the contributing factors, albeit an important one. If disorder were the sole determinant of differentiation, one would expect the appearance of differentiations wherever the members of a society experience themselves as threatened; and yet in the case of cosmological empires, social crisis does not lead to a break with the compact mode of symbolization, but rather to the development of the cosmological symbolism of historiogenesis.[41]

Both the material conditions of a given society and the level of differentiation already attained by that society are factors influencing whether or not there will be further differentiation. In the following passage Voegelin speaks of how these two factors mutually condition one another to create situations in which "experiences of transcendence" are possible:

> The context in which the experience of transcendence was supposed to appear turned out to be not a rigid set of institutions, customs, and beliefs but a medium that could be softened by unsettling disturbances to the point of receptivity, while the experience occurred not just once and fully actualized but repeatedly and in various deficient modes. The setting furthermore affected the expression of the experience, and the expressive symbolism became, through communication, part of the setting, thereby increasing its receptivity for future and more articulate experiences. Setting and experience thus lost their identity as they dissolved into a medium in a state of fermentation.[42]

Differentiation and the setting in which it occurs tend to merge, the setting affecting the manner in which experience of the divine

41. *New Science of Politics*, 70–71; *Israel and Revelation*, 413–14; Voegelin, "Anxiety and Reason," in *Collected Works*, vol. 28. See also Barry Cooper, *The Political Theory of Eric Voegelin*, 134–44.
42. "What Is History?," 33.

ground is articulated and the symbols thus articulated conditioning the setting, making it more receptive to further differentiation.

When conditions are fortuitous, that is, when both setting and experience converge in such a way as to create a context in which further differentiation is possible, certain individuals may attain those epoch-making insights into the structure of reality whose intensity and importance are such that they are designated as "leaps in being," "spiritual outbursts," or "differentiations of consciousness." Why it is that only certain people and communities are the recipients of such insights is, as Voegelin saw it, part of the mystery of history.[43]

With a differentiation, the structure and movement of reality comes to be understood more clearly. The individuals in whom the differentiation emerges become more conscious of the truth of order, since to become more fully aware of the structure of reality is to be illuminated as to the standard by which societies are to be judged in their attempts to attune themselves to the ground of being. The differentiation, however, is not the private possession of the recipient; what has differentiated in the consciousness of the individual is the structure of reality in which *all* participate; what is evoked is the *xynon* in which all people share.

Individuals in whom a differentiation of consciousness takes place receive it on behalf of all humanity, whether or not they are aware of it at the time: "Inasmuch as by the outbursts a truth about human existence is discovered, the human vessels of the spirit discover it representatively for mankind; and inasmuch as they realize the truth in their existence, they become the carriers of representative humanity." Nor is this experience merely "subjective," for what is revealed is the very tension toward the divine ground that constitutes humanity. According to Voegelin, "The experience of transcendence is representative by its essence," and it is discovered to be "valid not only for the man who has the experience but for every man, because the very idea of man arises from its realization in the presence under God."[44] Understanding this point is crucial to our correctly understanding Voegelin's project. If a social order is to be just and coherent, it must seek as far as possible to incarnate the truth of divine

43. *Ecumenic Age,* 316; "History and Gnosis," 76.
44. Voegelin, "What Is History?," 46–47, 49. See also *World of the Polis,* 6; and "History and Gnosis," 76.

order in its own order and structures. To do this, though, the members of society (or at least their representatives) must not lose contact with the experience of participation in the ground in which the truth of order is encountered, whether that experience be compact or differentiated. A great deal of Voegelin's work was precisely an attempt to recover these experiences by moving through symbols to the experiences underlying them. Far from mere "subjective theorizing," he would maintain that he was engaged in the most empirical and "objective" pursuit of all—the recovery of reality. As evidence he would appeal to the trail of symbols found in cultures of every age, all of which seem to indicate an awareness of participation with varying degrees of differentiation. If a person is to be intellectually honest when confronted with this data, he or she must be willing to ask the further questions as to what it is that lies behind and beyond this plethora of overlapping symbolic expression. To dismiss such omnipresent, cross-cultural phenomena as "subjective" experiences, in the sense of their being private or illusory, without seeking to analyze the experiences behind them would be, for Voegelin, an example of intellectual obscurantism and a dangerous eclipse of reality.[45] It is the underlying equivalence of experiences and their symbolizations that enables the person in whom a differentiation of consciousness occurs to serve in the capacity of representative humanity.

The role of representative humanity carries with it a responsibility to communicate the fruits of the differentiation, so that one's society might better attune itself to the order of being now more clearly differentiated. To the extent that the recipients of these important insights into the truth of order are able to communicate their vision to others and have it accepted by them, they and their communities can be said to constitute a new "social field." A social field is neither an area nor an empirical object; rather, it is a process in which communicated experiences of order are "understood by other concrete men who accept them as their own and make them into the motive of their habitual actions."[46]

A question that naturally arises is, What is the relationship between a social field and a society? Social fields are called societies "if

45. *Autobiographical Reflections*, 93–101; *New Science of Politics*, 64; "Equivalences," 115–33.
46. *World of the Polis*, 6; *Anamnesis*, 202. See also *In Search of Order*, 25; "The Nature of the Law," 56; and "Gospel and Culture," 190.

their size and relative stability in time allows us to identify them." The key here is the notion of "relative stability in time." Remember that, for Voegelin, a crucial constitutive dimension of a "society" is an effective organization that enables it to endure in time by providing for the defense and the flourishing of its members. The stability, size, and duration of this organizational structure would seem to be what distinguishes a society from a social field. Yet while this may be the case, Voegelin acknowledges that a social field, even if it is not a full-fledged society, must also possess a certain degree of durability and must be able to attract adherents if it is to have any influence.[47] It is thus the "relative" stability of a social entity that can help us to differentiate between society and social field. Where a group of people united by a common social field are able to structure their life together in such a way so as to meet both the pragmatic exigencies of life and the experienced need for attunement to the truth of order, and when the arrangement they have evolved is able to endure in time, then we have the case of a social field whose effectiveness in striking a balance between mundane and transcendent concerns enables it to be recognized as a society. Every society, then, is sustained by a social field that has attained a sufficient degree of stability to maintain its existence in the world, albeit imperfectly. From this distinction between society and social field it follows that while every society is supported by a social field, not every social field constitutes a society.

Further questions arise, though: What is the relationship between the sustaining social field of a society and other social fields that develop within that society? Is it the case that the social field underpinning an organized society exhausts the possibilities of social reality for that society? Voegelin explains:

> The social fields of concrete consciousness are not identical with organized societies, even though the ideologists of power like to assume that social organization exhausts all political reality. We are in the realm of freedom of the concrete consciousness. True, every organized society is sustained by a social field of consciousness expressed in the respective civil theology, but that sustaining consciousness is not the only social field in society and many of the other fields far transcend the area of social power. One may refer to the danger to

47. *Anamnesis*, 202; *In Search of Order*, 25.

the national consciousness constituted by the ideological social fields in our time and also to the precarious compromise of pluralistic democracy, by means of which one hopes to maintain a balance between the potentially disruptive fields and the sustaining field of an organized society. Furthermore, the fields of consciousness are not personally and mutually exclusive, as they must be in organized societies with their basis in corporeality; rather a concrete consciousness may belong to several fields at the same time. A Greek living in the fourth century B.C., for instance, can be simultaneously an Athenian and a Hellene, a Sophist or philosopher, and a member of a mystery cult.[48]

While it is true that all social fields arise within the context of a particular society whose level of development both materially and spiritually may condition their emergence, they are not determined or bound by the limitations of that society. While they may be influenced by pragmatic factors, social fields emerge on the level of consciousness, and on the level of consciousness one can belong to a number of social fields simultaneously. Problems may develop, however, owing to the fact that consciousness is also always concrete, that is, embodied. A social field may originate on the level of consciousness, but from differentiated consciousness it moves toward communication and ultimately to action. The truth of order is not only discovered; it is to be communicated and acted upon. It is at the level of action that the newly emergent field may come into conflict with the sustaining field of the society that has given rise to it, because the level of action is the level of corporeality where concrete choices are to be made as to how society is to be structured. The fields of consciousness may not be "personally and mutually exclusive," but in organized society, with its "basis in corporeality," not every social field can prevail. This problem of competing social fields may also force individuals to choose one way of life over another because of the mutually exclusive claims of each field.

What happens, then, when a differentiation of consciousness occurs in a society and engenders a new social field? The truth discovered in the differentiation represents an advance in knowledge into the structure of reality, and as such it serves as a new standard by which to judge the society in which it arises. In some cases it is the obvious corruption of the present society that gives rise to the pur-

48. *Anamnesis*, 202.

suit of true order, which, when discovered, becomes the criterion for judgment as to the deficiencies of the present social order. In other instances it is simply a matter of coming to recognize the inauthenticity of one's society in the light of the new differentiation. The communication of this differentiation of consciousness constitutes the new social field, which may come into conflict with the dominant social field.[49]

The new differentiation represents a more exacting standard by which to evaluate the attunement of the society in which it occurs. The increase of clarity as to the structure of reality is accompanied by an increase in the tension between the more clearly illuminated truth of order and the present social order. The bearers of the differentiation may then come into tension both with the existing representatives of the society and with the populace as a whole. If this happens, the society may become embroiled in a contest between competing claims to authority. The bearers of the "new" truth are obliged to call their societies to live in its light, and the societies have an obligation to heed. Tradition, custom, and the weight of ancestral authority, however, often prevent the truth of order from finding a welcome reception. What results, then, is a conflict as to who will be recognized as representative of public order and a struggle for social effectiveness.[50]

The representatives of the newly discovered truth pose a challenge to the prevailing structures of their society as they call upon society's present representatives to implement the vision of order arising from the differentiation of consciousness. In the light of differentiation, the imperfections of a given society may come to be viewed as intolerable by the new bearers of truth, and the truth imperfectly embodied in that society may be disdained as falsehood. If the new representatives of the truth of order can create suitable symbols, if they can find a sufficient number of adherents to their vision, and if they can devise durable forms of social organization, then they may create a new social field. From this fresh perspective, older social fields may come to be viewed as representative of falsehood, but adherents of the older way of life may react strongly

49. *In Search of Order,* 25.
50. Voegelin, "What Is History?," 48. See also *New Science of Politics,* 67; and *Plato and Aristotle,* 38–39.

against the new vision. Of equal concern to the new representatives of order are the spiritual dullness and apathy of the majority, and the skepticism engendered by the appearance within society of competing "truths."[51]

The question arises, then, as to why anyone would acknowledge the authority of a new witness to the truth of order. Why place one's faith in the vision of a person at odds with the venerable traditions of one's society? The only possible answer is that the philosopher or prophet who gains the faith of the people appeals to that level of reality in which even social authority and traditions are grounded, that is, the level in which humans are constituted by their relationship to the ground: "Using the Heraclitian distinction of public and private, we may say, the appeal will be no more than a private *(idios)* opinion unless the questioner finds in the course of his quest the word *(logos)* that indeed speaks what is common *(xynon)* to the order of man's existence as a partner in the comprehending reality; only if the questioner speaks the common logos of reality can he evoke a truly public order."[52]

If the new insights are communicated in such a way as to inspire others to make them the basis of their actions, if the newly discovered truth can evoke a positive response among a relatively significant number of people, and if the group thus constituted is able to organize itself so as to endure even in the hostile environment of the status quo that it challenges, we then have the emergence of a new and effective social field. When only some of these conditions are fulfilled, the truth of order may shrink into a tightly knit but socially ineffective group; when none of the conditions are met, order may contract into the soul of the rejected individual who represents humanity. But if, instead, the new social field eventually prevails in the battle for representation and becomes the dominant and lasting social field, it would then be a case of a social field achieving the requisite stability and size enabling it to be designated a society.

To conclude, what can be said of the relationship between differentiations of consciousness and the societies in which they occur? To begin with, all differentiations are responses to individuals' being

51. *In Search of Order,* 25.
52. Ibid., 26.

moved or drawn by the It-reality. Such responses always take place within a society, because the differentiations of consciousness emerge in the concrete consciousness of human beings, and human beings are social beings. What this means is that the possibility of differentiation is conditioned to some extent by the type of society in which it occurs; some social and cultural situations seem more conducive to differentiation than others. The particular conditions of a society, then, establish the context within which a differentiation takes place. If a differentiation does take place, its recipients, as bearers of a newly found standard of order, may challenge the prevailing order from which the differentiation emerged. The tension resulting from the conflict of competing social fields sets new social conditions that may result in further differentiations. It is this constant interplay between differentiation, social field, and society that marks the unfolding of human existence. Society sets the conditions for differentiation; in turn, differentiations give rise to new social fields, which may or may not develop into new societies setting the conditions for further differentiations. Propelling the entire process is the inevitable tension between the truth of order and its attempted realization in social order. The crucial issue, then, is the degree to which the discovered truth can be made effective in society. I believe this question to be at the heart of Voegelin's work: Can the truth of order become socially effective? Or, in other words, Is the good society possible?

F O U R

D E R A I L M E N T
Society and Disorder

CONCRETE CONSCIOUSNESS AND THE
POSSIBILITY OF DISORDER

Asking the question Can the truth of order be implemented effectively within society? implies the possibility that it could fail to be realized. For Voegelin, such a scenario was more than a possibility; he had been exposed firsthand to the consequences of society's failure to take seriously the need for attunement to the ground. Indeed, it was the experience of just such a failure and the ensuing emergence of socially effective and murderous carriers of disorder that served as an important catalyst in his philosophical enterprise.[1] It is to the problem of the social effectiveness of disorder that we now turn. We will proceed by tracing the source of disorder to its origins in concrete consciousness, followed by an analysis of the loss of reality stemming from such aberrations, and concluding with a discussion of the consequences of this loss for social life.

Were all people to acknowledge and respond with openness to the tensions experienced through participation in the It-reality, the human story would consist of a series of ever more accurate attempts to bring social and political life into harmony with the differentiating truth of order. But such is not the case. There is in society disorder as well as order. And just as the pursuit and discovery of order has its source in human consciousness, so too the basis of disordered existence is to be found in this same consciousness

---

1. Voegelin, "Autobiographical Statement," 117. See also Voegelin, *Autobiographical Reflections,* 93.

gone awry. What is it, then, about consciousness that enables this to happen?

Consciousness is free. It is in the freedom of consciousness that the potential for derailment can be found, since participation in reality does not automatically generate a correct understanding of that participation. Voegelin explains, "Consciousness has a dimension of freedom in the design of images of reality in which are found such disparate phenomena as mythopoeic freedom, artistic creation, gnostic and alchemistic speculation, the private world view of liberal citizens, and the constructions of ideological systems." The questioning unrest that marks a truly human response toward the ground can be blocked, ignored, led astray, or rejected. Opportunities for attunement can be and often are missed. People choose whether or not to follow the unfolding of their questions and the attraction of the ground; "it does not follow that, because man is by nature responsive to reason, he will, in fact, allow himself to be governed by it when faced with a concrete, historical situation."[2]

This ambiguous freedom of consciousness accounts for the "dualism" of the psyche: "However multifarious the desires may be, and however many of them may be distinguished by psychological description, they are overshadowed by the sense of basic dualism in the psyche: Autonomous man can order himself and society either by orienting himself toward transcendence or by emancipating himself as a world-immanent existence. In Augustinian language: Man can live either *secundum Deum* or *secundum hominem*." The potential for derailment is always present in consciousness. "Madness" and "reason" are not simply alternative types of existence or the normal sequence of stages through which every individual or society must pass; each is an ever-present possibility within the structure of consciousness. It should be noted here as well that the passions and desires are not the primary causes of disorder, although they may contribute to a state in which the recovery of reason is difficult. While the passions may be very much a part of human existence and may indeed exercise a disruptive influence on individuals and society when not intelligently ordered, their ability to dominate human life is the *result* of a distortion in the unfolding of questioning unrest.

2. *Anamnesis*, 168; "On Readiness," 270, 282. See also *Anamnesis*, 100–101; and *In Search of Order*, 39.

Diseases of the spirit have their origin in "man's freedom to actualize the meaning of humanity potentially contained in the unrest or to botch the meaning"; aberrations of the passions proceed from these prior disturbances.[3]

The danger present in the freedom of consciousness is that the tension toward the ground, which is constitutive of humanity, may be effectively blocked. The differentiation of consciousness is accompanied by the possibility of deforming the structure of consciousness engaged in the differentiation. The articulation and experience of the Beginning and the Beyond can be so overwhelming as to result in a loss of balance, a rejection of existence in the metaxy. As noted in Chapter 2, the pneumatic differentiation of the divine Beyond is particularly liable to this kind of deformation. The unfolding of our questioning unrest, which propels us toward the discovery of that truth of order in light of which we structure human existence, contains within itself the potential for derailment. The Beyond that is the goal of questioning may be deformed into a thing whose parousia can be realized within history by human means.[4]

Voegelin traces the source of these problems to the freedom of consciousness in its mode of "imagination."[5] By means of imagination human beings move from experiences of participation to symbols that reveal those experiences. Yet this very power to create images of reality can be mistaken for the ability to create or alter the structure of reality. Instead of clarifying the metaleptic tension by creating images that reflect the openness of consciousness toward reality, "the metaleptic tension can be obscured by letting the reality that reveals itself in imaginative truth imaginatively dissolve into a truth that reveals reality." The great philosophers and religious figures have always sought to improve upon the symbols they have inherited so as to enable these symbols to speak more effectively of reality. Differentiating consciousness finds in earlier symbolizations inadequate attempts at articulating the truth of order. While this may very well be the case, the thinker in whom the differentiation

3. Voegelin, "What Is History?," 32; "Wisdom and the Magic," 329; *Anamnesis,* 101.
4. *In Search of Order,* 33.
5. Ibid., 37–38. Imagination, for Voegelin, was not primarily a "faculty" enabling people to create symbols, but a structure of concrete consciousness, sharing in both intentionality and luminosity.

occurs must scrupulously avoid the temptation to assume that his ability to better symbolize the structure and movement of reality means that he possesses the power to alter that structure or to escape the tension of existence.[6]

There are a number of reasons that some questioners succumb to this "imaginative oblivion." Often the catalyst is to be found in their dissatisfaction with present reality. When the truth of order has differentiated, and in particular when the eschatological Beyond reveals itself, the tension of living in a society and in a world in which this order is not adequately realized can become difficult to bear. In addition there is the uncertainty that comes from no longer living in a world full of gods and having only the tenuous link of faith to connect oneself with the divine. For some, this uncertainty can become unbearable, in which case the tension of existence must be overcome. The contrast between newly revealed truth and the imperfection of human life, with its disease, hunger, labor, and injustice, can lead to a profound disaffection with and even rebellion against the order of existence: "At this point, when the resistance to disorder transforms itself into a revolt against the very process of reality and its structure, the tension of formative existence in the divine-human movement and countermovement of the metaxy can break down." What is important to understand is that the resistance to reality often has its origins in the quite valid resistance to disorder that accompanies the differentiation of consciousness; "regarding the tension between dream and reality the activist's consciousness does not differ from the philosopher's." Deformations of consciousness stem from the impulse to embody order in society. In cases of deformation, though, we have attempts at attunement that have gone awry because of a refusal to live within the tension between the imperfection of society and the perfection of order. The crucial point of divergence between resister and philosopher is that the former believes in his own power to transfigure the structure of reality.[7]

THE ECLIPSE OF REALITY

The refusal to acknowledge the structure of reality and the desire to escape the tension of existence result in an "eclipse" of reality. While

6. Ibid., 39, 40–41. See also Voegelin, "Wisdom and the Magic," 317–18, 338–39.
7. Voegelin, *Science, Politics, and Gnosticism*, 107–8; *In Search of Order*, 36–37, 39, 40–41; "Wisdom and the Magic," 323–24.

it is within our power to either obscure our participation in reality or allow it to be brought to the clarity of consciousness, we have no choice as to whether or not we participate. We may rebel against existence in the metaxy, but even in rebellion we remain within the tension of existence. Dissatisfaction with the human condition does not abolish it. What often happens, though, is that the rejection of reason through acts of imaginative oblivion becomes a pathological condition in the resister, resulting in a distortion within the structure of consciousness. From Cicero, Voegelin recovered the symbol *aspernatio rationis* to describe the rejection of reason (understood as openness to the divine ground), and from Heimito von Doderer, he borrowed the symbol *Apperzeptionsverweigerung* to speak of the refusal to apperceive reality.[8] Related to and falling within the range of meaning of these symbols for the eclipse of reality are numerous other common subphenomena, including "selective conscience," "defensive obtuseness," and "a variety of disorderly phenomena ranging from the intellectual crookedness of political activists, through the semiliteracy of trendy career opportunists and the profounder illiteracy imposed by the educational system, to plain stupidity." In any given case of deformed consciousness "it is difficult, if not impossible, to determine . . . whether the suspension is an act of intellectual fraud or of persuasive self-deception."[9]

Voegelin describes the consequences of this eclipse of reality:

> There is no other reality than that of which we have experience. When a person refuses to live in existential tension toward the ground, or if he rebels against the ground, refusing to participate in reality and in this way to experience his own reality as man, it is not the "world" that is thereby changed but rather he who loses contact with reality and in his own person suffers a loss of reality. Since that does not make him cease to be a man, and since his consciousness continues to function within the form of reality, he will generate *ersatz* images of reality in order to obtain order and direction for his existence and action in the world. He then lives in a "second reality," as this phenomenon is called, since Musil's *Man without Qualities*.[10]

We then have a situation in which consciousness acts in such a way as to block one's knowledge of participation. At the same time, this

---

8. "Wisdom and the Magic," 322; *Anamnesis*, 101; *In Search of Order,* 46–47.
9. *In Search of Order,* 47; "Wisdom and the Magic," 316.
10. *Anamnesis*, 170.

obscuring of the consciousness of reality abolishes neither consciousness nor reality. The "form" of consciousness remains despite the loss
of "content," that is, the loss of reality. Imagination will continue to
bring forth images and symbols as a means of orienting the person
within the world. But since contact with the structure of reality has
been lost because of the refusal to apperceive, the images generated
will not correspond to the truth of order. Under such conditions
human existence becomes a matter of meanings and actions structured in accordance with the "second realities" thus generated in
opposition to the "first reality" of "common experience," that is,
existence in tension toward the ground.[11] The foundation is thus
prepared for those utopias and "dream worlds" that are the products
of minds that can insist on the possibility of realizing perfection on
earth because they refuse to acknowledge the tension of existence
and the limitations it imposes on human possibility.[12]

A number of consequences flow from disordered consciousness
and its creation of "second realities." The suspension of existential
consciousness does not make the problems of living in the metaxy
disappear—human existence remains a matter of striking a balance
between the exigencies of life in the world and the truth of order
discerned in differentiations of consciousness. Voegelin maintains
that at some level the resisting dreamer is aware of this tension. The
dreamer, like the philosopher, can distinguish between first and second realities, but out of either pride or ignorance the dreamer blocks
out that knowledge of reality that would interfere with his dream of

11. Voegelin, "The Eclipse of Reality," 114. See also Voegelin, "Extended
Strategy: A New Technique of Dynamic Relations," 199–200; as well as *Science,
Politics, and Gnosticism,* 35; and "German University," 16.

12. Voegelin, *Science, Politics, and Gnosticism,* 53, 88–92. See also "Wisdom
and the Magic," 316–23; and "What Is History?," 51. Voegelin describes a utopia
as a "model of a perfect society that cannot be realized because an important
sector of reality has been omitted from its construction, but its author and
addicts have suspended their consciousness that it is unrealizable because of the
omission" ("Wisdom and the Magic," 316). Voegelin refers to incomplete models
of society in which only certain evils are specified for elimination, e.g., private
property, as "ideals." He makes a further distinction between utopias and the
vision of the activist mystic or dreamer. Utopias offer images of what ought to be
without spelling out clearly the means by which it is to be realized. In the vision
of the activist this image of perfection is joined to a teleological notion of
progress toward the goal of perfection in time (derived from the Christian goal
of perfection *beyond* time) in which the means of attainment are known to the
activist (*Science, Politics, and Gnosticism,* 88–92).

perfection. The dreamer must somehow acknowledge the reality he wishes to change or abolish, because, however much he may rebel against mundane imperfection, he still remains within the world. The dream of perfection thus presupposes at least some recognition of the first reality that is to be transformed. The resister is also reminded of the eclipsed tension because the first reality, eclipsed but not abolished, continues to make its presence felt in consciousness.[13]

The metaxy, then, must somehow be reproduced within the boundaries of the second reality. What happens is that the tensions of the metaxy are transposed to the domain of deformation, and new kinds of cognition and language must be constructed to reproduce the tension of existence under these disordered conditions.[14] The dreamer and the philosopher both seek to orient themselves within reality, a reality with the structure of metaxy. Since this structure has been blocked from consciousness in the mind of the dreamer, the result is a situation in which the metaxy is reconstructed in terms of the deformation. However, even deformed consciousness seeks to offer an intelligible account of reality, so the dreamer will create an account of consciousness that makes sense within the conditions of the second reality. In addition, the continued presence in consciousness of the eclipsed first reality increases the pressure on the "imaginators" (another Voegelinian term for those who block reality from consciousness) to reconcile their images of reality with the unacknowledged truth of order: "As the world of common experience can be eclipsed but not abolished, it will resist its deformation and, in its turn, force the imaginators to revise their Second Realities. Imaginative projecting will not be given up as senseless, but specific projects will be changed in detail or replaced by new ones. During the period under discussion, revisionism is a common phenomenon, caused by the refusal to dissolve the contracted self and to stop projecting."[15] The new account of consciousness involves a rejection of consciousness as luminous and its replacement by an intentional consciousness that is better suited to describe a reality that has become "objectified" through the loss of the tension of existence. In these unfortu-

13. Voegelin, "Wisdom and the Magic," 243; "Eclipse of Reality," 114, 116.
14. "Wisdom and the Magic," 266–67.
15. "Eclipse of Reality," 116.

nate tendencies, Voegelin finds the origins of propositional meta-physics and dogmatic theologies.[16]

The hypostatization of the poles that structure reality is a result of the eclipse of reality in consciousness. At times Voegelin wrote as if in the process of deformation the hypostatization of the tensional poles precedes the emergence of intentional consciousness, and in other instances he wrote as if intentional consciousness is the prerequisite for the objectification of reality. Yet if we recall Voegelin's account of the relationship between reality and consciousness, we will be re-minded that, to his mind, to even raise such a question is to already begin to separate and objectify what is inseparable. It is not a matter of first eclipsing reality and *then* changing one's consciousness; the eclipse of reality is simultaneously a deformation of luminous con-sciousness and an obscuring of the structure of reality illuminated in consciousness.

While it is the case that hypostatization of the tensional poles that structure reality is the product of an eclipse of reality, it is not simply a matter of cause and effect. Voegelin maintained that the possibility for such an eclipse often originates in a social climate already marked by hypostatization and doctrinalization. This interrelationship be-tween eclipse and social conditions should come as no surprise, given Voegelin's insistence that the state of a society vis-à-vis the truth of order and the level of attunement it has achieved will always condi-tion both the possibility of and the type of differentiation that will emerge. Some societies are ripe for crucial differentiations; others, because of the ambiguities of concrete consciousness and the resul-tant possibility of losing the way in the quest for order, may be ripe for deformation.

The origin of the problem lies in the very process of differentia-tion and symbolization. Once a symbol has been articulated it is liable to deformation. It may become dissociated from the engender-ing experience. Voegelin is aware that this may happen for quite valid reasons. A genuine symbol emerging at the point of differentia-tion may be mistaken for a final truth to be preserved forever. In that case it may be formulated as a metaphysical principle or theological doctrine. Under stressful and threatening historical conditions, bear-ers of insights into the truth of order may seek to preserve those

16. "Wisdom and the Magic," 266.

insights from destruction by means of a canon of scripture or through the creation of the terms and relations for a propositional meta-physics. Such a well-intentioned act may, in the long run, turn out to be counterproductive:

> When doctrinal truth becomes socially dominant, even the knowledge of the processes by which doctrine derives from the original account, and the original account from the engendering experience, may be lost. The symbols may altogether cease to be translucent for reality. They will, then, be misunderstood as propositions referring to things in the manner of propositions concerning objects of sense percep-tion; and since the case does not fit the model, they will provoke the reaction of skepticism on the gamut from a Pyrrhonian suspense of judgment, to vulgarian agnosticism, and further on to the smart idiot questions of "How do you know?" and "How can you prove it?" that every college teacher knows from his classroom. . . . When the real-ity of truth has declined to the traditionalist belief in symbols, the scene is set for the appearance of unbelief and reasoned objection to belief. For belief, when losing contact with truth experienced, not only provokes objection but even gives aid to the enemy by creating the doctrinaire environment in which objection can become socially effective.[17]

In the ensuing "dogmatomachy," as Voegelin refers to the situa-tion, one doctrinal orthodoxy battles another. The outcome of these controversies may be wars of religion, skepticism, the privatization of belief, and the discrediting of the search for the truth of existence. What follows is an ideological rebellion in which all orthodoxies are rejected. In one sense, Voegelin views the criticism of socially oppres-sive orthodoxies by the ideologists as a move toward authenticity; societies dominated by doctrine need to be transformed and to re-capture the experiences that gave rise to the symbols they hold dear. The problem with the ideologists, however, is that in rejecting the prevailing orthodoxies they also reject the experiences of reality from which these traditions grew. In this regard, they are distinctly mod-ern.[18] The conflicts that marred the development of earlier symbol-

17. *Ecumenic Age*, 43–58; "Immortality," 54, 66.
18. *Anamnesis*, 188; "Immortality," 55. Voegelin does acknowledge, however (especially in his post-*Anamnesis* writings), that such revolts against reality have occurred in earlier periods as well; e.g., note his treatment of the Sophists in "Wisdom and the Magic of the Extreme," 348–57. As his theory of consciousness evolved and with it the notion of "equivalences of experience and symboliza-

izations were most often due to overinflated claims to have adequately articulated the mysterious process and structure of reality. Concerning the existence of such a reality, however, there was generally little doubt. The advent of modernity, however, is characterized by the prevalence of a closure against reality itself and a prohibition of any questions that would challenge the deformed consciousness of the dreamer.[19]

The extent of the deformation can be seen in the dangerous aberration of consciousness that comes about when the attempt is made to reproduce the tension between the divine and human poles of the metaxy in a consciousness in which that tension has been eclipsed. Since existence is no longer understood as being constituted in terms of orientation toward the divine ground, the tension between the Beginning and the Beyond must be reconstituted in the consciousness of the deformer. The creative Beginning and the transfiguring Beyond are contracted into the consciousness of the dreamer. This contraction of consciousness, combined with the dissatisfaction with reality that prompted the rebellion in the first place, results in a lethal combination: "The transfiguring reality of the philosopher's noetic response to the divine presence must become the sorcerer's human-divine power to force reality, through the 'magic of the extreme', into transfiguration here and now." Voegelin has given the name *egophany* to this phenomenon whereby the tension of existence is contracted into the consciousness of the imaginator.[20]

The suspension of existential consciousness has, then, destructive consequences in the social realm. Since the balance of consciousness has been lost and the metaxy contracted into the consciousness of the imaginator, it is society, and not the Beyond, that becomes the place

---

tion," certain aberrant phenomena were found to be constants in the struggle for order and the sharp distinction between modern and ancient varieties of deformation tended to decrease. In general, though, Voegelin would, I believe, find the modern period to be marked by the social effectiveness of disorder to a degree that simply was not present in earlier ages. This is so because of a parallel history of deformation accompanying the emergence of differentiation. As differentiation increases, so does the possibility and prevalence of derailment. See *In Search of Order*, 34, 39.

19. Voegelin, "On Debate and Existence," 37–39. See also *Science, Politics, and Gnosticism*, 21–22.

20. *Ecumenic Age*, 254–55; "Wisdom and the Magic," 267; *Ecumenic Age*, 260. See also Voegelin, "On Hegel: A Study in Sorcery," in *Collected Works*, vol. 12, 222–55; and *In Search of Order*, 48–54.

where perfection is to be realized. The "turbulence" created by the theophanic event, prompting the movement of questioning unrest, is replaced by the turbulence of revolutionary action designed to force a recalcitrant reality into conformity with the vision of the dreamer. Unlike earlier utopian thinkers (such as Thomas More), who, in their dreams of perfection, were sufficiently aware of the presence of first reality to criticize their own constructions as being "nowhere," activist dreamers experience no such constraint because of the fact that in their consciousness the structure of reality has been almost completely eclipsed: "In the activist's language, Utopianism has become the great symbol that is supposed to justify any action, whatever its human cost, if it pretends to overcome the imperfection of man's existence."[21]

THE SOCIAL EFFECTS OF DISORDER

It remains to be seen how and why the perspective of deformed existence can become an effective force in society. What is the appeal of such second realities? Voegelin suggests two reasons for their being attractive enough to become effective: first, that second realities mirror the true structure of reality closely enough to be accepted by a sizable segment of society, and second, that they be analytically obscure enough to mask their true character as deformations.[22] The dreamer must incorporate into his account enough of the actual structure of reality to make his second reality plausible to the members of the society he is addressing. The degree of adjustment necessary will depend upon the preexisting level of their attunement to the truth of order; "projecting, in order to have social appeal, must include a hard core of First Reality, changing with the social and historical situations." He must also "equip his project with symbols of authority in matters of truth." The pool from which these symbols may be drawn is strictly circumscribed by the fact that these symbols have not arisen haphazardly, but have emerged from the struggle for attunement. Thus, to be effective the dreamer must refer to his cre-

21. *Ecumenic Age,* 253; "Wisdom and the Magic," 316–17. See also Voegelin, "More's *Utopia,*" 258, 263–64; and "World Empire," 182.

22. "Wisdom and the Magic," 318–19; "Eclipse of Reality," 133–34. Voegelin often criticized Marx in this regard, but one should not get the impression that his critique was directed only at the Left. See, for example, his article "Extended Strategy," 194–95, where he attacks the Nazi use of "screen patterns" to employ the formal elements of democracy to undermine democracy.

ation as a science and clothe himself in the mantle of a messiah or prophet. In addition, the great imaginators are often people of tremendous intelligence, and their insights into First Reality are often quite perceptive. Because of this, otherwise clear-headed people may be captivated by certain dimensions of the dreamer's system and in the process fail to recognize the point at which First Reality ends and Second Reality begins.[23]

As tempting as the imaginative construction of the activist may be, the probability of its becoming socially effective would decrease sharply were it not for the all-too-common absence of spiritual substance in the society in which the derailment occurs. We have already observed how societies in which one doctrinal orthodoxy is opposed to another create the conditions under which an eclipse of reality is easily possible due to the skepticism engendered by such dogmatomachy. But visions of deformed existence are often successful simply because they fill the void created by personal and social indifference toward the promptings and pulls of the divine ground. Commenting upon the abdication of responsibility by German universities during the Nazi and postwar eras, Voegelin wrote:

> A lack of seriousness in spiritual matters is by no means harmless. For a society cannot renounce the order of the spirit without destroying itself, and when the institutions which are to serve the life of the spirit through their educational efforts cease to be serious, then their function will be taken over by men and institutions who do take their work seriously. Who these men and institutions are in our own time we are well aware: the *abdicatio* of the university is the *translatio imperii* of the spirit onto the ideological mass movements.[24]

Such apathy in spiritual matters leads not to a tolerant and benign state, but to social chaos:

> When the organizing power of the spirit becomes weak, the result is not a peaceably happy despiritualized society, but a chaos of instincts and values. Despiritualized happiness is the twin brother of despiritualized brutality; once the spiritual order of the soul is dissolved in happiness, it is only a question of time and circumstances when and from which quarter the attack on an order without dignity will begin.[25]

23. "Eclipse of Reality," 134, 144–47.
24. Voegelin, "German University," 29.
25. Voegelin, "Nietzsche, the Crisis and the War," 180.

Into a situation marked by spiritual dullness and an unwillingness to engage in the struggle for attunement there march those in whom the tension toward the ground has been almost completely eclipsed. Depending upon the extent to which the tension of existence has already been dulled in a given society, the dreamers will meet with varying degrees of success in their attempts to make their dreams socially effective. Every society consists of people at various levels of attunement; thus each society will embody a unique configuration of tensions, ranging from those genuinely attuned to the structure of reality to those in whom reality has been eclipsed. If those who reject the tension of existence come to dominate a society, the public life of that society will suffer, for those estranged from reality are de facto estranged from the *xynon,* that commonality constituted by tension toward the ground that makes public life possible at all:

> Through the life of the spirit, which is common to all, the existence
> of man becomes existence in community. In the openness of the com-
> mon spirit there develops the public life of society. He, however, who
> closes himself against what is common, or who revolts against it, re-
> moves himself from the public life of human community. He becomes
> thereby a private man, or in the language of Heraclitus, an *idiotes.* . . .
> Now it is possible, however, and it occurs all the time, that the *idiotes*—
> that is, the man estranged from the spirit—becomes the socially domi-
> nant figure. The public life of society is thus characterized not only by
> the spirit, but also through the possibility of estrangement from it. Be-
> tween the extremes of the spiritually genuine public life and the disin-
> tegration of a society through the radical privatization of its members,
> lie the actual concrete societies with their complex field of tensions
> between spirit and estrangement. Every concrete society, therefore,
> has its own particular character of public life through which the genu-
> ineness or sickness of its spirit can be recognized.[26]

To become socially effective, the dreamer's proposal must satisfy the same criteria as the philosopher's; it must be clear enough to be communicated to—and attractive enough to be accepted by—a substantial number of people or at least by their representatives, and "the organizing center must at least be comprehensive enough to provide for the self-sustaining, defensive, and lasting order of society."[27] Of course, for the imaginator, it is difficult to create a pro-

---

26. Voegelin, "German University," 7.
27. Voegelin, "What Is History?," 31.

posal like this, given the fact that tremendous tension is created when one attempts to impose a Second Reality construction upon a First Reality that refuses to be distorted. For this reason the dreamer often achieves social effectiveness only through terror and violence; reality must be "forced" into conformity with untruth. The chances for the dreamer's success also depend a great deal upon how much of First Reality he has been able to incorporate into his perspective. In cases where little compromise is made with First Reality, those with a deformed consciousness may constitute an isolated sect. More commonly, though, those estranged from reality will achieve a certain degree of social influence through the creation of a prevailing "climate of opinion."

A climate of opinion is a by-product of the work of the great imaginators. Voegelin distinguishes between a primary process of deformation in the work of the deformation's major exemplars and the secondary movements that emerge in the course of its unfolding. The eighteenth through the twentieth centuries in Western culture are, Voegelin believed, a time in which the various possibilities in eclipsing reality have been tested in numerous ways by the major thinkers of modernity. As the limits of deformed existence come to be more clearly understood, while the truth of order remains out of reach, the modern age becomes more and more nihilistic. Throughout this process, the major imaginators engender many secondary movements among intellectuals of lesser mind. Pale reflections of the great eclipsers of consciousness, these second-rate thinkers "determine an intellectual climate of such force that it can be, and frequently is, mistaken by the unwary for the 'age' to which they must conform if they want to be up-to-date 'modern men'." Such secondary deformers are, in fact, blind guides whose lack of insight into the process unfolding around them prevents them from understanding the truth about the intellectual climate they have helped to create: that it is "the secondary, epigonal, stagnant, and obsolescent aftermath of a primary process that has run its course and belongs to the past."[28]

The continuous pressure exerted by the eclipsed First Reality sets limits to the imaginators' projects and forces them to continuously revise and re-adapt their systems in a futile attempt to lend the proj-

28. "Eclipse of Reality," 151–52.

ects some plausibility and to get them to "work." Yet the simple fact remains that they will never work because they are not attuned to First Reality; thus, as the process unfolds and the deficiencies of the constructions become apparent we find a progression from the optimistic rationalism of the Enlightenment to the crisis of Western culture identified by Nietzsche. This primary process of deformation leaves in its wake a series of secondary movements that emerge from the ranks of less creative minds. Some may come under the spell of the imaginators because they too exist in a state of estrangement. Others may be unsuspectingly drawn into the imaginators' orbit because they find themselves attracted by the insights into First Reality that the imaginators have incorporated into their systems:

> If he is not on his guard, agreement on points that overlap with First Reality may suck him into the vortex of existential deformation. The great projectors of Second Realities are social forces because they are able to transform rational agreement on an unexceptional point into sweeping existential assent to the deformation of humanity. They are surrounded by the social fields of secondarily deformed humanity in their schools, adherents, admirers, vulgarizers, followers, fellow-travelers, and so forth.[29]

It is possible for the secondary deformations to flourish because of the "blocking effect" created by the imaginators' "new truth." As we noted earlier, Voegelin acknowledged that this "new truth" of imaginators arises to a great extent as a reaction to dogmatic theology and propositional metaphysics. Like every newly discovered truth it has a tendency to relegate previous truths to oblivion, to "block" them from consciousness. However, in their rejection of doctrinal orthodoxy, the dreamers "pushed below the horizon of awareness not only the degenerative dogmatisms of the eighteenth century but all representative expressions of existential truth in the history of mankind." We have, then, in the ascendancy of Second Realities, the paradox of a "new truth" without substantive content. In its secondary manifestations the "new truth" has the effect of "legitimating ignorance with regard to the truth of existence, be it expressed in the languages of Myth, Philosophy, Revelation, or Mysticism. It has established what I shall call the authority of ignorance."[30]

29. Ibid., 134.
30. Ibid., 154–55.

The authority of ignorance leads to a situation in which opinion, rather than the truth of existence, comes to dominate a society. This comes about not primarily through society's political representatives, but more subtly and in some ways more effectively through the institutions dominated by the secondary movements. Certain intellectuals, believing themselves enlightened, but in fact suffering from secondary deformation, exert a disproportionate influence in society because of their presence within universities and the mass media. An important result of their influence is that

> the right to be ignorant of the reality and truth of common experience has become, in the twentieth century, the most remarkable and characteristic institution of Western societies. The institution is firmly established and recognized, has entered public consciousness, and has even been elevated to something like a principle of social order by the self-interpretation of Western societies as "pluralistic societies." The intellectual climate deriving its character from the authority of ignorance has achieved a certain degree of stability that repeats, on the level of secondary deformation, the compulsiveness of imaginative projecting.[31]

In this fashion a relatively small number of individuals suffering from deformed consciousness may come to have an inordinate influence in society—not by becoming socially effective in the technical sense, that is, by taking responsibility for society and its continued survival, but by fostering a public unconsciousness that vitiates rational discussion concerning the effective ordering of society or gives tacit approval to murderous dreamers.

As long as there exists either a dominant "substantial public"—a public that remains conscious of the tension of existence—or a strong governmental authority, the disturbances of public order caused by the institutions in which deformation prevails will be kept to a minimum. However, as institutions such as universities continue, under the influence of educators suffering from secondary deformation, to destroy students' consciousness of the ground, there emerges an ever-growing mass of people who have been educated to nonpublic existence. The reason for this is that the loss of tension toward the ground is also the loss of *xynon*, the "common." In place of social responsibility rooted in the acknowledgment of a common participa-

31. Ibid.

tion in reality, we find a narcissistic and apolitical emphasis on individual development, self-expression, and originality because of the fact that where the ground of reality has been denied it will be replaced by the notion that the individual is the ground of his or her own existence. When those trained in this way attain a critical mass within a society, a climate is created in which social movements of estrangement can assume power.[32]

Where such estrangement from reality comes to dominate public consciousness, it is no longer proper to refer to the resulting configuration of individuals as a political society, but rather simply as a mass:

> Even when a man has been deformed to nonpublic existence—that is, not a subject through political status, but an *idiotes* through estrangement—he doesn't cease to be a member of society and a politically willing person. When, however, the existentially nonpolitical "subject" is to function as a citizen in an industrial society with a democratic constitution, there exists for him vis-à-vis the ruling authority only the two alternatives of tradition-conscious subordination or antitraditional opposition. The alternative of subordination leads to the attitude which today we call national conservative; that of opposition to the peculiar attitude of the intellectuals who protest against the regime without themselves being able to develop viable political alternatives. . . . A clear understanding of these two basic varieties of nonpolitical politics seems to me to be indispensable for an understanding of National Socialism and its rise to power. You will often hear the view expressed that National Socialism was a national movement. . . . This view I believe to be false, since in order for a political nation to exist, there must be a substantial public of sufficient social dominance, and it was just this which was missing in the German case. What Hitler brought to power was not a political nation (for had such existed, the phenomenon of Hitler would not have been possible) but the masses of existential subjects with national-conservative mentalities, who could turn with enthusiasm to a new, humanly so grotesque authority, when a regime, which in a political sense tries to be national, appears to fail at a moment of crisis.[33]

The loss of reality, then, is not merely a problem on the level of philosophical debate; it also has quite serious and detrimental effects on the political process. Without the truth of the ground as a standard in the creation of social order, one is confronted with the

32. Voegelin, "German University," 18–26.
33. Ibid., 26–27.

possibilities either of acquiescing in the face of present authority for the sake of social order and/or nationalism, or of expressing one's dissatisfaction by rebelling against that authority in the name of impractical ideals. In both cases the truth of the ground as the criterion by which to judge authority has been lost, along with the possibility of a rational public discourse rooted in that ground.

When reality is eclipsed, public language is destroyed as well; "in place of language symbols which relate to the reality of the tension towards the ground, there appear the various idioms of estrangement." The dominant literature and culture of the age may succumb to this deformation of language, and rather than serving to criticize the prevailing climate of opinion they may become the instruments of its most ardent apologists. In such cases members of the minority substantial public find themselves in the position of always having to stand as an opposition movement. Instead of being able to create in freedom, their energies are spent primarily in discerning, analyzing, and exposing deformation; "the shadow of the socially dominant estrangement lies over the works of men whose life has been spent in an effort to work their way free from it." Nor is this easy to do, given the prevalence of corruption:

> Anybody who is exposed to this dominant climate of opinion has to cope with the problem that language is a social phenomenon. He cannot deal with the users of ideological language as partners in a discussion, but he has to make them the object of investigation. There is no community of language with the representatives of the dominant ideologies. Hence the community of language that he himself wants to use in order to criticize the users of ideological language must first be discovered and, if necessary, established.[34]

The difficulty of the problem becomes clear when we recall that the critic himself is always a social being who "in his turn may have succumbed to one or the other of the dominant deformations of existence which characterize the age. He may be inclined to use as his instrument of interpretation one of the so-called theories which themselves are symbolizations of deformed existence." When the common ground of reality has disappeared, the universe of rational discourse collapses; "behind the appearance of rational debate there lurked the difference of two modes of existence, of existence in truth

---

34. Voegelin, "German University," 32, 28; *Autobiographical Reflections*, 93.

and existence in untruth." Under these circumstances an appeal to *xynon* is futile, for it is precisely this experience that has been eclipsed in the minds of the imaginators and their adherents. In place of rational discussion there are the threats of violence characteristic of totalitarianism; in democratic societies, the threats are social boycott and ostracism, and, most insidious of all, in both cases there is a prohibition of questioning itself.[35] If allowed to unfold in accordance with its own exigencies, questioning unrest would at least point the seeker in the direction of the ground. But it is just this movement that is obscured, either consciously or unconsciously, by the dreamers. In order to protect their Second Realities they must prohibit, ignore, or denounce any questions that would remind them of the ever-present, vaguely sensed, yet firmly resisted, First Reality.

EVALUATING VOEGELIN'S ACCOUNT OF SOCIAL REALITY

In the previous chapter the structure of social reality was analyzed along with its relationship to the process of differentiation. What we find in our discussion of deformation and its social effects is a process that runs parallel to that of differentiation. This should not come as a surprise, given the ambiguities of a concrete consciousness in which the possibilities exist of acting in accordance with the truth of order, of missing the opportunity, or of rejecting the quest. In addition there is the fact that the emergence of both the philosopher and the dreamer stems from the same process of differentiation. A differentiation in itself represents an advance in knowledge into the structure of reality. But there is always the danger that this advance may be misunderstood. In some cases differentiated consciousness, confronted with a hostile social milieu, will attempt to preserve the advance by transforming the symbols of experience into propositions and dogmas, thereby creating a situation in which the "new truth" of the imaginators may emerge. In other cases, the overwhelming impact of the differentiation (particularly in the case of pneumatic differentiation) may lead to a loss of balance and rejection of the tension of existence. The point is that when we speak of the process of deformation as being parallel to that of differentiation, what is

---

35. Voegelin, "On Henry James's *Turn of the Screw*," in *Collected Works*, vol. 12, 152; "On Debate and Existence," 36; *Science, Politics, and Gnosticism*, 20–22; "Eclipse of Reality," 135.

meant is not that there exists a stream of deformation and a stream of differentiation flowing side by side but originating in two separate sources. Rather, the source of both advance and deformation is the one spring of consciousness. The possibility of derailment is intrinsic to the process of differentiation.[36]

This is why, regardless of the existential response chosen by concrete consciousness, the essential dynamic between social reality and consciousness remains the same. A person suffering from estrangement lives in a society just as does the individual who seeks order. Human existence is always social existence, whether accepted as such or not. Both dreamer and philosopher are conditioned by the societies in which they live. Where a substantial public is dominant, the probability will be greater that members of society will be habituated to pursue the truth of order. Where public unconsciousness holds sway, it is far more difficult for someone to break free of the reigning deformation. In short, then, the process of deformation follows the same pattern as that of advancing differentiation: (1) A society sets conditions which are favorable to either further differentiation or derailment. (2) When differentiation occurs, new social fields arise in response to the present imperfect attunement of society. These social fields represent a movement either toward greater attunement or toward greater deformation. (3) From the interaction between society and conflicting social fields there arise new configurations of social forces which may result in restructured societies and/or new social fields. (4) The new configurations create a new set of social conditions representing either a better approximation to the truth of order or a further degree of deformation.

The process, then, is not simply a repeating cycle. With each new social configuration society moves closer to order or closer to an eclipse of reality. Nor is a society's development or decline an uninterrupted movement forward or backward. Periods of development may be followed by periods of stagnation in which society may succumb to a smug complacency that saps its strength and sets it on the path toward estrangement from reality. On the other hand, the deformation of a society may become so unbearable that it serves as the

36. Anibal Bueno, "Consciousness, Time, and Transcendence in Eric Voegelin's Philosophy," in Opitz and Sebba, eds., *The Philosophy of Order,* 109. See also Franz, *Spiritual Revolt,* 1–38.

catalyst for renewed efforts to recapture reality. And of course there is always the possibility that the evolution or demise of a society may be cut short by a natural or man-made catastrophe. To follow this struggle between order and disorder is to concern oneself with history. I will introduce this subject in the next chapter. However, I believe some reflections on Voegelin's account of social reality may be in order first.

One of the great strengths of Voegelin's approach is his refusal to reduce social/political reality to an inventory of institutions and a description of how they function. The humanly constructed meanings that underpin a social order are of equal, if not primary, importance in any social analysis. For Voegelin, the analyst obtains access to these meanings through a meditative exegesis of the symbols that reveal a community's ultimate orientation within reality. As this orientation is always expressed in terms of participation, the symbols will lead back to experiences of the creative and transcendent ground, whether rendered compactly or in more differentiated form. To speak of participation and the symbols engendered by such experiences is to advert to the role of consciousness. Thus any account of social reality, when pursued to its origins, will also involve an account of consciousness; indeed, the ultimate source for a theory of society is a theory of consciousness.[37] Likewise, an aberration in consciousness will have detrimental effects in the social realm. We find in Voegelin, then, a rejection of any obscurantism that would interfere with the unfolding of the questioning unrest that constitutes the human. We have a philosopher who insisted on probing the structures of reality and consciousness not with the intention of discovering final answers, but rather to recapture the constitutive human orientation toward mystery.

One may be in agreement with Voegelin's basic stance and still raise questions concerning particular areas of his analysis. I find this to be the case when considering his approach to social reality. It is my view that there are tensions in Voegelin's analysis that stem (at least to some degree) from tensions present in his description of concrete consciousness. This is to be expected, as social reality has its basis in concrete consciousness.

I have already noted in Chapter 1 and again in Chapter 3 how, according to Voegelin, the substantive unity of body and conscious-

37. Voegelin, "Consciousness and Order," 35.

ness is "objectively inexperiencable."[38] While we can experience the various levels of being "objectively" in their ontic differentiation, we do not have an experience of their unity as rooted in the ground. In other words, while we can readily distinguish among inorganic, plant, and animal life, and while we are aware of ourselves as being in some sense constituted by and dependent upon the lower levels of life (to use Voegelinian language), the foundation, the ground of this "basis-experience," can never be known as it "really" is; it remains an ontological hypothesis, "indispensable for grasping the 'ensemble' of consciousness and bodily process in the total process of human existence."[39] Consciousness itself is experienced as noncorporeal and nonmaterial; it is a process *illuminated from within* and is not known in the same fashion as the levels of being upon which it is founded. The unity of the human person, then, depends upon the ultimately unknowable and mysterious ground, which in its unfolding provides for both the existence of the various levels of being and their unification.

This relationship between body and consciousness is reflected in the language Voegelin uses to describe concrete consciousness. Human consciousness is "founded on" bodily existence; it is "corporeally localized," and the "subject of consciousness is *located in* a physical-concrete human being" (italics mine). Human beings are said to "have bodies" and "through their bodies participate in the organic and inorganic externality of the world."[40] Are body and consciousness distinct entities forming one "ensemble," or does such language refer only to a theoretical distinction? Are we dealing here with a contemporary version of Platonic or Cartesian dualism? It is likely that Voegelin did not intend to create the impression that consciousness is separate from the body. Indeed, he insisted that consciousness is always the consciousness of a concrete individual. There is also a sense in which it is true to say that the underlying theme of his entire enterprise is the *integration* of consciousness and bodily existence, "the interpenetration of society and psyche."[41] Voegelin's elaboration of a theory of consciousness and reality is never an end in itself, but is always presented with an eye toward transform-

38. *Anamnesis*, 31.
39. Ibid., 31.
40. Ibid., 200; *New Science of Politics*, 31. See also Voegelin, "Meditative Origin," 49.
41. Dante Germino, *Beyond Ideology*, 168.

ing the social/political sphere. It is for just such reasons that I believe his choice of language in describing the body-consciousness relationship is unfortunate; it is the type of language that is more likely to inhibit than to foster the integration of consciousness and pragmatic existence. Why employ such language if it does not aid in the effort to integrate consciousness with the social/political reality in which it occurs? I believe the answer can be traced, in part, to Voegelin's account of intentional and luminous consciousness, which I shall examine shortly.

The ambiguity that marks the relationship between the body and consciousness carries over into Voegelin's account of society, for the structure of society reflects the fact that consciousness is bodily grounded. Society has *externality* as one of its important components. In similar fashion it is society's *corporeality* that *compels it* to provide for the material care of its members and for the control of the passions.[42] Now, it may very well be that what is meant here is simply the obvious fact that humans are not angels, but incarnate spirits, and that a society must provide for the physical protection and sustenance of its people. But might it not also be the case that a language that speaks of an external, corporeal "component" of society "compelling" it to address such needs and to restrain passions stemming from this corporeality can also contribute to an understanding of society as consisting of two distinct realms? Is social reality a "two-tiered" entity, consisting of a level of meaning emerging from consciousness and another level concerned with meeting the demands of bodily existence? And if so, how are the two related? These questions are not necessarily meant as criticism; they arise spontaneously when one considers the connection between the order of consciousness and the order of pragmatic existence. It was just this issue that occupied Voegelin's energies during most of his life, and it is his exploration of this problem that will occupy us in the next two chapters. At this stage, however, I would suggest that ambiguity concerning the relationship between consciousness and corporeality in his account of social reality and the primacy he gave to the role of consciousness pointed Voegelin in a definite direction when it came to resolving this issue.

The problem with Voegelin's position becomes evident when one raises the question as to how the truth of order is to be mediated in

---

42. *New Science of Politics,* 27; *Anamnesis,* 200.

social form.[43] When differentiation occurs, the tension between the newly discovered truth and the present social order increases. In the consciousness of those who receive the new truth there is experienced a pressure to bring about its realization. Yet how does one mediate between experience in the metaxy and the pragmatic situation of one's society? What is the relationship between the order of pragmatic existence and the order of consciousness?[44] The strength of Voegelin's analysis lies in his ability to move from symbols of participation back to their origin in the divine ground. But how does one make the corresponding movement from the experiences of transcendence to pragmatic existence? How is the discovered truth to be translated in social form? Human reason as *nous* may raise to consciousness human participation in the ground, but how is this experience to be translated back into the social sphere?

To a great extent the responsibility falls upon the representative men and women in whom differentiation occurs, who must then create effective social fields. But how are they to effect this transformation of society? One possible means of mediation would be through clarifying and developing a systematic understanding of such transcendent experiences. Of course this must not be taken to mean that those involved in such clarification should seek to abolish mystery or to put an end to the wonder that is our ultimate orientation. What it does mean is that they must move from *experiences* of participation in which the truth of order is apprehended to an *understanding* of those experiences that could be formulated in a philosophy which could serve as a basis for discussion concerning what it is that constitutes a good society. Such a philosophy would consist of a set of terms and relations which do not seek to displace transcendent mystery or reduce it to merely economic or social phenomena, but which would seek to develop a common, systematic language with which to mediate between experiences of transcendence and the social reality in which these experiences occur. The importance of such a philosophy

43. Other places where this question is raised include: J. M. Porter, "A Philosophy of History as a Philosophy of Consciousness," 96–104; Cooper, *The Political Theory of Eric Voegelin*, 161–64; Gerhart Niemeyer, "The Order of History and the History of Order," 407–9.

44. See John William Corrington, "Order and History: The Breaking of the Program," 115–22; and "Order and Consciousness/Consciousness and History," in McKnight, ed., *Eric Voegelin's Search for Order in History*, 155–95.

would be to ground a social theory wherein one could speak of social reality within a context in which questions of transcendent reality are integrated, not excluded from consideration. In other words, what is required is a social/political philosophy whose horizon is open to questions concerning the transcendent ground and which can serve to mediate between human experiences of this ground and the societies in which they occur. Such a philosophical language could serve as a bridge between experiences of transcendence and their transformative influence in social life. In themselves, experiences remain just that—experiences. There is a need for reflection upon those experiences so that the structure of reality, that is, the truth of order, might be better understood and might thus provide criteria by which to distinguish between those accounts of human existence that indicate attunement and those that are the products of derailment. And is this not precisely what Voegelin himself was engaged in doing? Is not his work an extended effort to move "beyond" experience—not in the sense of transcending experience, but rather to provide an understanding and theory of experience by which to judge the authenticity of both individual and social order?

The fact that Voegelin indeed sought to conceptualize a set of terms and relations and to develop a language by which to evaluate symbolizations of order makes his overall attitude toward conceptualization and doctrine somewhat perplexing. For there is in his work a tendency to equate conceptualization and systematization with the hypostatization of experience. Conceptualization tends to be associated with consciousness in the mode of intentionality, in contrast to symbolization, which is associated with consciousness as luminous. Yet certainly Voegelin does not remain on the level of experience and symbol in his own work; rather, he moves toward "a new science of politics" and a theory of order. It can scarcely be doubted that Voegelin was himself involved in developing a systematic set of terms and relations with an aim toward mediating between experiences of transcendence and society. One might even go so far as to say that what "broke" the original plan of *Order and History* was the realization that, from within the events that constitute history, there emerged certain patterns or "configurations" of meaning that could be elucidated and then employed as criteria by which to evaluate other theories of order. The results of this process can be found in the fifth volume of *Order and History,* where the "case study" approach is for the most part abandoned in favor of a presentation of the essential structures of reality and consciousness.

It would seem, then, that Voegelin was himself engaged in an effort to develop a normative and systematic philosophical language with which to distinguish between social authenticity and aberration. This creates a tension in his thought, to the extent that he also tends to view doctrinal formulations with suspicion. Of course, Voegelin would claim that there is a role for doctrine as a preserver of important insights into the truth of order, and that his criticism is directed at doctrines that have become separated from their engendering experiences. But while he acknowledged the important role that doctrine can play in preserving the truth gained through differentiation, one also gets a sense from his writings that the positive role played by the emergence of doctrine is largely overshadowed by the inherent danger of reification in such an enterprise.[45] As soon as one begins to move from experiences expressed symbolically toward a more conceptual or systematic rendering of those experiences, one has somehow already "lost" the originating experience. Might it not be possible that part of the reason for Voegelin's reaction is that, in associating "concept" with intentional consciousness, it tends to be understood as a kind of mental "object" with connotations of "thingness" and externality, and since experience can never be adequately articulated in this fashion, that any attempt at conceptualization will inevitably fail to do justice to the reality of experience?

In his own defense, Voegelin would point out to his critics that his "theory" was an exegesis of the originating experiences in which *he* had preserved the "reflective distance" necessary to avoid the doctrinalization and hypostatization of experience. Others may not have been as attentive in this regard, and Voegelin certainly was not shy in pointing out and judging the defects of others' accounts in light of the criteria emerging in his own work. Yet, in doing so, did he not open himself to the same charge as that which he leveled against the originators of "scripture," "doctrinal theology," and "propositional metaphysics"? My sense is that in reacting against the excesses of a theology and/or a metaphysics that *had* often become disconnected from the engendering experiences, Voegelin perhaps went too far in the opposite direction, at least in his criticism of others. I would

45. *Ecumenic Age*, 36–58.

argue that his own work demonstrates that it is quite possible to speak about transcendence without doing violence to mystery. It is regrettable that he was unable to recognize this process at work in himself as well as in some of those he too quickly labeled as doctrinalizers.

This hesitancy in regard to conceptualization and doctrine can present a problem when one desires to bring one's social milieu into conformity with the truth of order revealed in the experience. For without the mediating role of understanding and, I would contend, without some type of conceptual framework, it is difficult to move from experiences of transcendent order to social institutions that reflect that order. The great strength of symbols is that they function at an evocative, preconceptual level, engaging our feelings in profound ways. In this regard they are tremendously important to any social order, a fact constantly emphasized in Voegelin's work. But their very lack of precision calls forth the complementary strengths of a conceptualization and systematization that seek to understand and articulate symbolically expressed experience, with an eye toward recognizing the difference between attunement and derailment, and the goal of mediating between experiences, symbols, and concrete social life. Performatively, Voegelin did this; but his cognitional stance contributed to his tendency to view conceptualization and doctrine with deep suspicion. He viewed with wariness as a potential cause for derailment any attempt to enunciate doctrines or principles that would perform a mediating function between transcendent experience and social realization. Voegelin would likely have cautioned anyone attempting to translate the truth of order discovered in the luminosity of consciousness into social form, with the aid of a conceptual and systematic set of terms and relations, that in doing so one was heading down the path toward hypostatization. How, then, are experiences of reality to be communicated to the wider community with an aim toward its transformation?

The tensions and ambiguities present in Voegelin's account of social reality are connected, to some extent, to his distinction between consciousness as intentional and consciousness as luminous. At the conclusion of Chapter 1, I raised some possible difficulties concerning the manner in which Voegelin articulates this distinction. These problems do not disappear in his analysis of social reality; in some ways the tensions engendered by this distinction are made even more apparent.

Voegelin's division of consciousness into an intentional and a luminous mode would seem to be mirrored in the structure of the world in which this consciousness occurs. There is a world of things corresponding to and known by consciousness as intentional, and a world of experience in the metaxy corresponding to consciousness as luminous. This split is ultimately traceable to the fact that consciousness is always concrete. For Voegelin, the intentionality of consciousness is attributable to its embodiment in individual human beings. As noted in Chapter 1, though, the dimension of intentional consciousness that Voegelin explicitly identifies as "intentional" is that which renders the world in terms of what is external to the consciousness so embodied:

> When we construe the subject as the knowing subject, then we are following a speech usage that I believe is usual in the West: we have a consciousness of something, we speak about something, we think, we imagine something. In English it is always 'something', and so I name this state of affairs a reality in the mode of thing-reality, which corresponds to a consciousness of something. I make the supposition that this thing-reality, which this 'something' is, this 'something' about which one is thinking, of which one speaks, and so forth, is a consequence of the fact that human consciousness is corporeally localized and that, in relation to our corporeal localization, everything of which one has consciousness, this 'something' is co-experienced as an 'outside' of this corporeal existence. The object of consciousness has to it, therefore, an aura of externality.[46]

Consciousness as intentional, then, is interpreted in terms of a biological extroversion in which all data, including the relationship of one's own body to one's consciousness, are rendered or conceived in terms of externality, and where *object* means whatever is so rendered. It is almost as if because we have bodies we are forced to contend with the "problems" associated with intentional consciousness, since it is due to the bodily dimension of consciousness that what is not in reality "objectifiable" gets rendered as "something" anyway. What is perplexing about Voegelin's description of intentional consciousness in these terms is that it tends to obscure the fact that the incarnate status of consciousness is quite compatible with an account of intentional consciousness in which intentionality is specified in terms of "questioning unrest" rather than as extroversion.

46. Voegelin, "Meditative Origin," 49.

In describing intentionality as he did, Voegelin was led to contrast consciousness as intentional with consciousness as luminous. Corresponding to these different modes of consciousness are the dimensions of reality that they apprehend. It is by means of consciousness as luminous that the truth of order comes to be more clearly known through an exegesis of participatory experience. The meanings that ought to inform social existence arise within this mode of consciousness. By contrast, intentional consciousness is geared toward the objects that surround us, including the external apparatus of society. Every society, then, consists of two dimensions. There is the external dimension of society accessible to and corresponding to intentional consciousness. More importantly, society is constituted through symbols emerging from the luminosity of participatory consciousness. Society as external is to be ordered in accordance with the truth of order discovered in luminous consciousness. The question becomes one of mediating between the two modes of consciousness in one social reality. How does one make the transition from reality apprehended in the mode of luminosity to the social embodiment of this reality?

In Voegelin's account, social reality is, to some degree, a divided reality, part of which is the object of consciousness as intentional and part being apprehended through consciousness as luminous. This kind of division leads to a certain degree of awkwardness for the conscientious political philosopher or social theorist, who may find himself or herself wondering what the relationship is between the "external" dimension of society encountered intentionally and the level of meaning emerging in luminosity. For some, the dilemma is easily resolved by limiting one's horizon in these matters to a political "science" or a positivist social science in which one simply deals with the data accessible to sense, that is, institutions, demographics, tabulation of voting, and the like. For others, though, such an approach represents an impoverishment of the study of social/political reality that does not take sufficient account of the meanings and values that inform these realities. Voegelin would certainly have allied himself with the latter position, but one might wonder whether his epistemological stance does not in some fashion undermine that position through its division of consciousness. The problem arises because, by nature, social reality does not lend itself to the type of division operative in Voegelin's cognitional theory; institution and meaning are too closely interwoven to be understood using disparate modes of consciousness.

Of course, one might correctly point out that, as noted in the preceding chapter, Voegelin affirmed the inseparability of meaning and structure. He insisted that the institutional order of every society is always informed by meaning, even when those meanings are distorted forms of transcendent truth. However, rather than resolving the problem, this assertion on Voegelin's part serves once again to highlight the tension in his thought between his insistence that social reality is a compound constituted by concrete structures illuminated by meaning, and a cognitional framework that seems to undermine this affirmation by making a sharp distinction between intentional and luminous consciousness. This is not to imply that the tensions in Voegelin's account of social reality and social change are solely attributable to his cognitional position. Voegelin's cognitional theory is not the only cause of what might be perceived as dualistic tendencies in his thought; my point, however, is that the language he employed in speaking of intentionality/objectivity does reinforce such tendencies, and that this complicates matters for anyone (including Voegelin himself) who would attempt to mediate between the truth of order experienced in luminous consciousness and the concrete, institutional order of society. Voegelin's way of thinking about society was not simply a consequence of his cognitional stance. However, even if a philosopher's thinking about social reality is not a direct function of his/her cognitional position, one's approach to these matters will nevertheless have a significant impact upon one's entire philosophical approach—how one understands cognitional structure will have a profound effect upon one's thought concerning objectivity and reality. I believe this to be true in the case of Voegelin's theory of consciousness and its impact on his analysis of social reality.

Perhaps what is required in order to alleviate some of the tensions in Voegelin's thought is a terminology that preserves his insight into the integral nature of social reality while simultaneously avoiding language that establishes sharp distinctions between luminous and intentional consciousness, and between reality as "external" and as "luminous." Instead of a division juxtaposing externality and luminosity, there is a need for a language that can articulate the unity of social reality as a composite of structure and meaning while avoiding any dualistic tendencies. Rather than a distinction between the "external" and the "luminous," might not a possible alternative be to speak of the relationship between reality as "intelligible" and reality as "intelligent"?[47] As understood, the lower levels of being, that is, the inorganic, the vegetative, and the biological, can all be considered intelligible; that is, by an act of understanding there is grasped in the data at these levels a pattern and unity. Again, what is important to note in this regard is that the intelligibility discovered in the data is *understood*, it is not "seen." The same holds for understanding the "synthetic unity" of the human person. In Voegelin's account this unity is somewhat problematic; we really don't know in what our unity consists, because all our "finite experience is experience of levels of being in their differentiation." All that we can infer is that "there must be something common which makes possible the continuum of all of them in human experience." Further, "the differentiation of the experienced levels of being can be made understandable only by interpreting it through the category of process as a series of phases in the unfolding of the identical substance that attains its illumination phase in human consciousness."[48] The unity Voegelin spoke of in this instance is the result not of an act of understanding grasping intelligibility in the data, but rather understanding as somehow analogous to looking or picture-thinking, in which unity is attributable to a "something" or an "identical substance" that somehow links together the various levels of being. In Voegelin's account, unities grasped in the external world of "things" are not grounded in the apprehension of abstract intelligibility discoverable in relations among data, but in the positing of an underlying substance or "something" to account for the fact of understanding. Certainly Voegelin did not conceive this "something" as in any way material; but his language suggests that, at least in this case, the real as intelligible had not yet been fully distinguished from the real as imaginable. To the extent that this is the case, it contributes to an understanding of intentionality conceived in terms of an analogy with ocular vision.

In the distinction I am suggesting, the intelligibility discovered in the data on these lower levels of being is not invented or projected

47. I am indebted to Dr. Patrick Byrne for suggesting this distinction as a possible way of addressing these matters.
48. *Anamnesis,* 28–29.

onto the data by human beings; natural science formulates its "laws" not on the basis of wishful thinking or subjective feeling, but by appealing to data for verification of its hypotheses. But as appropriated by human beings and employed in human schemes of social, political, and cultural activity, these lower levels are invested with meaning in terms of human design and purpose. At this level human intelligence is not only insightful but also creative, in that technology, economy, polity, and culture are not discovered but rather constituted by human acts of meaning. As the products of human acts of intelligence, reflection, and action, these humanly constituted schemes can be said to be both intelligible *and* intelligent.[49] The realm of meaning is still distinguishable from those lower orders to be used and transformed by human beings in their attempts to realize the good, but the distinction here does not lie between an "external" reality grasped by intentional consciousness and the truth of order apprehended in luminosity. Instead, we find consciousness specified in terms of the intentionality of questioning—a consciousness which, by raising and answering questions, comes to understand the intelligibility to be discovered in the data at the lower levels of being, but which also goes beyond the discovery of intelligible order to transform that order to serve human needs in accordance with that same process of questioning as it intends truth, beauty, and the good.

This suggested revision of terminology with which to speak about consciousness and reality is consonant with the broader understanding of intentionality mentioned in Chapter 1, where I suggested that intentionality might be better understood in terms of the primordial wonder animating all inquiry. I also noted that, for Voegelin, faithfulness to this questioning unrest is at the very foundation of the move-

49. In this regard Bernard Lonergan has written that "there are human schemes that emerge and function automatically, once there occurs an appropriate conjunction of abstract laws and concrete circumstances. But, as human intelligence develops, there is a significant change of roles . . . . Man does not have to wait for his environment to make him . . . . The advance of technology, the formation of capital, the development of the economy, the evolution of the state are not only intelligible but also intelligent. Because they are intelligible, they can be understood as are the workings of emergent probability in the fields of physics, chemistry, and biology. But because they also are increasingly intelligent, increasingly the fruit of insight and decision, the analogy of merely natural process becomes less and less relevant" (*Insight: A Study of Human Understanding*, 236).

ment to recapture reality. Such a reappropriation of intentionality would be in keeping with the spirit of Voegelin's thought. Indeed, this notion of intentionality is already present in his work; the problem has been that by accepting a model of intentionality in which knowing is likened to "taking a look" and in which "object" means "external," he has introduced an ambiguity into his account that tends to obscure this broader and more encompassing conception of intentionality. The effects of this ambiguity are detectable in his analysis of social reality; especially concerning the question as to how the truth of order emerging in luminosity is to be related to society's institutional, "external" dimension.

Intentionality, understood as questioning rather than as looking, would perhaps offer a better model by which to interpret social reality. Voegelin was well aware of the important role questioning plays in coming to know reality; he was particularly sensitive to its role in philosophy and religion. What might be helpful is a more explicit recognition in his work as to how this same questioning is operative on the cultural, economic, technological, and institutional levels. The division between society's "externality" and the constitutive meanings discovered in luminosity would be replaced by an understanding of society in which social authenticity is the product of attentiveness to the normative yet multifaceted unfolding of intentionality. Faithfulness to this questioning unrest might then develop in such a way that insights as to what is good for me in a particular instance give rise to further questions and insights into the common good, the good of order. As question follows question, there would eventually arise the question of the ultimate and sustaining good, the question of God and transcendent value. On this level there exists the possibility of a profound transformation and higher integration of human life; in Voegelinian terms, it is to follow one's questioning unrest in its orientation to the Beyond and to allow that experience to inform every aspect of one's life. Throughout this process, what is operative is the unfolding of the human capacity to wonder. The distinction would not be drawn between those dimensions of social reality known through intentionality and those known through luminosity, but rather social reality would be conceived as having been shaped through a single and continuous unfolding of intentional consciousness, originating in wonder, moving among religious experience, reflection upon that experience on a theoretical level, and the concrete insights necessary to bring that theory to bear on particular social/political problems. If intentionality were to be understood in this fashion, there could then be a valid role for doctrine and for metaphysics as a means of mediating among transcendent experience, its communication, and its social implications. Doctrines would no longer be understood as mental "objects" distanced from the luminosity of experience, but as the conceptual rendering of insights into the truth of order, specified through intentional acts of understanding and judging, but having as their source that same primordial wonder that Voegelin described as "luminosity." In such cases conceptualization could contribute toward a theory that might help to translate the truth of order into a communicable and effective form.

The purpose of these suggestions has been to raise some questions concerning possible areas of development in Voegelin's thought. *Development* is, I believe, the proper word to use in this case, since what I am proposing is not the introduction of themes and perspectives alien to Voegelin's work, but rather the further explication of what is already present there. The notion of the Question is central to Voegelin's project; my intention here is to indicate some possible ways in which it might serve as a comprehensive and unifying framework for his thought. As such, these reflections should be understood as pointing to areas of further possible exploration; they can scarcely be considered exhaustive. It remains to be investigated how Voegelin applied his understanding of social reality to the actual process in which differentiations have given rise to social fields that in turn have set the conditions for new social fields and new differentiations. This will be our concern in the following chapter, as we turn our attention to the emergence of history out of the struggle for order.

FIVE

THE STRUGGLE FOR ORDER
Israel and the Prophets

There is a sense in which the preceding chapters have assembled the elements necessary for a philosophy of history. We began by trying to understand what Voegelin meant by the terms *reality* and *consciousness*. Within reality we specified the epoch-marking differentiations of consciousness. Having thus elucidated the dynamic process that is reality, it was possible to situate social reality within this broader context. Earlier chapters, then, have sketched the framework in which Voegelin's thought concerning history can be understood. This chapter and the next will focus more specifically on the actual struggle for order as it has unfolded historically.

Voegelin's analysis of historical materials is wide ranging; here the concentration will be upon two representative figures and their societies. One reason for this is practical: to examine all the societies and civilizations with which Voegelin concerned himself would be a sizable undertaking. And it really is not necessary, given the fact that Voegelin himself, in his later work, moved away from the idea of history as a sequential "course," toward a concentration on the constant structures and configurations evident in every historical period. I have chosen to focus on the struggle for order as it manifests itself in Israel and in Hellas. Within these societies, particular attention will be given to Isaiah and Plato. The reason for this choice is that the lives of these two men and their relationships to their societies exemplify the differences between those societies shaped by the pneumatic differentiation and those shaped by the noetic differentiation. After a brief discussion concerning the structure of history, we will turn to the struggle for order as it unfolds in the life of Isaiah and his society. The following chapter will focus upon the Platonic approach to problems of political/social order. Having analyzed the struggle for order and its inherent problems, I will consider in Chapter 7 the question as to what extent the good society is realizable at all.

HISTORY

For Voegelin, a theory of political society led to a theory of history. Indeed, while he saw his work as being motivated by the political situation, he maintained that it culminated in a philosophy of history. It is not difficult to see why this so, given the relationship between social fields and differentiations. We have already described the process by which social fields give rise to differentiations, and differentiations help to set the conditions in which new social fields emerge. Implicit in this account of social reality as dynamic process is a theory of history. Its most succinct and classic formulation can be found at the very beginning of *Order and History,* in the famous motto "The order of history emerges from the history of order."[1] If it is the task of each society to attune itself to the structure of reality, that is, to the truth of order, then we may speak of history as the series of attempts by which societies struggle to live in accordance with that order:

> The primary field of order is the single society of human beings, organized for action to maintain itself in existence. If, however, the human species were nothing but a manifold of such agglomerations, all of them displaying the same type of order under the compulsion of instinct as do insect societies, there would be no history. Human existence in society has history because it has a dimension of spirit and freedom beyond mere animal existence, because social order is an attunement of man with the order of being, and because this order can be understood by man and realized in society with increasing approximations to its truth. Every society is organized for survival in the world and, at the same time, for partnership in the order of being

1. *New Science of Politics,* 1; *Autobiographical Reflections,* 93; *Israel and Revelation,* ix. With regard to the question of whether Voegelin repudiated this principle in his later work, a negative answer must be given. What *is* changed is that the principle is no longer interpreted as referring to a *single, unilinear* course of differentiation; but it remained true for Voegelin that order has a history and that history is constituted by the emergence of that order. This may involve a change in his conception of *history,* but not in the underlying principle that supports his enterprise. According to Voegelin, his change in approach stems not from any inherent limitation in his original principle, but rather from its conscientious application to the data. See *Ecumenic Age,* 2.

that has its origin in world-transcendent divine Being; it has to cope with the problems of its pragmatic existence and, at the same time, it is concerned with the truth of its order. This struggle for the truth of order is the very substance of history; and in so far as advances toward the truth are achieved by the societies indeed as they succeed one another in time, the single society transcends itself and becomes a partner in the common endeavor of mankind.[2]

Order has a history because the relationship between pragmatic conditions and differentiations of consciousness varies from society to society. Not only does the relationship vary among societies, but, as we have seen, it is a dynamic one within each society. What propels the process is the tension of existence, motivating at least some people in every society to order their lives in truth. There is history because the effort to attune human existence to the truth of order depends upon concrete consciousness, whose response to transcendence may range from a genuine openness toward the promptings of the Beyond to an eclipse of reality in consciousness. This struggle for attunement, conditioned by the particular configurations of pragmatic exigencies and differentiations of consciousness present in each society, constitutes history.[3] It can thus be said that the order of history emerges from the history of order.

As might be expected from the preceding considerations, history's structure mirrors that of society, for history is constituted by societies' attempts at attunement. Like society, it is founded in the external world, in humanity's biophysical existence. The historical process is likewise conditioned by the pragmatic situation in society. However, as was the case with social reality, the most significant dimension of history is the meaning it acquires in relationship to the transcendent ground. Indeed, in Voegelin's work one can only recognize social data as "historical," that is, as meaningful, in relation to transcendence. From a myriad of data, some are recognized as historically significant because they allow the structure of reality to be more clearly understood and in so doing advance the process of differentiation. History is constituted through consciousness, be-

2. *World of the Polis*, 1–2. See also *Israel and Revelation*, 128.

3. Unless otherwise specified, what is meant by *history* in this chapter is history not as written, i.e., as a specialized field of inquiry or specific subject, but rather history as that which is written about. I borrow this distinction from Bernard Lonergan, *Method in Theology*, 175.

cause it is in consciousness that advances in the understanding of reality occur, and it is by consciousness that they are recognized as such.[4]

The criteria for historical relevance are derived from the encounter with transcendence that characterizes existence in the metaxy. Human existence becomes "historical" when the transcendent pole within reality casts its light upon society. The differentiations that eventually crack the earlier, compact symbolizations create a situation in which human beings stand in relation to the Beyond, which, while always present, is not until that point clearly distinguished. Human efforts to cope with such "disturbances in being" are what fashion history:

> The Within-Beyond tension of divine being, compactly present even prior to its differentiation and articulation, is the driving force in the movement that culminates in epochal outbursts. Once an experience of transcendence has actually occurred that is sufficiently intense and articulate to disintegrate the primary experience of the cosmos and its symbolism, events can be discovered as affecting the order of man and society in its relation to eternal being. The index that events receive because they concern the realization of eternal being in time is the *historical index*. The events that receive this index shall be called *historical phenomena.* . . . This process of phenomena in breadth and time we shall call *history* [emphasis Voegelin's].[5]

Of course this description of history is not in any way meant to imply that prior to differentiation there were no "events." People in cosmological societies gave birth, lived and died, and made war and peace just as those living in post-differentiation societies. Their horizons, though, remained bound by compact symbolisms. As long as this was the case they cannot be said to have been living a "historical" existence. What this distinction reveals is how closely intertwined are the notions of "transcendence" and "history" in Voegelin's work. By definition, *historical* meant, for him, to be related to differentiated, transcendent being. According to this criterion, existence in cosmological form can never be "historical," because it is just this differentiation of transcendent being that is absent.[6]

---

4. *Ecumenic Age,* 304, 333, 305; *Anamnesis,* 158. See also "What Is History?," 11–12, 23, 36.
5. "What Is History?," 35.
6. This distinction is not to be confused with the distinction between "cyclical" and "linear" time. When he wrote *Israel and Revelation,* Voegelin still tended

History, then, consists of a "phenomenal" dimension that receives its meaningful, "historical" dimension from the experience of transcendence in differentiated, luminous consciousness. The same distinction between a phenomenal, "external" sphere and luminous participation, which was found to characterize social reality, also marks the historical process. And this should not be surprising, considering that there is no history apart from the societies in which the struggle for order unfolds. This distinction results in what Voegelin refers to as the "double constitution of history":

> We thus arrive at something like a double constitution of history: On the one hand, the phenomenal objects can be recognized as historical only through tracing their meaning to the sphere of encounter; on the other hand, the phenomena must be explored by methods that, in principle, are the same as those used in other sciences of the external world. The question can be further clarified by applying to historiography the Kantian language of *phenomena* and *noumena*, originally developed for the case of physics. Using this language one might say: History has a phenomenal surface that can be explored by an objectifying science, but the enterprise of science makes sense only as long as the facts ascertained can be related to the noumenal depth of the encounter. This proposition, if it is thought through, shows the point at which the analogy with physics will prove untenable. The natural phenomena envisaged by Kant, it is true, have a noumenal depth, but the ontic underground of the external world is that part of the constitution of being that is hidden from man, so that the manner in which the phenomenon depends on the noumenon is unknown. What is accessible to knowledge is only the definitely constituted surface of phenomena. One might define *given*, therefore, as the *pre-given definiteness of constitution*. This is the sense in which one can speak of objects as given. In history, on the contrary, the noumenal depth of the encoun-

---

to view history as a "course," and he attributed to Israel both the discovery of existence as historical and the understanding that history was a meaningful, linear course of events, as opposed to cosmological empires and their view of time as cyclical. By the time he came to write *The Ecumenic Age,* he had discovered the presence of linear symbolizations of time in the writings of the cosmological empires. This led him to revise his understanding of history as being constituted for the most part by a series of ever-advancing differentiations. While it was still possible to speak of advances, he no longer viewed them as falling along a single linear course of historical development. However, even though the creation of the symbol of linear time could no longer be attributed solely to Israel, Voegelin never seems to have abandoned his original thesis that it was in Israel that existence in *historical form* first arose.

ter involves man in the constitution of being; and the process leading
from the encounter, through the experiences, to their expression,
again involves man in its constitution at every step. As a consequence,
the surface of the process does not have the *pre-given definiteness of
constitution;* it is not *given* at all but constitutes itself in the acts of symbolic expression. Still, we cannot escape the earlier insight that history has a surface that is phenomenal in character; history, if it is
not a given object, at least partakes of givenness in one of its strata.
The resulting relationship between the two factors of what we have
called the double constitution of history can be formulated as follows:
The historiographer's work is essentially a part of the expressive
surface of history, while the subject-object dichotomy of the phenomenal surface is a secondary stratum within the primary expressive surface. Hence, if a philosophy of history were reduced to a methodology
of exploring the phenomenal surface, its essential part would have
been abandoned.[7]

I have quoted this passage at length because I believe it reveals the
ambiguities into which Voegelin was led in his account of society and
history by adopting the Kantian notions of phenomena/noumena
and subject/object dichotomy. The same tensions noted in his language describing social reality carry over into his discussion of history. It is not that Voegelin applied the Kantian language uncritically
to the problem of history; on the contrary, he explicitly distinguished
between the "givenness" of the data for the natural sciences and the
fact that history is not "given" in the same fashion, but is in some
sense constituted by human beings through their symbolization of
noumenal experience. At the same time, he was also aware of a
"phenomenal" dimension to history which does indeed partake of
givenness, and which is to be investigated according to the methods
of the empirical sciences. We have, then, a single reality, history, with
phenomenal and noumenal strata. One gets the impression that the
constitutive dimension of history, arising from the encounter with
transcendent being, and its external, "phenomenal" dimension are
not completely integrated, resulting in a "double" constitution of
history. Again I believe it to be a case of Voegelin's correctly recognizing and defending the position that human history is to a great
extent constituted through human acts of meaning, but at the same
time his laboring to do so within a cognitional framework that never

7. "What Is History?," 12–13.

sufficiently breaks with the positivist views he wished to oppose. The idea that history has a double constitution can lead to a situation in which history is understood as being divided into two realms whose relationship to one another is not altogether clear. As I hope to illustrate in the following chapters, this temptation was one to which Voegelin was susceptible.

ORDER AND PROPHECY IN ISRAEL

According to Voegelin, Israel came into existence through a differentiation of consciousness from which there could be no returning to existence in cosmological form. Through this differentiation there emerged an awareness of the gulf between transcendent God and mundane reality. From that point on, to be human meant to stand in relation to the divine Beyond and to live out the implications of that orientation within the concrete social order. Human existence, now interpreted as a response to transcendence, had become historical existence.[8]

From the very beginning, the historical path of this people constituted by the pneumatic differentiation was fraught with ambiguity. The intensity with which the transcendent God manifested himself in the Israelite experience had a quite salutary effect in differentiating divine from mundane reality. The insight into the structure of reality gained thereby brought to greater clarity the truth of order by which all societies were to be judged. As Israel was to discover, however, divine order is not easily translated into the mundane sphere. No social arrangement seemed able to bear the power of the pneumatic experience. Its intensity tended to overwhelm any attempts at social embodiment. At the same time, there was experienced a need to structure society in accordance with this truth in order to secure a foothold within reality. This tension between worldly and transcendent order was the central issue of Israelite history.

The ambiguous nature of the Israelite experience found expression in the symbol "Canaan." As discussed in Chapter 2, a danger peculiar to the pneumatic differentiation is that the radical disengagement of transcendence can result in a state of imbalanced consciousness in which there may be a tendency either to denigrate life

---

8. *Israel and Revelation,* 132. Subsequent page citations from this source will be given parenthetically in the text.

in the world or to expect one's transcendent vision to be realized in present society. From the very start, this was a danger for Israel:

> It was a people that moved on the historical scene while living toward a goal beyond history. This mode of existence was ambiguous and fraught with dangers of derailment, for all too easily the goal beyond history could merge with goals to be attained within history. The derailment, indeed, did occur, right in the beginning. It found its expression in the symbol of Canaan, the land of promise. The symbol was ambiguous because, in the spiritual sense, Israel had reached the promised land when it had wandered from the cosmological Sheol to the *mamlakah*, the royal domain, the Kingdom of God. Pragmatically, however, the Exodus from bondage was continued into the conquest of Canaan by rather worldly means; further to a Solomonic kingdom with the very institutional forms of Egypt and Babylon; and finally, to political disaster and destruction that befell Israel like any other people in history. . . . The promised land can be reached only by moving through history, but it cannot be conquered within history. The Kingdom of God lives in men who live in the world, but it is not of this world. The ambiguity of Canaan has ever since affected the structure not of Israelite history only but of the course of history in general. (pp. 113–14)

The symbol "Canaan" represents the specific form that the tension between the truth of order and pragmatic existence, found in all societies, assumed in the Israelite context. Particular to Israel was the fact that the search for order was marked not only by a profound experience of the Beyond, but also, paradoxically, by an awareness that the divine had intervened concretely in specific temporal events; God was both absolutely transcendent and salvifically at work in Israel's pragmatic existence. For Voegelin, this linkage between divine presence and pragmatic event lent to the Israelite experience a degree of compactness in which the line between transcendent order and its earthly incarnation was sometimes blurred. In its Exodus, Israel understood itself to have been liberated from slavery through divine intervention. Because the experience of divine power and graciousness was so tied to this specific event, there arose in Israel the frequent tendency to identify its own pragmatic advances and reversals with the will of God. On the one hand, this allowed Israel to deal effectively with the exigencies of mundane existence; the growth of the Kingdom of Israel was identical to the growth of the Kingdom of God. On the other hand, this identification caused Israel to sometimes lose the consciousness that the saving encounter also served as the criterion by which to judge Israel's pragmatic policies and that it implied a responsibility to reflect the experienced graciousness and saving justice in the social order. Voegelin refers to this unfortunate tendency on the part of Israel to confuse the Kingdom of God with the Kingdom of Israel as the "mortgage of Canaan," that is, the "perpetual mortgage of the world-immanent, concrete event on the transcendent truth that on its occasion was revealed" (p. 164).

In the "mortgage of Canaan" we have, then, the Israelite variation on the dilemma confronting every society—how to satisfy both the demands for attunement to transcendent order and the demands of pragmatic existence. The difficulty in satisfying both requirements is evident in the paradox of Israel's development, particularly in the emergence of the monarchy. To insure pragmatic survival, Israel instituted a monarchy, which was understood by most as the fulfillment of the Covenant. Was it not God's will, after all, that Israel survive and occupy the land? But as soon as the monarchy was established it became increasingly clear to some that the new social order represented a falling away from the original Mosaic vision of society. Thus, the prophetic movement arose to confront Israel with the fact that the pragmatic power politics of Israelite society were to be identified neither with the will of God nor with faithful adherence to the Covenant (pp. 179–80).

The case of Israel raises the quite serious question as to what degree it is possible for a society to successfully integrate pragmatic social/political effectiveness with attunement to transcendent being. As noted in Chapter 3, there will always be some discrepancy between society's present condition and the truth of order. It remains to be considered how much of the truth of order a society can be expected to incorporate in its structures. Is it true, as seems to have been the case in Israel, that every socially effective solution to the pragmatic situation involves a society in a defection from the truth of order? And if that is the case, by what criteria are we to evaluate how much weight is to be given to pragmatic and transcendent concerns? Or might it actually be possible to strike a balance between social effectiveness and faithfulness to divine presence?

It was to this problem that the prophets addressed their message. Was it possible to embody revelatory experiences in social existence? Was this embodiment to be identified with the historical Israel? If

not, how was the meaning of existence in historical form to be car-
ried on when and if Israel as a nation ceased to exist? What did the
prophets expect from their people and their God? And how did they
react when their hopes were disappointed? As an example of prophetic response to a concrete question of order, let us turn to an
instance that Voegelin analyzed extensively—the situation of Isaiah
at the time of the Syro-Ephraimic War.

The scene from Isaiah, chapter 7, is a familiar one. As Ahaz is
inspecting the water supply for Jerusalem he is confronted with the
prophet's admonition to trust in Yahweh. In this faith lay the salvation of the city. Alliance with Syria and the Northern Kingdom or
appeal to the protection of Assyria were vain efforts and could only
come to nought.

In Isaiah's counsel to Ahaz, Voegelin perceived a return to the
reliance upon God alone that characterized the holy war tradition of
the Archaic League. There is a significant difference, though, between Isaiah and his Israelite predecessors. Israel during the period
of the judges displayed a ready willingness to fight even while relying
on God, whereas the citizens of Jerusalem are advised to do nothing
but wait for the intervention of Yahweh. In light of the impending
catastrophe facing Judah there is to be no divine-human synergism,
no reliance upon military means, and no dependence on political
craft—redemption lies in the Lord alone, as his will is revealed in the
word of the prophet. Voegelin found this stance unsatisfactory: "That
is a correct description as far as it goes—but it does not touch the
crucial question how the prophetic charisma can be considered by
anybody an effective substitute for weapons on the battlefield"
(p. 450).

In Isaiah's confidence that his words revealed the only true choice
for Israel (since they expressed the will of God) and in his unyielding
demand for faith, Voegelin detected a strong magical element—
magic in this case referring to the belief that human words accompanied by an act of faith can alter reality. In *Israel and Revelation*,
Voegelin admits that he tempered his assessment of Isaiah's position
as magical after encountering resistance from professors Von Rad,
Glatzer, and Bultmann (p. 452), but in his later *Autobiographical Reflections* (p. 89), he reasserts his former belief that Isaiah was indeed
engaging in magic. His judgment concerning Isaiah is based on the
fact that Isaiah's message was oriented toward earthly victory and not

a merely spiritual triumph. What Voegelin discovered in Isaiah is not trust in the inscrutable will of God but certain knowledge that the divine plan and the Isaianic prescription are the same: "The divine plan itself has been brought within the knowledge of man in as much as Isaiah knows that God wants the survival of Judah as an organized people in pragmatic history" (p. 451). Voegelin saw such knowledge of the divine mind as weakening human freedom and paralyzing action in the world: since the Lord will act on our behalf there is no need to do anything; in fact, to act in any way would be presuming upon divine initiative. Voegelin went so far as to label the attitude of Isaiah as incipient gnosticism (p. 451).

The problem faced by Isaiah and the other great prophets has its origin in the differentiation of consciousness that takes place in the separation of the historical from the cosmological form of existence. Within the cosmological form the divine order infused the existing civilization by way of cult and myth. The order of the cosmological empire was a reflection of the heavenly realm. The stability of the social order mirrored that of the cosmos. Under the historical form of existence, the transcendent is differentiated from the mundane; the correspondence between social and cosmic order has been fractured. It is now only the tenuous link of faith that binds the divine and the human. How, then, is the relationship between the transcendent and the mundane to be understood?

In the royal theology of the Jerusalem temple, the cultic restoration of order was enacted in an annual festival in which the enthronement of Yahweh in the person of his representative, the Davidic ruler, was celebrated liturgically. Isaiah, Voegelin believed, develops this notion even further: the cosmic divine order has become the knowable divine plan, requiring only the trust of God's chosen people in order to become effective in pragmatic history. Isaiah's solution was to effectively ignore the limitations and strictures of mundane existence and to attempt by way of a magically manipulated knowledge to bring about a divinely transfigured realm. He thereby violated the laws that govern pragmatic existence and displayed a marked lack of common sense. Ignoring the restrictions imposed by the tension of existence, the prophet attempted to find a way out of the tension through an act of faith. In doing so he tried to abolish the structure of reality, "to make the leap in being a leap out of existence into a divinely transfigured world beyond the laws of mundane existence." Voegelin explains in *Israel and Revelation:* "Through the intervening 'knowledge,' thus, the recurrent restoration of order through the cosmological cult becomes, when it enters the historical form of existence, a unique transfiguration of the world according to the divine plan. A gulf opens between the world as it is and the world as it will be when it has been transfigured" (pp. 451–52).

Since there is no technical term describing this change in reality anticipated by the prophets, Voegelin offers the term *metastasis,* which means "the change in the constitution of being envisaged by the prophets" in which "the experience of cosmic rhythms, in the medium of historical form, gives birth to the vision of a world that will change its nature without ceasing to be the world in which we live concretely." One can then speak of "metastatic experiences, of metastatic faith, hope, will, vision, and action and of metastatic symbols which express these experiences" (pp. 451–52). Metastasis would seem, then, to derive from a dissatisfaction and impatience with present reality stemming from an intense experience of the world-transcendent God. It differs from gnosticism in that metastasis emphasizes the *transfiguration* of the present world, rather than an escape from it. In later writings Voegelin allowed the term to be used to describe those thinkers who deliberately reject any notion of God or transcendent reality, but in the present case he is dealing with religious figures for whom God is the author of metastatic transformation.

The problem created by metastasis is that the constitution of being is not altered by the whim of the prophet: "The constitution of being is what it is, and cannot be affected by human fancies. Hence the metastatic denial of the order of mundane existence is neither a true proposition in philosophy, nor a program of action that could be executed. The will to transform reality into something which by essence it is not is the rebellion against the nature of things as ordained by God" (p. 452). By rebelling against reality, Isaiah, far from serving the divine plan, is actually setting himself in opposition to God. It is Ahaz who is said to possess "common sense," while Isaiah has disregarded the "laws of mundane existence" (p. 452). His rebellion is undoubtedly sublime, but it is rebellion nonetheless. One might also note that such metastatic derailment was not the invention of Isaiah; it was implicit from the start of Israel's history in the idea of the kingdom of God as being in some way present in the life of the chosen people. But with the passage of time the discrepancy between the empirical Israel and the anticipated Kingdom became too blatant to be ignored. The "mortgage of Canaan" eventually took its toll. It was the prophetic task to address this defection. This the prophets did; but the translation of the prophetic critique into concrete political and social structures was always in danger of failing because of the fact that mundane reality stubbornly refused to conform to the demands of the Kingdom. In this regard we find Voegelin able to praise Isaiah for his recognition and denunciation of Israelite disorder while simultaneously criticizing him for choosing the path of metastatic faith.

The problem confronting Isaiah and the other prophets was how to deal with and interpret a situation in which there was widespread refusal to heed the prophetic word. Israel had become largely impervious to the call for change; the prophets understood correctly that this self-satisfied apathy would rot the nation from within and leave it susceptible to destruction by both its enemies and its own shortsighted leaders. Certainly the prophets experienced disappointment when the word they delivered went unheeded and the empirical Israel remained recalcitrant. At the same time, from the prophetic point of view, there could be no return to cosmological existence once the transcendent God had been revealed. The question then became, How was life in the present under God to continue if the historical Israel was doomed? Israel may have chosen defection from God, but that did not mean that the divine promises had been canceled. And while it may have failed to heed the revealed word of God, this revelation, as the basis for a new form of existence, was an irrevocable breakthrough. What form would the human response to revelation assume if the chances for its social effectiveness were almost nonexistent? This was the crucial question: "If the Kingdoms of Israel and Judah are doomed, the question becomes ever more burning: who will be the carrier of historical order in the future? If it is no longer the people and the king of Judah, who then will be Israel? What kind of 'people' and what kind of 'king' will emerge from the imminent destruction as the new Israel under the new Covenant?" (p. 472). Following historiographic convention, Voegelin would refer to this as the "messianic problem."

Isaiah realized that to move from existence within the cosmological form of existence to existence in the present under God would require symbols that had been radically recast. One such symbol significant to Isaiah was that of the *kabhod,* or glory of Yahweh. In his inaugural vision Isaiah became aware of the *kabhod* as the divine substance that permeates all creation. In order for the *kabhod* to permeate human society and history, people must remain open to the divine substance and allow themselves to be penetrated by its light. This relationship constitutes the dynamic of history in Isaiah's thought. In Voegelin's work, such a dynamic is, of course, metastatic, for the same reasons given above, that is, that Isaiah looks for the transfiguration of mundane reality by means of an act of faith, believing that the process would begin in his person and radiate outward to the rest of society. Essential to the realization of the *kabhod* would be the trust of the king, Ahaz. Yet the king refused to listen and the prophet was forced to consider the possibility that the present occupant of the Davidic throne was not to be the vehicle of divine transfiguration. The role of the king was crucial—Isaiah was not about to reject the Davidic covenant; but it now became clear that the intended ruler would be a future member of the House of David (pp. 476–77).

The Immanuel prophecy that followed Isaiah's disillusionment with Ahaz may have triggered a hostile backlash from the royal court. Whether frightened or dispirited, or both, Isaiah withheld his prophecies from the public and entrusted them to a group of disciples, who, along with himself and his children, formed a faithful remnant awaiting the righteous king. Unable to become socially effective, the bearers of representative humanity shrank to a small circle. Though their numbers were few, it was they who were the center of order in society (p. 483).[9]

Voegelin understood the next prophecy (Isaiah 9:1–6), describing

---

9. With the prophet Jeremiah, the truth of order had shrunk to his own person. Voegelin had a far more favorable impression of Jeremiah. Although Voegelin found him too to be a metastatic visionary (*Israel and Revelation,* 490), unlike Isaiah, his response to the messianic problem was not to engage in futuristic projections, but to address the untransfigured present. He did this by transferring many of the important symbols from Israel's past onto himself; if order was nowhere to be found in the world, it would take shape in the life of the prophet. In the person of Jeremiah, "the human personality had broken the compactness of collective existence and recognized itself as the authoritative source of order in society" (p. 485). Voegelin considered this step to be an important advance in Israel's development. My suspicion is that he viewed it as such because it approximates, in the Israelite context, the differentiation of the psyche that occurred with Plato and Aristotle.

the coming Prince of Peace, as evidence of a change in Isaiah's position. While there is clearly a reference to a Davidic ruler, royal descent is no longer stressed. More importantly, Voegelin found in the phrase "the zeal of Yahweh of the hosts will perform this" evidence that Isaiah had come to believe that the time for response by ruler and ruled had come to an end. The Lord would act decisively to raise up a messianic figure of his own choosing. This could explain why the message had been "bound up and sealed" (p. 479), since it would be of no use to the faithless but only to the remnant.

Voegelin's interpretation is confirmed, as he saw it, by what he viewed as the "last of the great metastatic prophecies," Isaiah 11:1–9. In this case, there is no reference to any particular situation. Clearly, the awaited ruler would be of the root of Jesse, but he would resemble no previously imagined historical figure. Unlike Immanuel, he would not be leader because of his ability to discern good and evil but because he would be filled with the "*ruach* Yahweh." We have more than a David here, for he would not judge as mortals do, by way of sight and hearing, but with divine understanding: "The *kabhod* has penetrated the structures of the world indeed and the metastasis is complete. . . . Yahweh himself will be the judge between the nations. Governmental institutions and their human incumbents are no longer mentioned" (p. 480).

One can detect a progression in Isaiah's vision. He moves from an appeal to the present king, to a future ruler anticipated by the sign of Immanuel, to a Prince of Peace ruling over a remnant. From there, he makes a leap to a figure of Davidic lineage, but one who is animated by the very spirit of God and in possession of superhuman qualities of judgment and wisdom. The final stage finds the world enjoying an era of universal peace without the need or benefit of distinct institutions at all, "for the *ruach* of Yahweh has transfigured human nature, so that the order of society and history has become substantially the order of the *kabhod*" (p. 481).

With the complete unfolding of Isaiah's metastatic vision, prophetism has reached an existential impasse. The transfiguration of social and cosmic order will take place through an act of God—the only possible human response is to wait in the hope that events will occur as the prophet has said. Among a remnant this hope is maintained and passed along. How long will it take, though, before the group of believers begin to question or reinterpret their expectation? The problem becomes especially acute when the long-awaited metastasis is predicted for a certain date. Modern metastatic movements, which reject the notion of divine order and anticipate a transfiguration of mundane existence by purely human means, can indefinitely postpone their disappointment by interpreting each new stage of historical development as another "installment" toward a final metastasis that is still "in progress" (pp. 481–82). Isaiah foreshadowed this metastasis by installment in his description of a remnant who, as bearers of the secret concerning the future messianic ruler, represent the first stage in the development of the final divine transfiguration.

Voegelin saw the prophetic impasse as bringing to light the ambivalence at the heart of the pneumatic differentiation. In Isaiah he recognized this ambivalence in its most striking form. Certainly Isaiah's experience of God's holiness and his insistence that society reflect this holiness represents a genuine continuation of the great Israelite leap in being. And yet the overpowering impression made by this experience is also responsible for the imbalance that marks Isaiah's vision. Consequently, Voegelin was puzzled by the prophets; one might even say that he seemed irritated by their refusal to adjust to the world:

> If one isolates the complaints of the prophets, one is inclined to wonder what the servants of Yahweh wanted. Should Israel have submitted to the Philistines instead of creating a king and an army? should the ships of Tarshish stay in port? should the cedars of Lebanon grow only half size? and should the daughters of Zion be dowdy? It is important to realize that no prophet has ever answered a question of this kind. . . .
> The prophets wanted to overcome the externalization of existence; and the texts reveal the remarkable degree of success their efforts achieved: They disengaged the existential issue from the theopolitical merger of divine and human order; they recognized the formation of the soul through knowledge (Hosea) and fear (Isaiah) of God; and they developed a language to articulate their discoveries. . . . Nevertheless, the rejections of the mundane order remain as an oddity. The prophets apparently were not only unable to see, but not even interested in finding, a way from the formulation of the soul to the institutions and customs they could consider compatible with the knowledge and fear of God. The attitude of the prophets is tantalizing in that it seems to violate common sense. (pp. 444–47)

In Voegelin's opinion, the positive contribution of the prophetic movement is balanced or even overshadowed by the prophets' refusal to come to terms with mundane existence. What society did the prophets have in mind when they spoke of a future age of justice and peace? They all saw clearly that the social structures and cultural institutions that had nourished them were no longer able to bear the meaning of the true order of existence under God. But could any concrete society do so? And if so, what kind of order would that society have? Such seemingly unanswerable questions gave Voegelin cause to wonder about the meaning and purpose of the entire prophetic effort:

> The concern of the prophets goes beyond the Chosen People, orga
> nized as a kingdom for survival in the pragmatic power field, toward a
> society which, though in some manner derived from the present people
> through survival and expansion, is certainly not identical with it. There
> is no answer to the question: Of which society are the prophets speak
> ing when they envisage the carrier of true order? It certainly is not the
> society in which they live; and whether any concrete society that has
> formed in history since their time would be recognized by them as their
> object may be doubted. . . . Nor is there an answer to the second ques
> tion: What kind of order will the society have? For it will be the trans
> figured order of a society after metastasis. And a transfigured order
> was no object of knowledge to the prophets, nor has it become an ob
> ject of knowledge to anybody since their time. Since neither the identity
> of the society nor the nature of its order can be determined, the suspi
> cion will raise its head: Does the movement of the prophets make sense
> at all? (pp. 490–91)

Since the prophetic demands seem to be unrealizable, "it will be come clear that the sense of the movement can be found only if the apparent nonsense be taken as the starting point in the search for its motives." Indeed, in the Israelite experience and the prophetic im passe, Voegelin saw an important lesson concerning the relationship between the truth of order and its concrete realization in any society. If one accepts as fact that the society envisioned by the prophets is unrealizable in history, then their metastatic faith can be seen in a new light. For implicit within such metastatic imagining is a true insight— that there will always exist "a gulf between true order and the order realized concretely by any society, even Israel," and that "no Chosen People in any form will be the ultimate omphalos of the true order of mankind." Voegelin believed that at some level the prophets were aware of this truth, and that in Israel's history one can detect a move ment in which the differentiation of the Beyond was able to disengage itself from Israelite society and its institutions:

> The fact must be accepted that the questions can find no answer. The *terminus ad quem* of the movement is not a concrete society with a recognizable order. If the concern of the prophets with this apparently negative goal makes sense nevertheless, it must have been motivated by the insight, though unclear and insufficiently articulate, that there are problems of order beyond the existence of a concrete society and its institutions. . . . When Abram emigrated from Ur of the Chaldeans, the Exodus from imperial civilization had begun. When Israel was brought forth from Egypt, by Yahweh and Moses his servant, and constituted as the people under God, the Exodus had reached the form of a people's theopolitical existence in rivalry with the cosmological form. With Isaiah's and Jeremiah's movement away from the concrete Israel begins the anguish of the third procreative act of divine order in history: The Exodus of Israel from itself. (p. 491)

Israel's historical existence in the present under God had been a series of stages each of which involved a further exodus from existence in cosmological form. With the prophetic insight that Israel's status as the Chosen People was no assurance or guarantee of its ability to embody true order, and that in fact Israel's defection had reached a point of no return, came a glimmer of understanding that perhaps the divine intention to save was able to encompass even the disappearance of the empirical Israel. During and after the Babylonian Exile, this latter insight found expression in the prophecy of Deutero-Isaiah, in which Israel's sufferings were incorporated into a wider vision of universal redemption.[10]

In conclusion, what might we say about Voegelin's interpretation of the prophets? Above all, Voegelin saw in the prophets vigorous witnesses to the God beyond the gods. To the extent that the prophets overcame Israelite chauvinism and were able to appreciate the universalism implied by the encounter with God, and in the degree to which they were able to understand that the Kingdom of God did not coincide with the Kingdom of Israel, Voegelin has only praise for the prophetic effort. Unfortunately, the "mortgage of Canaan" was never completely eliminated from the prophets' preaching, and their message continued to reflect metastatic hopes for the restoration of Israel in some form.

The sharpest criticism that Voegelin aims at the prophets has to do with what he perceived to be their failure to deal adequately with the

---

10. *Israel and Revelation*, 491–515; *Ecumenic Age*, 26–27, 212–14.

demands of worldly existence. In this regard he chastises them on two levels. First of all, there is, particularly with Isaiah, the charge of passivity and apoliticism; confronted with a threatening political situation, Isaiah cautioned Ahaz to wait for the Holy One of Israel to intervene. Second, Voegelin charges Isaiah and the other prophets with *doing and expecting too much;* they offer counsel and interfere in matters best left to the king and look forward to a transformed social reality. Both criticisms center on the prophetic failure to strike a balance between the exigencies of the pragmatic situation and transcendent truth. In the first instance they refuse to acknowledge what is necessary in the pragmatic situation; in the second instance they wish to go beyond what is possible in the political realm.

Whether the prophetic counsel was naively utopian or a proper response to the pragmatic situation in which they found themselves is an issue that cannot be settled here.[11] To begin to deal with this question would require detours that would take us far afield. Our concern is with how *Voegelin* understood the prophets; and clearly he found their prescriptions to be unrealistic. It remains for us, though, to examine the possible reasons for his conclusion. Is there an inherent dimension to Voegelin's thought that would lead to such a judgment? The prophets have been found lacking in their ability to reconcile transcendent experience with pragmatic existence. In particular, they stand accused of being inattentive to mundane concerns and of adamantly refusing to accommodate their vision to the exigencies of life in the world. By what standard have they been judged? This question will occupy us more fully in Chapter 7. For now, let us summarize the results of Voegelin's analysis: The gap between the truth of order and society is indeed wide; advances in the order of consciousness can rarely, if ever, be translated into lasting social form. If there was any doubt as to the irresolvability of the tension of existence, it has been dispelled. Israel's great achievement did not

---

11. This is not to imply that the question is unimportant. One could find a number of biblical scholars who might call Voegelin's interpretation into question, or at least offer an alternate view of prophecy, e.g., Bernhard W. Anderson, "Politics and the Transcendent: Voegelin's Philosophical and Theological Exposition of the Old Testament in the Context of the Ancient Near East"; Paul Hanson, "Jewish Apocalyptic against Its Near Eastern Environment," 31–58; "Old Testament Apocalyptic Reexamined," 454–79; and *The Dawn of Apocalyptic,* 10–26; Gerhard Von Rad, *Old Testament Theology,* vol. 2, 160; and R. E. Clements, *Isaiah 1–39,* 16–17.

consist in a successful reconciliation of transcendent truth with mundane exigencies; quite the contrary, such an enterprise was doomed to failure, as Israel's pragmatic history amply demonstrated. In Voegelin's interpretation, Israel's contribution lies instead in serving as an example of the fact that no society is an adequate vessel for the truth of order and that the goal of history can only be reached beyond history.

SIX

THE STRUGGLE FOR ORDER
Plato and the Polis

The problem confronting Plato was much the same as that faced by the prophets—how to order society in light of transcendent truth. The main difference, of course, was the context in which Plato's response took shape. Prophecy arose in a social milieu that was both formed by and formative of the pneumatic differentiation of consciousness. An intense awareness of God's majesty and transcendence characterized Israel's existence. In Plato's Hellas, however, it was the noetic differentiation that figured more prominently. Among the reasons for this was the Hellenes' rather flexible stance toward the existence of intermediate, minor divinities, from which there could eventually emerge the notion of an individual soul.[1] Regardless of which differentiation dominated, it was the same transcendent reality that was encountered in both Israel and Hellas. Thus, the task of attunement remained the same in both societies, despite the fact that in Hellas the emphasis was placed on the questioning unrest characteristic of human nature, while in Israel it was the transforming presence of the Beyond that was most prominent. Following Voegelin's procedure, we shall examine Plato's response to the tension of existence by tracing the development of his thought concerning order and society as it unfolds in the course of several dialogues spanning his entire career.

---

1. *Israel and Revelation*, 234–42. In "The Meditative Origin of the Philosophical Knowledge of Order" (1981), this explanation no longer appears as a possible reason for the difference between Israelite and Hellenic formulations of order. Israel and Hellas have become "ethnic variants" stemming from the same experience. It is interesting to consider whether this represents a movement on Voegelin's part away from his more clearly drawn distinctions in the first three volumes of *Order and History*.

Like the prophetic effort, Plato's philosophy arose as a reaction to surrounding social disorder.[2] Earlier philosophers, such as Parmenides, Heraclitus, and Xenophanes, were concerned with establishing the truth of divine being as transcendent in opposition to the people, the polis, and its myth. Plato continued this effort, but his primary concern was to overcome the corrosive effects of the Sophists, whose influence had so permeated the social milieu that society itself could be described as the greatest of Sophists. The prevailing disorder served as a catalyst, moving the philosopher to resist the distorting forces: "From this act there emerged the *nous* as the cognitively luminous force that inspired the philosophers to resist and, at the same time, enabled them to recognize, the phenomenaof disorder in the light of a humanity ordered by the *nous*. Thus, reason in the noetic sense was discovered as both the force and the criterion of order."[3] The rightly ordered soul, then, in its capacity as site and sensorium of reality, became the standard by which society was to be judged. We turn now to the dialogues themselves, which preserve for us a record of the Platonic soul's struggle with society.

The *Gorgias* is Plato's declaration of war against corrupt society, his judgment on Athens. The stakes in this war are high: Who will form society's leaders? Who will shape the souls of the young? In the *Gorgias,* we find Plato transferring authority from Athens to himself. The revolutionary character of this move stems not from the fact that a new political force has arisen to challenge older ones, but that Plato calls Athens to a profound *spiritual* regeneration. Voegelin understands Plato as having deliberately placed himself in competition with the leading statesmen of his day, "not with regard to political action, but with regard to the spiritual authority." As we shall discover, though, Plato did not conceive of his spiritual authority apart from political authority. The polis had lost its way; the reason for its existence, that is, to reflect wisdom in its institutions and practices, had largely disappeared. In Voegelin's view, "the *Gorgias* is the death sentence over Athens."[4]

If it is the case that Plato was in competition with the political leaders of his day, it would seem reasonable to ask why he would

2. *Anamnesis,* 89; *Plato and Aristotle,* 24; *New Science of Politics,* 61–62; "Nietzsche, the Crisis, and the War," 197–98.
3. *Plato and Aristotle,* 70–79; *Anamnesis,* 89.
4. *Plato and Aristotle,* 89, 39.

engage in such a struggle if Athens was so hopelessly corrupt. Why expend one's energies trying to reform an apparently irredeemable society? A partial answer to this question may be found by noting that, just as Israel was burdened with the "mortgage of Canaan," Plato had to contend with the "mortgage of the polis." In Hellas, with its differentiation of the psyche, the leap in being "assumed the form of personal existence of individual human beings under God," in contrast to Israel, where it remained the historical existence of *a people* under God. Voegelin believed that the universality of transcendent truth could be more easily disengaged in the Hellenic context, where there existed a consciousness of the individual soul as sensorium of the ground, than in the more compactly structured Israelite context. When this new truth came into view through the differentiation of the soul, the moral and spiritual authority of the polis could be called into question, but for Plato it still remained the context within which questions of social order were to be decided:

> For the discoveries, though made by individuals, were made by citizens of a polis; and the new order of the soul, when communicated by its discoverers and creators, inevitably was in opposition to the public order, with the implied or explicit appeal to reform their personal conduct, the mores of society, and ultimately the institutions in conformity with the new order. Hellenic philosophy became, therefore, to a considerable extent the articulation of true order of existence within the institutional framework of an Hellenic polis. . . . At any rate, the institutions of the polis were distinctly a limiting factor in the Hellenic exploration of order, down to the great constructions of paradigmatic poleis by Plato and Aristotle.[5]

Plato labored under the mortgage of the polis. Even when he despaired of Athens, he continued, in his later work, to formulate his experience of order within the conceptual framework provided by the polis:

> Human existence meant political existence; and restoration of order in the soul implied the creation of a political order in which the restored soul could exist as an active citizen. As a consequence he had to burden his inquiry concerning the paradigm of good order with the problem of its realization in a polis. We have no means to go back of this motive. That Plato conceived his spiritual authority as political must be accepted as the impenetrable mystery of the way in which his

---

5. *World of the Polis,* 169–70.

personality responded to the situation. In the history of symbols the fact of his response has burdened the philosophy of order with the "mortgage" of the polis that we discussed in an earlier context.

If human life was inherently political, then the soul could only flourish in the best possible polis. It was the philosopher's role to supervise its realization. While moving beyond the polis in his own soul, and creating the reflective language with which to articulate the structure and movement of consciousness, Plato never completely abandoned the quest for a regenerated polis. To a certain extent this had to do with the fact that the fullness of differentiation, in which the individual soul was able to break through to an awareness of a universal humanity beyond the boundaries of any particular time or place, was only possible after the epiphany of Christ and the resulting differentiation. Just as the presence of the pneumatic differentiation did not lead the prophets of Israel to a full understanding that the God they worshiped was the God of all the nations, in similar fashion the presence of the noetic differentiation did not empower Plato to move beyond the cultural/social horizon of the Hellenic polis. Full differentiation had to await the advent of the Christian Gospel. Plato could not know that the problem with which he labored would be addressed in the Christian era through the division of human affairs into temporal/spiritual spheres along with the accompanying emergence of the Church.[6]

If the *Gorgias* was Plato's challenge to Athenian authority, the *Republic* found him involved in creating the paradigm of true order for society. The crucial advance in the *Republic* was the noetic differentiation of the soul as site and sensorium of the ground and the insight that social order reflected the order or lack thereof in the souls of its constituents. The *Republic* makes clear that the substance of society is psyche and that society can destroy the souls of its citizens because social disorder results from a disease in the psyche of its members. Through noetic exegesis of psyche and its relationship to reality, Plato was able to articulate a paradigm by which the present polis could be evaluated and possibly renewed. For Voegelin, it was very important that the term *paradigm* not be confused with *ideal*. Above all, Voegelin wished to make it quite clear that whatever

6. *Plato and Aristotle,* 90; *Anamnesis,* 34; *Plato and Aristotle,* 225–27. See also *Ecumenic Age,* 249–50.

Plato may have had in mind, he had no intention of creating an "ideal state."[7]

How then, does a "paradigm" differ from an "ideal"? First of all, one is confronted with the fact that there is, in Greek, no equivalent to the word *ideal*. It has already been noted in the preceding chapter that Voegelin considered an "ideal" to be a model of society in which a particular evil to which all humanity is subject is designated for elimination, often through institutional means. Voegelin's verdict on such ideals is not entirely negative; as instruments of social critique, they may help to stigmatize and call attention to evils that are very much present in a given society. Nonetheless, the overall result of social ideals is to lead people to imagine that realities such as private property, labor, sickness, human pride, and so forth can be done away with and that this can be accomplished by human means. Spiritual order is renounced in favor of an unrealizable ideal of social perfection. In short, then, the problem with an ideal is that an important dimension of reality must have been omitted in its creation.[8]

In contrast to an ideal, a paradigm, or model, is characterized by a sensitivity to the structure of reality in all its dimensions. The paradigm has its source in the philosopher's attunement to the truth of order: "The paradigm is not a construction of social order on the same level as the other types known, only better. Nor is it a utopia or ideal. It is the paradigm of order in the Metaxy, on the new spiritual level achieved in Plato's noetic consciousness." The paradigm is a secondary elaboration, a mediating model between the truth of order illuminated in consciousness and its practical realization in society. The philosopher does not discover a blueprint when reflecting upon the truth of order. The philosopher allows himself or herself to be formed by these experiences of transcendence and attempts to articulate their relevance for society by devising models that reflect something of the experience: "The weight of the work lies, therefore, in the inquiry into the nature of true order. The model projects, while more than literary devices, have the character of secondary elaborations and must not be taken as rules with autonomous validity." For Plato, it is the divine ground that is truly real; it is the responsibility of

7. *Plato and Aristotle*, 69–70. See also Voegelin, "The Oxford Political Philosophers," 109; "More's *Utopia*," 459; and *Plato and Aristotle*, 82–83.

8. Voegelin, "Oxford Political Philosophers," 109; *Science, Politics, and Gnosticism*, 91; "More's *Utopia*," 459–68.

society to attune itself to this reality as well as it can: "The word 'ideal' has no meaning in a Platonic context. The Idea is Plato's reality, and this reality can be more or less well embodied in the historically existing polis."9 In Voegelin's view, adherence to social ideals can often lead to a loss of contact with reality. What characterizes the philosopher, though, is an awareness of reality's structure and the knowledge that it is only in relationship to the ground that one is truly human.

The paradigm, then, emerges from the philosopher's experience of reality. It is a model that attempts to render the truth of order arising from luminous participation in terms of the society in which the philosopher lives:

> Platonism in politics is the attempt, perhaps hopeless and futile, to re-generate a disintegrating society spiritually by creating the model of a true order of values, and by using as the material for the model real-istically the elements which are present in the substance of the society. The *Politeia* as well as the *Nomoi* have their superb richness because Plato built them out of the best materials of Hellenic society, of the mythical law-givers and the enlightened tyrants, of the martial virtues of Sparta and the civilizational refinements of Athens, of the hum-ble Attic peasants and the craftsmen and traders of the cities—all wrought together in an order glowing with the spiritual light that per-vades it from the mystical source in the Idea of the Good. If not man, the *Politeia* at least is Hellenic man written large.10

While Voegelin could admire Plato's faithfulness to the truth of order and could oppose the Platonic paradigm to the social ideal, the ambiguities stemming from the mortgage of the polis make themselves felt in the passage just quoted. The paradigms are marvelous and balanced constructions, yet their articulation may be for nought, considering society's seemingly impenetrable corruption. The Hellenic materials ingeniously interwoven with the truth discovered in participation are also the chains that bind Plato's vision to the unregenerate polis, preventing him from moving beyond Hellenic to universal humanity.11

Although refusing to break completely with the notion of a regenerated polis, Plato was not naive when it came to estimating the

9. *Ecumenic Age*, 227; "The Nature of the Law," 53–54; *Plato and Aristotle*, 218.
10. Voegelin, "Nietzsche, the Crisis, and the War," 195.
11. The notion of "universal humanity" will be explored further in Chapter 8.

likelihood of its realization. Certainly in the *Republic* he expresses grave reservations as to whether the paradigmatic polis in which philosophers preside will ever come to pass. The reason, however, is not that the paradigm is an impractical, utopian dream; rather, it is because the people lack the desire and willingness to bring it about. One can appeal to the people, but one cannot force their consent.[12]

Confronted with such an intransigent situation, how is the philosopher to respond? Regrettably, the philosopher may be forced to withdraw from political life. What makes this choice particularly poignant is that for Plato it is only within the polis that the human person develops most fully; to leave the corrupt polis to its own devices may indeed help to preserve the truth of order in one's soul, but only at the price of a diminution in one's human stature. As Voegelin notes, "The withdrawal from politics is heavy with resignation, for the fullness of growth, the maximal augmentation (497a) of man, can be achieved only through participation in the public life of the polis." Likewise, in his reading of the *Republic*, Voegelin observes that the philosopher's duty to the polis depends upon its condition; "return is a duty only in the polis of the *Republic*, not in the surrounding corrupt society."[13]

To turn away from the polis may be the best way to resolve the impasse between a recalcitrant social order and the truth of the ground. Voegelin comments upon the passage in the *Republic* (592b) in which Socrates speaks of the paradigm as existing in heaven:

> Without change of terminology, through a slight switch from metaphor to reality, the inquiry into the paradigm of a good polis is revealed as an inquiry into man's existence in a community that lies, not only beyond the polis, but beyond any political order in history. . . . To be sure, the paradox is dissolved. The statesman in the philosopher, who feels his stature diminished when the proper field of action is denied to him, has disappeared. Sliding through the metaphor to reality, participation in politics now means concern with the transpolitical politeia that is set up in heaven and will be realized in the soul of the beholder. . . . The dissolution of the paradox must, therefore, not be understood as an intellectual solution of a puzzle, but as the spiritual "augmentation" of existence produced through the process of the *zetema*. The paradox remains intact at its own stage of the

---

12. *Plato and Aristotle*, 91–92, 136.
13. Ibid., 91, 116.

inquiry. To live in an age of social corruption and to be denied one's proper field of action in public is really a misfortune; and the honoring of Arete is no substitute for the inevitable diminution of stature. Yet the price must be paid, because in the hierarchy of goods political life ranks lower than eternal life. . . . The paradox, thus, remains as unsolved intellectually as it was, but the bitterness of renunciation is spiritually overcome through the growth of the soul into the transcendent politeia.[14]

The paradox of having one's human, that is, political, stature diminished while the order in one's soul increases is resolved by looking beyond the polis. The apparent impasse stemming from the failure of the truth of order to become socially effective only existed as long as Plato remained focused on the Athenian polis.[15] It would seem as if Plato largely abandoned the attempt to realize the truth of order in society; what he gained was an insight into that community which lies beyond any historical attempt at embodiment and which one enters through the attunement of the soul to the divine ground. The tensions in Plato's thought, according to Voegelin, arise when the tendency that pushes his vision beyond the historical polis comes into conflict with the equally strong tendency to embody the truth of order in his society.

The philosopher continues to be repudiated by society, and society's institutions and practices remain unchanged. The polis, the arena in which the philosopher might exercise his authority, has been closed to him through the obduracy of its members; the only effective change is that taking place in the philosopher's soul and in the souls of those influenced and molded by his wisdom. It is in this form that true order will become socially effective. The paradigmatic evocations of order may find a response in other souls in which the ground has not been eclipsed and who experience the philosopher's word as a saving tale. New social fields may emerge, not tied to the institutions of the polis, but formed by a mutual responsiveness to the ground. These new communities would far outlast the polis and its problems. The historical Athens may have lost its authority to represent the truth of order, but new carriers of truth, in the form of philosophical schools, offer hope for the eventual renewal of society.[16]

14. Ibid., 92–93.
15. *New Science of Politics,* 70–71.
16. Voegelin, "Gospel and Culture," 180; *New Science of Politics,* 75.

In Plato's case this new community would be perpetuated through the creation of the Academy. Even here, though, the ambiguous pull of the polis is still present in Plato's work. On the one hand, Voegelin saw in Plato's Academy a tendency toward apoliticism, "a withdrawal from the sphere of power, if not into solitude, at least into the restricted community of those who are responsive to the appeal of the spirit." On the other hand, it seems evident that "the Academy is conceived as the institutional instrument by which the spirit can wedge its way back into the political arena and influence the course of history."[17] Again, Plato was never able to completely disengage himself from the polis.

While it may be true that Plato never completely broke with political life, Voegelin saw in the *Phaedrus* a decisive shift in Plato's thinking. In the *Phaedrus,* Plato announces the emigration of the spirit from the polis. The public order of Athenian society has ceased to be normative. Philosophy has disengaged from the setting that gave it birth. The *Phaedrus* bears witness to a situation in which the noetic differentiation, having arisen within a particular society with its own institutional and political structures, begins to challenge the corruption of that society, only to find that the society rejects the very insights to which it gave birth and which, if taken to heart, might have stemmed its decline. Plato's response was to disengage himself further from the institutional and political life of the polis. The denizens of the cave have proven to be incorrigible; hence Plato has left the cave for good. In the *Phaedrus* the parallel between soul and society is overshadowed by an emphasis on the relationship between the soul and the idea. At the same time the borders of the soul become blurred; rather than the individual human soul, the "soul" comes to be identified as a "cosmic substance" that is "articulated into nobler and less noble souls which, according to their rank, animate parts of the cosmos itself or merely human bodies" (p. 136). The reality of human existence has moved from life in the polis to life in the metaxy. The problem of an unregenerate polis is solved by removing reality from the hands of politicians and denying the status of ultimate reality to the body politic:

> The Idea when it leaves the polis, does not leave man. It goes on to live, in individuals and small groups, in the mania of the erotic soul. . . .

17. *Plato and Aristotle,* 88, 225–26. Subsequent page citations from this source will be given parenthetically in the text.

The Idea is reborn, and the position of the philosopher is authenticated, through the communion with a nature that is psyche. That is the ontological foundation for Plato's late political theory; and the communion is the source of the "truth" of the mythical poems in which the late Plato symbolizes the life of the Idea. (pp. 140–41)

In the *Statesman* we find Plato's reformulation of the political problem from within the new perspective gained in the *Phaedrus.* The rejection of the polis does not mean that one ceases to live in the polis. What has changed is that the problem must now be formulated with the understanding that the polis sketched in the *Republic* will never be realized. The philosopher-king of the *Republic* has become "a savior with the sword, who will restore order to society in its time of troubles" (p. 150). In the *Republic,* there was still some hope, however slight, that through proper education and with the guidance of philosophical rule the paradigmatic polis might yet come into existence. The integration between soul and society among the inhabitants of the polis was still within the realm of possibility. By the time the *Statesman* is written, such hope is gone. The ruler described in the *Republic,* who fit as an integral part into the harmonious polis of the idea, has been replaced by the royal ruler who, possessing true rule, the *logos basilikos,* within himself, confronts a degenerate polis and is called upon to bring order to a chaotic social situation. True rule is the possession of those who have ordered their souls in accordance with wisdom—it matters not whether they rule in fact. In the *Statesman,* "the nature of true rule has been disengaged from the problem of institutional forms as well as from that of actual rule" (p. 160). This is not to say that it is apolitical; rather, it means that true order has shrunk into the soul of the royal ruler. The royal ruler remains, however, a "savior with the sword," ready to restore external order, by violent means if necessary.

The royal ruler of the *Statesman* must be understood within the context of Plato's disillusionment with the polis. The actually existing polis is now viewed as a *mimesis,* an imitation of the paradigmatic polis. All actual societies are a falling off from the paradigm, and as they develop through time, whatever truth they may have possessed degenerates until the chaos reaches the point where the royal ruler must intervene forcefully in order to prevent total disorder. As for the possibility of somehow renewing the society through an appeal to the core of truth still present, Plato is skeptical: "According to the *States-*

man, the mimetic character of actual politics is inevitable and cannot radically be abolished. All one can do is to inject as much of 'true' reality as possible into the actual polis at times and then let it run its course until the misery has become great enough so that, let us hope, the people will prove amenable to another injection" (p. 163). Because most people are lacking in the knowledge necessary to recognize and desire true order, royal rule will never become a permanent achievement. The royal ruler may put a temporary end to social chaos, and he may even experience some success in weaving a certain degree of order into the floundering society if he is able to eliminate those who are unfit for political life; but any order thus embodied will inevitably begin to expend itself until another crisis is reached.

Faced with such a situation, Plato suggests adherence to written law as a means by which social order may be sustained among those in whom attunement to the truth of order is tenuous. But if the situation is already impervious to reform, how is a society to enact good laws? From what source are they to be derived? How are laws reflecting the true substance of order to gain a foothold? The answer lies in the precarious process of persuasion:

> Such good as there is in the laws of the mimetic polis has come into it because the people at some time have listened to the wise legislators in their midst. Plato is not elaborate on this point but we may assume, from the references in other contexts, that he considered Solon one of the wise legislators who injected into the polis an order that lasted for a while. The laws would have to be copies of the truth *(aletheia)* which comes from those who have knowledge (300c). And once the substance of the law is acquired, the best a polis can do is not to do anything against the written laws and national customs. (p. 164)[18]

The law, though, is not simply an alternative to royal rule. It is only because royal rule is so precarious that one turns to written law as a far less adequate response in sustaining social order. Law is a poor substitute for the wisdom of the royal ruler, who, because he possesses knowledge of order, has an authority above that of the law, which he may alter or suspend as he sees fit (pp. 161–64). The royal ruler, however, is not a tyrant; while both the royal ruler and the

---

18. More will be said concerning the notion of "persuasion" when I discuss the *Laws.*

tyrant may exercise an authority that is above the law, the crucial difference is that the royal ruler is actually wise and just. He alters the law for the human good. The specificity and rigidity of the law must be adapted and made more flexible in responding to changing circumstances, through the judicious application of the *logos basilikos*. In their ignorance, the common people cannot distinguish between tyrant and royal ruler, hence the need for written laws. In any case, whether guided by royal rule or relying upon law and tradition, the order of society will inevitably decline.

The *Timaeus* finds Plato continuing to concern himself with a problem that was at the heart of the *Republic*—the status of the Idea. The *Republic* still offered some hope that the idea might be realized; in the *Timaeus* such hope has vanished. Was the paradigm, then, merely an impractical program or a subjective opinion? The *Republic* described the paradigm laid up in heaven and its formative influence on the politeia in one's soul. But when it came to translating this model into social form the *Republic* left many questions unanswered (pp. 173–74).

Plato's solution, as developed in the *Timaeus*, was to move beyond society and to project the soul against the much larger canvas of the cosmos. Naturally, one may wonder whether this wider projection in any way solves the problem of the embodiment of the idea in historical reality, since "the projection of the psyche into the order of the polis was the point of doubtful legitimacy in the *Republic*, and it does not become less doubtful by a projection of the psyche on a still larger scale" (p. 184). Voegelin believed that Plato solved this dilemma through his ingenious use of myth. In Plato's hands myth articulates the experience of psyche as it ranges from the conscious awareness of an individual to the unconscious depth of the cosmos. Psyche provides continuity along this spectrum, and it is myth that renders this psychic mediation symbolically. The myth links noetic consciousness to the process of reality in which it occurs. Through the myths of the *Timaeus* the drama of the soul is connected with the drama of the polis, the rising and falling of civilizations, and the very life of the cosmos itself: "The idea of the polis has grown into its fullness, not because it has gained overtly the dimension of history, but because in the life of the soul the solitude of contemplation is now in harmony with the transpersonal rhythms of the people, of the human race, and of the cosmos" (pp. 178–79). The model polis may never take shape in history; but the paradigm as it exists in the soul of the philosopher has achieved its highest development by being integrated into the encompassing process of reality through its participation in a psyche that reaches from the depth of the primary experience to the articulation of noetic consciousness in the historical situation of the philosopher.

The resistance to the idea that was evident in the *Republic* is now seen as reflecting the eternal resistance to the idea permeating creation. As the royal ruler of the *Statesman* was called upon to impose order on the recalcitrant "matter" that was the citizens of the polis, so the Demiurge imposes order upon cosmic matter, forming the cosmic substratum in accordance with Nous, while at the same time acknowledging the limiting conditions, the Ananke, inherent to such matter. If the *Republic* emphasized ascent to the idea, the *Timaeus* focuses upon the idea's imposition on formless reality (p. 202). The emphasis in the *Timaeus,* though, is on the role of persuasion. The Nous of the Demiurge overrules Ananke by means of persuasion; in similar fashion the philosopher's soul, through its participation in the Nous, embodies noetic persuasion in social reality: "In the cosmos, at least, Nous has prevailed over Ananke and imposed the order of the idea. The task of the Statesman can now be conceived as the creation, in politics, of an order analogous to the order of the cosmos. This last step, the evocation of the polis as a cosmic analogue, was taken by Plato in the *Laws*" (p. 203).

For Voegelin, the *Laws* represents Plato's mature wisdom, rather than a falling off of his powers, as other critics have suggested (pp. 214–16). Indeed, the *Laws* finds Plato able to balance an appreciation for the primary experience of the cosmos with a sensitivity to historical and social change. Once again he accomplishes this feat through the use of myth. In the *Laws* Plato is at pains to convey something of the lastingness of the cosmos, while at the same time avoiding the impression that this cosmic lasting reduces history to a meaningless series of events that has happened an indefinite number of times in the past and will repeat itself in the future. He does this by introducing the myth of the last cataclysm and Deucalion:

> There is no reality but the reality of which we have experience and memory, and man's memory does not reach behind the last flood; by experience remembered we have knowledge only of the one history in which such meaningful events as consciousness becoming luminous

occur. The myth of the outlasting cosmos, thus, is confined to its function of keeping consciousness open toward the reality in which it becomes luminous while not converting the mystery into a "thing" that can be examined from all sides. As far as the historical course is concerned, the cosmos lasts long enough if it outlasts memory and meaning.

In this manner Plato was able to avoid those conceptions of history that close themselves to the encompassing mystery in which the process unfolds by making all previous movements a mere prolegomena to one's own historical present. Plato's vision was able to encompass both the recurrences of cosmic process and historical development. In Book 3 of the *Laws* he deals with the ages of Hellenic civilization and looks forward to a time when a federation of Hellenic poleis, conceived as a people, an *ethnos,* will be able to stand its ground against an ecumenic empire.[19]

Unfortunately, but perhaps inevitably, the envisioned federation fails to be realized because the lawgivers in two of the three member polities have committed "The Greatest Folly," *(megiste amathia)* by "not providing either a man guided by wisdom for the royal function or constitutional balances that would prevent the abuse of absolute power." The apex of this particular historical cycle has been reached; it is now the beginning of civilizational decline. While one may detect a certain degree of dismay in Plato's reflections, there is also, by the time the later dialogues are written, a new awareness that what is most real is that which takes place within a soul that remains young through its attunement to divine presence.[20]

From this perspective, we can understand why Voegelin identified the great theme of the *Laws* as the question of whether paradigmatic order will be created by "God or some man" (624a). A society structured in accordance with purely human standards will end in bickering and chaos; only when those who rule are aware that God is the measure will the community stand some chance of survival. In the *Laws* Plato writes as the one whose soul is attuned to the divine measure and who thus possesses the wisdom lacking in those shortsighted political leaders who have committed "The Greatest Folly." There is resignation here, but there still remains a strong desire to form the polis in conformity with the truth of order. While he is no

19. *Ecumenic Age,* 225, 220–23; *Plato and Aristotle,* 243.
20. *Ecumenic Age,* 221, 226. See also *Plato and Aristotle,* 243–44.

longer active in politics, Plato continues to conceive his reflections in political terms. The mortgage of the polis is never completely shed.

The key to understanding the Platonic position, especially in the dialogues that follow the *Republic,* is the realization that the idea is not invalidated by its rejection in society. Whether or not it ever takes shape in society is of secondary importance as long as it exists in the souls of those attuned to the divine measure. It is possible, even likely, that true order will never assume concrete form in social institutions, yet it is no less real because of its absence there: "If the historical polis resists its regeneration through the Idea, that is a misfortune for both the polis and the philosopher; but the historical resistance invalidates neither the Idea nor the position of the philosopher whose soul is ordered by the Idea." Reality is present in the highest degree where there is true order, and most often that means in those individuals who respond to the drawing from the Beyond. Of course it would be better if the truth of order were to radiate outward from this center and find social acceptance, but if it fails to do so the failure lies not with the philosopher but with the society that refuses to heed his words. Order continues to exist; it is simply not present in society at large: "The philosophers develop projects of order that they do not expect to be enacted as valid rules through the law-making process of their society. The work is done when the dialogue or treatise is finished. . . . The true order of society is living reality in the well-ordered soul of the philosopher, brought to sharp consciousness by the philosopher's refusal to succumb to the disorder of his environment."[21]

The *Laws* makes it clear that, in Plato's view, the vast majority of people are not capable of responding to the divine in such a way as to enable this experience to become the formative presence in their souls. Few can live the philosophic life.[22] Because the human material has been found incapable of appropriating the divine measure as revealed in the paradigm, Plato evokes a "second best polis," which is better suited to average capacities. Voegelin insisted, however, that this adaptation does not represent an abandonment of the Platonic paradigm. It is not a case of Plato's discarding an earlier, "utopian" model and adjusting to "reality." The Idea remains Plato's reality; it

21. *Plato and Aristotle,* 147; "The Nature of the Law," 52–53.
22. *Plato and Aristotle,* 163, 234, 249, 263, 288, 302; *Ecumenic Age,* 196.

is society that has proven deficient: "The idea remains the reality as before, and the good polis of the *Republic* remains the 'first best,' but the human raw material—which in itself is no reality at all—may to a greater or lesser degree prove fit to become the vessel of reality." The only compromise to be found in the *Laws* is an increased sensitivity and tolerance on Plato's part as to the degree of reality people can be expected to bear; unfortunately, their existential potency has proven to be low.[23] Once this fact has been accepted, the question becomes one of determining how order is to be embodied and maintained.

Law and creed, instituted by persuasion and backed by force when necessary, replace rule by those attuned to the truth of order. A profound shift has taken place from the *Republic* to the *Laws*:

> The *Republic* is written under the assumption that the ruling stratum of the polis will consist of persons in whose souls the order of the idea can become reality so fully that they, by their very existence, will be the permanent source of order in the polis; the *Laws* is written under the assumption that the free citizenry will consist of persons who can be habituated to the life of Arete under proper guidance, but who are unable to develop the source of order existentially in themselves and, therefore, need the constant persuasion of the *prooemia* as well as the sanctions of the law, in order to keep them on the narrow path. . . .
> On the lower existential level, which is presupposed for the citizenry, the divine measure cannot be the living order of the soul; God and man have drawn apart and the distance must now be bridged by the symbols of a dogma. From the vision of the Agathon man has fallen to the acceptance of a creed. Plato the savior has withdrawn; his polis cannot be penetrated by the presence of his divine reality; Plato the founder of a religion is faced by the problem of how the substance of his mystical communion with God can be translated into a dogma with obligatory force. . . . In conclusion we may say that the *Republic* and the *Laws*, while they both provide legal institutions for a political society, provide them for two different types of men; the differentiation of rank as the "best" and the "second best" is determined by the quality of men whom Plato envisages as the vessel of the Idea.[24]

In the polis of the *Laws*, the rulers, "though not philosophers themselves, are trained in the results of philosophy as a creed so that in the light of a philosophical minimum dogma they will make the

---

23. *Plato and Aristotle*, 218, 227, 247, 263. See also *Israel and Revelation*, 11; "Wisdom and the Magic," 320–21; "The Nature of the Law," 54–55.
24. *Plato and Aristotle*, 221–22, 263; *New Science of Politics*, 158.

laws as best they can." In place of philosophers in communion with the Good we have lawmakers in whom nous is sufficiently present to enable them to understand that God is the measure behind the *nomoi*. The *Laws* casts Plato in the role of the Athenian stranger whose communion with God gives him an authority above that of the lawmakers. If the polis is to flourish these legislators must avail themselves of his wisdom. The lawmakers, in turn, attempt, by means of *prooemia* attached to the laws, to persuade the citizenry of the laws' goodness. Persuasion mediates between God and the human material in whom the *nomoi* are to be incarnate. If nous is to be embodied in social reality with any degree of durability, then people must be persuaded to obey those laws in which it is represented. Persuasion would seem to presuppose that even in those whose souls are not capable of living in attunement with the truth of order there is still a residual capacity to respond to reason and to recognize its embodiment in law. In the *Laws* Plato develops the notion of persuasion beyond its articulation in the *Statesman* and the *Timaeus:*

> We recall the appearance of *peitho*, Persuasion, in the *Statesman* and in the *Timaeus*. The Demiurge cannot impose form on the formlessness of Becoming by force; he has to use persuasion to bend Ananke to Nous. Now Persuasion reappears as the means of bending man, the "material," to the *nomoi* of the *nous* and thus imposing on him the form of the polis. The gap between God and man has to be filled by Persuasion; in the organization of the dialogue the gap between the two parts on God and man is filled by the interlude on Persuasion.[25]

The dynamics that animate the cosmos are to be reproduced in society; Plato's vision of the community as cosmic analogue is complete.

As essential as persuasion might be in establishing and maintaining a stable polis, Plato also realized that it might not always be efficacious. In such cases the judicious use of force would be warranted. Of course, persuasion is preferable to force, but Plato still wanted the Idea to be embodied in the polis. Confronted with the unwilling, the resistant, and the obstreperous, he allows for the supplementing of persuasion with the proper application of force.[26] The Plato who, by means of the myth, has risen above politics still labors under the mortgage of the polis.

---

25. Voegelin, "The Nature of the Law," 54; *Plato and Aristotle*, 255.
26. *Plato and Aristotle*, 226.

Despite these ambiguities in the Platonic project, Voegelin could still applaud Plato's realism. Although Plato may have never completely abandoned the quest to make the truth of order socially effective, he also realized the limitations under which he labored:

> The classic philosophers had no illusions about their role in the process of reality. They knew their range of participatory action to be limited to a sensitive alertness to disorder in personal and social existence, to their preparedness to respond to the theophanic event, and to their actual response. They could not control either the revelatory movement itself, or the historical conditions which enabled them to respond; nor could they affect the order of the Plethos more deeply by their response than the method of dialogical persuasion, amplified by the literary work, would allow. The only flaw apparent in this otherwise impeccable realism is the philosophers' inclination to devise paradigms of order at all for a society which they knew to be spiritually unreceptive and historically doomed.[27]

Again Voegelin points out that the only flaw in the philosophers' realism stems from their refusal to break completely with the polis. There is a tension in Plato's thought; one finds there the insight that the reality of the truth of order is in no way diminished by its lack of incarnation in society, joined to an intense desire to employ this truth in the regeneration of the polis. In his soul Plato may have moved beyond the polis, but it was always with a backward glance toward the pragmatic political arena.

According to Voegelin, the key to Plato's realism lay in his ability to preserve a balance between transcendent experience and the exigencies of life in the metaxy. In *The Ecumenic Age* and in Voegelin's later writings he makes it quite clear that Plato was very much aware of the God beyond the Nous.[28] But Plato did not allow this experi-

27. *Ecumenic Age,* 218.
28. Whether this represents a shift in Voegelin's position from that in *Plato and Aristotle* is a good question. In that volume the emphasis seemed to be on Plato's *inability* to break with the primary cosmic experience and its myth (pp. 169, 200–201, 226), whereas in *The Ecumenic Age* it is evident that Plato was aware of the divine Beyond, but remained sensitive to the primary experience of the cosmos in order to maintain the balance of consciousness (pp. 231–32). Even in *The Ecumenic Age,* though, Voegelin would maintain that Plato's experience of the Beyond did not possess the same degree of intensity as that found in Isaiah or in Paul. As a result, the Platonic experience of transcendence was not powerful enough to dissolve the hold of the primary experience on the symbolization of the Beginning (p. 10). As far as the notion of a God beyond the Nous, what

ence to so overwhelm him that he lost sight of the limitations imposed by life in the cosmos. Plato consciously balanced these exigencies against the unbalancing tendencies of theophany: "He plays down the unbalancing reality of the theophanic event; his consciousness of the paradox is weighted toward the Anaximandrian mystery of Apeiron and Time, because he refrains from fully unfolding the implications of the directional movement." The obscurities and uncertainties found in Plato's later dialogues were placed there deliberately, so as to preserve the balance of consciousness from dogmatic, hypostatizing derailment. All this was done as a means of affirming life in the cosmos in the face of tendencies toward imaginative oblivion. Plato did not allow the theophanic event to distort the human condition.[29]

Plato's realism and balance can perhaps be best appreciated when contrasted with the approach of the prophet Isaiah:

> When Plato lets his analysis of right order in society culminate in the symbols of the Philosopher-King and the Royal Ruler, he is fully aware of the obstacles presented by human nature and the course of pragmatic history to the event of a paradigmatic polis ever becoming the institution of a society; he stresses both the improbability of its establishment and the inevitability of its decline if it ever should be established. When Isaiah lets his faith culminate in the vision of the Prince of Peace who will set the act of faith which the pragmatic king rejects, he believes in the magic power of an act that will transmute the structure of reality, as well as in his own advice as a Gnosis of transmutation.

While their experiences may vary somewhat in intensity, Plato was as much the recipient of revelation as was Isaiah. The difference lies in their response to theophany. Over the course of his life Plato came to understand the improbability of the paradigm ever taking shape in any concrete society. This led him toward a greater tolerance for human limitations and enabled him to adjust his vision in accordance with the level of attunement possible for the community in question. Reality was in the transcendent experience and could not

---

Voegelin seems to have had in mind is that, for Plato, the unknown God of the Beyond *reveals itself* as Nous, but that there remains a dimension of divine reality toward which we are oriented but which remains inaccessible to the human knower.

29. *Ecumenic Age*, 241, 234, 239. See also *In Search of Order*, 88–107; and *Anamnesis*, 90.

be affected by its failure to be embodied. In its social incarnation, however, the truth of order was subject to the restrictions imposed by existence in the cosmos. To live in the metaxy was to live in a permanent tension. It was this tension that Isaiah and the other prophets tried to obliterate. They attempted the impossible, "to make the leap in being a leap out of existence into a divinely transfigured world beyond the laws of mundane existence."[30]

While he praises Plato's realism, Voegelin's greatest reservation regarding the Platonic project concerns Plato's refusal to break completely with the polis. Plato stopped just short of breaking through to the notion of a universal humanity, because his conceptualization of the problem of order still tended to reflect the institutions of the polis.[31] The Platonic dream of a Hellenic empire, in the form of a federation under a hegemonic polis, infused by the spirit of the Academy, was never to be realized. Nevertheless Plato's effort could be counted a success "in as much as in his dialogues he created the symbols of the new order of wisdom, not for Hellas only, but for all mankind." Voegelin credits Plato (and Aristotle) with creating the language by which human beings can speak about the truth of order and the divine reality extending even beyond that order; although even this noetic language, while essentially sound, must be developed further. There is a need, then, to move beyond conceiving the good society along the model of the polis. "The Platonic-Aristotelian paradigm of the best polis cannot provide an answer for the great questions of our time—either for the organizational problems of industrial society or for the spiritual problems of the struggle between Christianity and ideology."[32]

The Platonic solution to the tension between the truth of order and its social incarnation would seem to have two dimensions. The first might be described as Plato's "realism." Society resists the truth of order, but Plato's realism enabled him to adjust the paradigm to accommodate what people are able to bear. This realism is also manifest in Plato's ability to maintain a balance of consciousness in the face of theophany; transcendent experience does not absolve one from following the laws that govern the cosmos. In both of these

30. *Ecumenic Age*, 27; *Israel and Revelation*, 452.
31. *Plato and Aristotle*, 227, 294; *Anamnesis*, 207.
32. *Plato and Aristotle*, 5–6; *Anamnesis*, 206; *Science, Politics, and Gnosticism*, 21. See also "Oxford Political Philosophers," 109.

areas, Voegelin could contrast Platonic realism with prophetic zeal, which seems unwilling to make concessions to either human weakness or cosmic structure.

The second important dimension of the Platonic solution has to do with the philosopher's realization that whether or not the paradigm is ever embodied in society, the truth of order continues to live on in the souls of those who are attuned to the divine ground. Order may never take lasting form in society; what matters more is that it remains present in the luminosity of noetic consciousness. Voegelin's Plato is a man conscious that the model *politeia* lives in his soul through his communion with the God; if society avails itself of this wisdom, so much the better, but if not, the truth of order continues to exist in the souls of the philosopher and his disciples.

As was the case in Israel, the tension of existence has not been overcome; there remains a wide gap between social order and the order discovered in experiences of transcendence. Voegelin faults the prophets for trying to eliminate or overcome this gap through metastatic faith and for expecting too much of their society and its institutions. In Plato's case, however, he finds a much greater sensitivity to the limits imposed by life in the metaxy, and also a tendency to dissolve the paradox on the level of luminous consciousness without as much concern for the institutional embodiment of the truth of order. Admittedly, Plato never completely abandoned his attempts at social regeneration, and we must recall that, for Voegelin, Plato's ongoing attention to the polis was more of a liability than a strength. In Voegelin's eyes, Plato's achievement consisted in his ability to recognize the *limits* to any social incarnation of transcendent truth, and in his knowledge that this lack of institutional embodiment did not detract at all from the preeminent reality of the paradigm as it existed in the philosopher's soul.

SEVEN

IS THE GOOD SOCIETY POSSIBLE?

Having followed the struggle for order in Israel and in Hellas as it manifests itself in the work of Isaiah and Plato, we are in a better position to consider the question of the degree to which the good society, that is, a society that reflects the truth of order in its practices and institutions, is possible. We have already noted that in both cases there remains a serious discrepancy between the truth of order known in consciousness and human attempts at its social incarnation, and this is not surprising. Voegelin was emphatic in stating that the tension of existence can never be completely overcome; human existence is always existence in the metaxy. Even at its best, social reality will not conform to the truth of order, and the most well ordered society will inevitably decline.[1]

In Israel, every adaptation geared to insuring the people's pragmatic survival, for example, the monarchy, seemed to seriously compromise the truth of order as expressed in the Covenant. On the other hand, the prophets' uncompromising adherence to the Covenant allowed no room for accommodation with the exigencies of life in the world. It appears that Israel was caught in an unsolvable dilemma: to survive in the world as an organized society meant a dilution of the Covenant strictures, while complete devotion to the Covenant was a recipe for political disaster. Failure to observe the Covenant by focusing primarily on pragmatic survival would bring about an inner weakness leading to political collapse, but observing the Covenant in its purity would result in political suicide.

Voegelin found Plato's approach to the tension of existence more

---

1. Voegelin, "Industrial Society in Search of Reason," 39; "Oxford Political Philosophers," 101.

satisfactory than that adopted by the prophets. Confronted with the same tension between order and society, Plato was willing to incorporate into society only as much of the truth of order as the people were able to bear and cosmic law would allow. And Voegelin did not see this compromise as an abandonment of the truth of order, since order lives on in philosophical souls. With Plato, the problem was transposed to a level beyond the vicissitudes of organized society.

In both cases, however, there remains an unanswered question: "To what extent can the truth of order be realized in society, and to what degree can society approximate this truth in its institutions?" In considering this question, I will reflect in the first part of this chapter upon the possibility of social change in relationship to the structure of reality, and in the second part, I will examine what Voegelin believed to be achievable in the social realm.

SOCIAL CHANGE AND THE STRUCTURE OF REALITY

In my discussion of the possibility of change in the structure of reality in Chapter 2, I noted that the development of Voegelin's theory of consciousness makes it amply clear that a "leap in being," or differentiation of consciousness, is not a change in the structure of reality, but a further illumination. The area that "changes" was very carefully circumscribed as pertaining to "man's consciousness of his humanity in participatory tension toward the divine ground, and to no reality beyond this restricted area." The differentiation does not alter the structure of reality or free one from the human condition. As one of Voegelin's interpreters has put it, "To be realistic means to acknowledge reality, all of it, beginning with the *realissimum* as the unseen source of order, and including the world's own stubborn order. Reality is not something within the power of man to change. It is something to live *within* and to live *with*."[2]

The stability that characterizes reality would seem to extend to that "area" within the whole referred to as "society":

> Human existence in natural societies remains what it was before its
> orientation toward a destiny beyond nature. Faith is the anticipation

2. *Ecumenic Age,* 8; Gregor Sebba, "Orders and Disorders of the Soul: Eric Voegelin's Philosophy of History," 282–310. See also Voegelin, "World Empire," 178–79.

of a supernatural perfection of man; it is not this perfection itself.
The realm of God is not of this world. . . . The result of the epochal
differentiation is not the replacement of the closed society by an open
society—if we may use the Bergsonian terms—but a complication of
symbolism which corresponds to the differentiation of experiences.[3]

The differentiation is a differentiation of consciousness; the structure of society, with its inherent imperfections and limitations, is not
changed. The world remains as it was after consciousness differentiates. In opposing gnostic and metastatic thinkers and their dreams of
a radically altered social reality, Voegelin underlines the stability of
order:

> No matter to which of the three variants of immanentization the
> movements belong, the attempt to create a new world is common to
> all. This endeavor can be meaningfully undertaken only if the consti-
> tution of being can in fact be altered by man. The world, however, re-
> mains as it is given to us, and it is not within man's power to change
> its structure. . . . It is likewise possible to assume that the order of be-
> ing as it is given to us men (wherever its origin is to be sought) is
> good and that it is we human beings who are inadequate.

Society participates in the wider It-reality; as such it is subject to the
Anaximandrian process of emergence and decline. It is the duty of
human beings to *understand* the place of the social order within this
process; in this regard a large part of philosophers' realism consists
in their understanding that their action is limited to "a sensitive
alertness to disorder in personal and social existence," as well as to
their response to theophany in consciousness. The structure of history is "not a project for human or social action, but a reality to be
discerned retrospectively." History is not primarily a matter of bringing about a changed social situation: "It rather reveals a mankind
striving for its order of existence within the world while attuning
itself with the truth of being beyond the world, and gaining in the
process not a substantially better order within the world but an increased understanding of the gulf that lies between immanent exis-

---

3. *New Science of Politics,* 157–58. See also *Science, Politics, and Gnosticism,* 87.
Voegelin has been criticized for his "otherworldly" interpretation of biblical
faith. See Anderson, "Politics and the Transcendent," 88–92; Douglass, "Gospel
and Political Order," 25–45; Russell Nieli, "Eric Voegelin's Evolving Ideas on
Gnosticism, Mysticism, and Modern Radical Politics," 93–102.

tence and the transcendent truth of being. Canaan is as far away today as it has always been in the past."[4]

It is the discovery of order that was Voegelin's primary concern. His philosophy of society and history is a philosophy of *order*, and he was wary of any human efforts that would seem to undermine the stability of order. Since the tension between true order and empirical order can never be abolished, "existence in an imperfectly ordered society, with numerous and even gross injustices in single cases, is preferable to disorder and violence."[5]

There are certain evils in human existence that are ineradicable; attempts to overcome them by institutional means are doomed to failure, because human nature does not change. Any suggestion to the contrary is utopian at best and at worst can make one an accomplice in totalitarian murder. Liberalism's notion of progress, expressed as a gradual and permanent revolution, is gnostic and is one in essence with totalitarianism. The notion that humanity might move beyond a world order sustained by a balance of military forces toward a more peaceful international order is like a gnostic dream. While insisting that Voegelin cannot be classified as "conservative" or "radical," Dante Germino argues that Voegelin "rejects as 'second reality' constructions any political views which hold out the hope or prospect of fundamentally altering domestic power relations—the power of elite rule—or of transcending the 'necessities' of international relations and the use of military force. It is unclear how much room for maneuver political reality affords in Voegelin's philosophy for the creation of a relatively more decent and humane world."[6]

---

4. *Science, Politics, and Gnosticism,* 86–87, 100; *Israel and Revelation,* 129. See also *World of the Polis,* 254; *Ecumenic Age,* 218, 174.

5. Voegelin, "The Nature of the Law," 61.

6. Voegelin, "The Origins of Totalitarianism," 74–75; Dante Germino, "Eric Voegelin's *Anamnesis*," 87–88. See also Voegelin, "More's *Utopia,*" 460–64; *Conversations,* 148; "Liberalism and Its History," 509–18; "Origins of Totalitarianism," 75, 84–85; "Oxford Political Philosophers," 109–11; *New Science of Politics,* 171–73. For a view similar to Germino's, see Nieli, "Eric Voegelin's Evolving Ideas," 101–2. Nieli suggests that Voegelin is not as susceptible to this criticism in his later (1960s and after) writings. To a certain extent this is true; Voegelin's attention turned from a critique of gnosticism and its corresponding political forms to an elaboration of his theory of consciousness. But it is also the case that there is nothing in his later writings to indicate that Voegelin had changed his mind on this issue, and the late essay "Wisdom and the Magic of the Extreme"

This observation highlights a tension in Voegelin's thought that underlies much of his writing on society. A reader may find himself or herself in substantial agreement with Voegelin's analysis of second realities and derailment. One might applaud his insights into the mentality of activist dreamers and the climate of opinion created by the eclipse of reality. Indeed, loss of reality *is* a serious danger to social existence. Yet one might also hesitate to agree with all of Voegelin's judgments concerning just what it is that constitutes deformation, eclipse, or activist dreaming. When does the effort to attune one's society to the truth of order derail into unreality? Are all efforts to make the social order more just and equitable by institutional means a revolt against God?[7] Is there no middle ground between the intolerant visions of activist dreamers and an uncritical acceptance of the status quo? No society may ever be able to fully embody the truth of order, but can they at least strive to approximate it to a significant degree, without this achievement being limited to the souls of isolated prophets and philosophers? Finally, by what standard is one to evaluate when and if a social movement or thinker has lost contact with reality?

Unfortunately, such a standard, while operative, is never made explicit in Voegelin's work. To illustrate the problem we return to the prophet Isaiah. When Isaiah advises Ahaz not to resort to expedient military alliances in defending Judah, Voegelin sees Isaiah's counsel as an example of metastatic faith or magic. Isaiah has lost the balance of consciousness; he has tried through faith to move beyond the structure of pragmatic social existence, and he has tried the impossible: "to make the leap in being a leap out of existence into a divinely transfigured world beyond the laws of mundane existence." Far from carrying out God's will, Isaiah's desire "to transform reality into something which by essence it is not is the rebellion against the nature of things as ordained by God."[8] In short, there has been an eclipse of reality in the vision of the prophet. Yet on what basis has this determination been made? How has Voegelin determined the "nature of things as ordained by God" in order to contrast them with the Isaianic vision? It will not do to declare that his advice is metas-

---

reveals the same caution with regard to the possible effects of pneumatic differentiation and a deep antipathy toward those he regards as activist dreamers.

7. *Science, Politics, and Gnosticism,* 53–54.

8. *Israel and Revelation,* 452–53. See also *Ecumenic Age,* 26.

tatic because it violates reality. What are the evaluative criteria by which this judgment is made? What is it about Isaiah's prophecy that places him at odds with reality?

I would contend that it is *on the basis of his political advice* that Isaiah is declared to have indulged in metastatic faith and thereby suffered a loss of reality. It is his political stance that earns him the accusation that he has ignored the structure of reality. Voegelin views Isaiah's exhortation that Ahaz eschew shortsighted political alliances and that he not resort to arms during this crisis as a violation of mysterious "laws of mundane existence." Unfortunately, he never makes clear exactly what these laws are, except that to transgress them is to attempt to move beyond the structure of reality. There are operative in Voegelin's judgment certain criteria as to what is possible in the social/political sphere, but he never makes these standards explicit. Are they a social manifestation of and participation in Anaximander's cosmic flux, revealing the inescapable hold of the primary experience? Are they perhaps the laws governing the external phenomenal world of a Kantian universe? Might they be the new "modes and orders" of Machiavellian power politics? Though politics may be the art of the possible, whose notion of possibility is to prevail? If we are going to distinguish those who acknowledge the structure of reality from those who do not on the basis of what they believe to be achievable in the social/political realm, then we must be very clear as to the evaluative standard being applied. We cannot simply declare someone to be detached from reality because their view of what is possible in the social and political sphere does not coincide with our own position. Lack of clarity on this point lends a certain degree of ambiguity to Voegelin's thought, because one person's obedience to the "laws" of mundane existence, in his words, may be for another an invitation to transform a disordered social situation.

Although it is impossible to say with certainty how Voegelin understood these "laws," we may gain some idea of what he had in mind by examining his attitude on related issues. We have already noted, in Chapter 3, Voegelin's observation that "the maintenance of an order will have always, human nature being what it is, to rely on the instrument of force." Isaiah failed to realize the difference "between the order of faith in Yahweh and the order of power in political existence." It is inconceivable that anyone would suppose that adherence to prophetic admonitions could be an effective substitute for armed force.[9] One must be attuned to both the truth of order *and* the order of mundane existence, where, it would seem, a different set of laws is operative. In the mundane sphere, force must at times be exercised in the interests of preserving social order, even if, regrettably, such action disturbs our moral sensibilities.

In a discussion between philosopher Michael Polanyi, economist M. M. Postan, physicist Robert Oppenheimer, and Voegelin, there arose the question of the relationship between ethics, governments, and warfare. Responding to Oppenheimer's concern that major political and military decisions were made without any ethical discussion, Polanyi suggested that the "cruelty and disdain of any moral consideration" during World War II may have been due "precisely to the fact that this war saw an unprecedented wave of moral passions which manifested themselves in this violent manner." Oppenheimer apologized for not making himself understood, and indicated that he did not maintain that a government must be influenced by ethical decisions: "We can ignore ethics; but it has to be there to be ignored. There is no need for man to act virtuously, but it is necessary that we discuss virtue." Postan, observing how easily moral passions can be manipulated by the state in service of its own ends, added:

> The trouble with our democratic society is not that moral or ethical stimulants are not widespread enough, but rather that it is easier to provoke them than get rid of them. And once they have been mobilized, not only are they a major force toward converting amoral intention into a public act, they may also serve as the justification for a whole range of cruel and destructive acts, to which our era seems especially prone. The problem is not to assess the depth or breadth of the ethical content in our civilization, but to study it from the institutional and sociological standpoint and define methods not only of mobilizing it, but especially of demobilizing it.

As part of this exchange, Voegelin maintained:

> The question of the use of arms was discussed long before the appearance of the atomic bomb—during the 1930's, for instance, when it was a question of gas or bacteriological warfare. In fact, this is a classic question of politics, which is part of the concept of the *bellum justum,* the "just war." One of the principal assumptions is that a war can begin as a "just war," become extremely unjust by the way it is

9. Voegelin, "Right and Might," in *Collected Works,* vol. 27, 86; *Ecumenic Age,* 27; *Israel and Revelation,* 450.

fought, and even more unjust by the type of peaceful settlement imposed after it is over. These are questions of the most elementary sort, and I do not believe anyone should complain if we refrain from constantly bringing them up in public. The question you pose is, I believe, essentially a sociological one. It concerns this type of society in which we live and in which an elementary knowledge perfectly acquired for centuries is not publicly efficacious. But there is a reason it is not; as you have quite rightly pointed out, an atomic bombardment is not a moral matter but depends on politics and questions of existence. And when a social process is involved, we cannot, in the name of morality, refuse to use certain types of weapons and make certain types of decisions. The classic treatise on this point is Thucydides' *Peloponnesian War*. The necessity of the process he terms *kinesis*, and he considers *kinesis* a kind of social illness. When you are caught in such an illness you cannot extricate yourself as long as you are a statesman; you can only get out of it personally. The Platonic attitude of withdrawal from "sick politics," in the Thucydidean sense of the term, is a personal possibility, but it does not eliminate the public necessity of taking on the sickness as long as it lasts.[10]

While one might appreciate the concern that animates this dialogue, that is, the danger of ethical feelings being inflamed and leading to further atrocities, there hangs over the exchange the aura of a political "realism" that is able to abstract from ethical concerns and to treat political affairs as the manipulation of forces to be mobilized or demobilized.

In relationship to the other participants', Voegelin's contribution to this exchange represents a more nuanced position, but one that still reflects the tensions in his own thinking concerning social change. First of all, there is Voegelin's observation that the most "elementary knowledge" concerning the possibility of a "just war" is not "publicly efficacious." This observation is quite consonant with his view that it is difficult for reason and order to become socially effective. At the same time, the next sentence in Voegelin's response indicates that he has learned well the lesson taught by Plato in the *Laws*. Order and reason are unlikely to become socially effective, so the philosopher must be willing to accept measures more applicable to the second, third, or even fourth best society. And in acknowledging that "an atomic bombardment is not a moral matter but depends on politics and questions of existence," perhaps Voegelin, following Plato, was

10. Raymond Aron, ed., *World Technology and Human Destiny*, 213–15.

attempting to strike that balance between persuasion and the judicious use of force that is an unfortunate fact of life in the metaxy. Nonetheless, Voegelin's approach still suffers from a tendency to find a certain degree of necessity operative in the institutional, "phenomenal" dimension of social reality. Even if one were to concede that Voegelin's remarks may have been directed against those who uncritically denounce the use of military might without having considered the possible consequences of not employing such force, the impression still remains that it is because of the *necessity* governing at least part of the social process that the use of force becomes compelling.

Voegelin's invocation of Thucydides supports this view, for in his treatment of the historian, Voegelin explains that while Thucydides may have rejected the Anaximandrian and Heraclitian doctrine of the "compensatory rise and fall of all existing things as the principle for explaining the course of human affairs," he still retained the notion of the necessity of social process. In Thucydides' case, however, Voegelin likens this necessity to the inexorable process of an incurable disease. This necessity may lead one to adopt measures that would normally be considered repugnant. In trying to explain the discrepancies between Plato's evaluation of Archelaus of Macedonia as a murderer and Thucydides' view of him as a benefactor, Voegelin adds: "The trouble is that probably both portraits are equally correct; there are situations where the nature of the opposition requires brutal means for the achievement of political ends desirable in themselves."[11] It would seem, then, that in dealing with a "social process" we must be prepared to separate moral from pragmatic considerations. There is an inexorable quality to social process that may require the suspension of one's ethical principles. In one's personal life, withdrawal from the ugliness of politics may be an option, but whatever is found repugnant to one's moral sense cannot be allowed to interfere with the pragmatic decisions necessary for the maintenance of social order. It would be marvelous if people lived in accord with reason, but since they do not, society depends upon a political realism that must sometimes compromise the truth of order to survive in a dangerous world.

We find the same ambivalence in Voegelin's assessment of the

11. *World of the Polis*, 354–58, 361.

early modern political philosophers.[12] While not uncritically advocating their approach, he seems to acknowledge their wisdom in dealing effectively with the problems of pragmatic existence. For example, Voegelin noted that Machiavelli correctly recognized the structure of reality and that he had been wrongly labeled an immoralist by "gnostic intellectuals." While admitting that Machiavelli's views on politics and human nature were distorted by the brutality of his age, Voegelin maintains that he is to be praised for his "healthy and honest" reaction to such experiences. In Hobbes, Voegelin recognized unfortunate gnostic tendencies and an attempt to eliminate the transcendent orientation from human nature and society. At the same time, Hobbes should be given credit for understanding the need for coercive and powerful measures to quell sectarian strife. In relationship to these sectarian, activist gnostics, Hobbes's approach, though one-sided in its rejection of transcendence, is to be preferred because his simplifications can be corrected while his clarification of the structure of political reality is a permanent gain. Even Locke, whose grounding of political order in a "psychology of desire" Voegelin views with contempt, must be given credit for presenting a better alternative to the problem of sustaining a social order than those Voegelin labels as activists or utopian thinkers.[13]

If these philosophers represent a falling off in quality from Platonic political philosophy, they are at least superior to utopians, gnostics, and ideologists in their acknowledgment of the structure of reality. They may lack Plato's emphasis on transcendent orientation as constitutive of human nature, but in their attentiveness to the mundane dimension of reality and their understanding of the coercive means that must sometimes be employed to maintain social

---

12. See, for example, the connection Voegelin makes between Thucydides and Machiavelli in *World of the Polis*, 364–65.

13. For Voegelin's references to Machiavelli, see *Plato and Aristotle*, 225; *New Science of Politics*, 170; "Machiavelli's Prince: Background and Formation"; and his review of *On Tyranny: An Interpretation of Xenophon's Hiero*, by Leo Strauss. For the view that Voegelin considered Machiavelli to be a gnostic, see Glenn Schram, "Strauss and Voegelin on Machiavelli and Modernity." For Voegelin's discussion of Hobbes, see *Political Religions*, 47–56; *New Science of Politics*, 152–62, 178–89; and "Oxford Political Philosophers," 106–7. Voegelin's references to Locke can be found in *From Enlightenment to Revolution*, 36–42; "More's *Utopia*," 463–64; "Oxford Political Philosophers," 105–7; "Industrial Society in Search of Reason," 36–37; and *Faith and Political Philosophy: The Correspondence between Leo Strauss and Eric Voegelin, 1934–1964*.

order, they are bearers of the Platonic insight that a society must first be pragmatically ordered "before it can indulge in the luxury of also representing the truth of the soul."[14]

The gap between the truth of order, the "Ought in the ontological sense,"[15] and the pragmatic realm of social order is indeed wide. The impetus to move society closer to the truth of order arises in the luminosity of differentiating consciousness. Such advances, however, enter into tension with the "laws of mundane existence" that seem to govern the realm of cosmic flux and political possibility. The notion of "laws of mundane existence" brings to attention once again the "two-tiered" quality of society noted in Chapter 4. On the one hand we have order revealed in consciousness, seeking embodiment in society, while on the other we are confronted with an external and pragmatic dimension of society, apparently sharing in the "laws" which govern cosmic, natural process. If there are hints of dualism here, they did not go unnoticed by Voegelin:

> The emphatic partnership with God does not abolish partnership in the community of being at large, which includes being in mundane existence. Man and society, if they want to retain their foothold in being that makes the leap into emphatic partnership possible, must remain adjusted to the order of mundane existence. Hence there is no age of the church that would succeed an age of society on the level of more compact attunement to being. Instead there develop the tensions, frictions, and balances between the two levels of attunement, a dualistic structure of existence which expresses itself in pairs of symbols, of *theologia civilis* and *theologia supranaturalis*, of temporal and spiritual powers, of secular state and church.[16]

Is it not possible that this distinction between levels of attunement reflects the "double constitution of history" described in Chapter 5? Might not the "laws of mundane existence" be applicable to the phenomenal realm of history and society, while the level of differentiating consciousness, the "sphere of encounter," corresponds to history as noumenal? Has Voegelin perhaps adopted a Kantian framework in discussing society and history, a framework in which we are confronted with a society operating simultaneously within two realms: one in which society is understood as phenomenal and as obeying

14. *New Science of Politics*, 162.
15. Voegelin, "The Nature of the Law," 42–44.
16. *Israel and Revelation*, 11.

the "laws of mundane existence," much as natural phenomena obey "inexorable laws," and another in which consciousness advances through differentiation? Voegelin's reading of Plato's *Timaeus* and *Laws* and his praise for the Platonic approach to the tension between the truth of order and society also point in this direction. For there we find society as cosmic analogue, faced with inevitable decline in conformity with cosmic rhythms, while the truth of order lives on in the souls of those who, through attunement to the divine measure, have moved beyond the flux.

What makes this account problematic is that social reality partakes of both realms. It then becomes difficult if not impossible to know where the boundary lies between those areas in which the laws of mundane existence are in effect and those in which a differentiation of consciousness might serve as a catalyst in bringing about the incarnation of true order in society. Society is one; there is no clear line between the meanings that inform social life and the institutional order in which they are incarnate. I believe that Voegelin understood this, but by framing his account within a context where society and history are understood as consisting of a luminous, noumenal core and a phenomenal surface operating in accord with laws of mundane existence, he introduces distinctions that obfuscate rather than clarify the structure of social reality and make it especially difficult to speak of genuine social change.[17] In other words, a "two-level" approach to social reality can easily lead to confusion because society does not lend itself to this kind of distinction. In Voegelin's case, I do not believe that he was always able to avoid this confusion.

What results is a view of social process that is at times indistinguishable from "phenomenal" process, that is, a process obeying cosmic and natural laws. Cosmic and natural rhythms blend with the "laws" governing what is possible in the social and political sphere. The "laws of mundane existence" would seem to reach from the natural order into the social order. The intelligibility that is characteristic of physical, chemical, and biological orders, interpreted by Voegelin as external "phenomena" acting in accordance with un-

---

17. Gerhart Niemeyer has raised similar questions. He wonders about the relationship between "social causality" and the "structure of philosophical order." See Niemeyer, "The Order of History," 403–9.

changing laws, is confused with those areas of human activity where people work to create social orders that better reflect human intelligence and transcendent goodness. "Laws" governing the natural world are extended to aspects of social and political reality. Voegelin did not carefully consider the distinction mentioned in Chapter 4 between process as intelligible and process as both intelligible and intelligent. Is poverty really in the same category as mortality when it comes to listing the ills that afflict the human race? Is it an equally unchangeable fact of human existence? In Voegelin's thought, the distinction between the realm of being as given and the realm of being as constituted through human action is not always clear.[18] The ambiguity becomes evident as he explains how, through encounter with the "noumenal depth," humans *are*, in some sense, involved in the constitution of being, but only as constituted in acts of "symbolic expression." There remains, however, a "phenomenal surface" to history which is "given" and which must be studied as one would study any other object in the external world.[19]

The language of phenomena/noumena, coupled with a failure to clearly distinguish between being as given and being as humanly constituted, leads, I believe, to encounters like the literary exchange that occurred between Voegelin and Hannah Arendt concerning Arendt's *Origins of Totalitarianism*. While finding much to praise in that work, Voegelin also notes some "theoretical derailments" in Arendt's account. From Voegelin's point of view, Arendt has focused too narrowly on the institutional and phenomenal surface of history, and in doing so she has failed to see the *essential sameness* between her own liberalism and modern-day totalitarianism. In her response, Arendt strongly insists that evaluating social and political movements in

18. Robert Doran has written: "Surely a distinction is in order here. . . . Human praxis is constitutive of being: not originally creative of its elemental structure, but responsibly constitutive of the character of the human world as good or evil. . . . Surely the movement from the real human world as it is to the good human world as it ought to be is grounded in a transformation of ourselves; but self-constitution is coincident with world-constitution. A philosophy of world-constitutive praxis need not violate the order of the soul masterfully disengaged in Voegelin's retrieval of classical sources" ("Theology's Situation: Questions to Eric Voegelin," 83). For the comparison of poverty and mortality, see Voegelin, *Science, Politics, and Gnosticism*, 91; *In Search of Order*, 35–36.

19. Voegelin, "What Is History?," 12.

terms of phenomena and essence tends to obscure some very real differences, which Voegelin seems to view as existing "merely" on the phenomenal level:

> Professor Voegelin treats "phenomenal differences"—which to me as differences of factuality are all-important—as minor outgrowths of some "essential sameness" of a doctrinal nature. Numerous affinities between totalitarianism and some other trends in Occidental political or intellectual history have been described with this result in my opinion: they all failed to point out the distinct quality of what was actually happening. The "phenomenal differences," far from "obscuring" some essential sameness, are those phenomena which make totalitarianism "totalitarian," which distinguish this one form of government and movement from all others and therefore can alone help us in finding its essence. What is unprecedented in totalitarianism is not primarily its ideological content, but the event of totalitarian domination itself. . . . Mr. Voegelin seems to think that totalitarianism is only the other side of liberalism, positivism and pragmatism. But whether one agrees with liberalism or not (and I may say here that I am rather certain that I am neither a liberal nor a positivist nor a pragmatist), the point is that liberals are clearly not totalitarians. This, of course, does not exclude the fact that liberal or positivistic elements also lend themselves to totalitarian thinking; but such affinities would only mean that one has to draw even sharper distinctions because of the *fact* that liberals are not totalitarians.[20]

Voegelin's concluding remarks illustrate how well he understood the real issue between himself and Professor Arendt. They also indicate the future direction his thought would take:

> It is the question of essence in history, the question of how to delimit and define phenomena of the class of political movements. Dr. Arendt draws her lines of demarcation on what she considers the factual level of history; arrives at well-distinguished complexes of phenomena of the type of "totalitarianism"; and is willing to accept such complexes as ultimate, essential units. I take exception to this method because it disregards the fact that the self-formation of movements in history, institutionally and ideologically, is not theoretical formation. The investigation inevitably will start from the phenomena, but the question of theoretically justifiable units in political science cannot be solved by accepting the units thrown up in the stream of history at their face value. What a unit is will emerge when the principles furnished by philosophical anthropology are applied to historical materials. It then

20. Voegelin, "Origins of Totalitarianism," 69, 75, 80.

may happen that political movements, which on the scene of history are bitterly opposed to one another, will prove to be closely related on the level of essence.[21]

In later writings Voegelin's language would change; the "level of essence" would yield to "equivalences of experience," while "principles of a philosophical anthropology" would be replaced by an analysis of consciousness and reality. But the project would remain the same: to get "behind" reality as phenomenal to the experiences of participation that give rise to social and historical meaning. A case could be made that this is Voegelin's greatest contribution to political philosophy. His refusal to allow political or social "science" to be reduced to an inventory of institutional practices and his insistence on the need for higher controls of meaning in ordering society are crucial insights for a genuine political and social theory. At the same time, one can detect in his exchange with Arendt some areas in which his greatest strengths left him susceptible to some of her criticisms.

Arendt's objection, that Voegelin tended to treat the "phenomenal" level of social and political reality as secondary while locating the "real" on the level of "essence," is, to a certain degree, a valid criticism. If anything, this tendency intensified in Voegelin's later work, where this concentration on "equivalence" of experience sometimes overshadowed not only differences on the phenomenal level, but even differences on the level of differentiation of consciousness.[22] What results from this tendency, as Arendt points out, is a failure to distinguish between political movements that, while displaying certain intellectual affinities, are in fact very different in their concrete social and political practices. Liberals are *not* totalitarians. Voegelin, in pushing beyond "phenomenal" differences to the level of essence, or equivalence of experience, perhaps did not give such differences the serious attention they deserve. As a consequence there is in his approach to social change a lack of differentiation between activist dreamers and those who, while not seeking to

21. Ibid., 84–85.
22. See Chapter 2 on the blurring of the distinction between pneumatic and noetic differentiation and the reduction of this distinction to "ethnic differences." For examples of this tendency in Voegelin's work, consult "Equivalences of Experience and Symbolization in History" and "The Meditative Origin of the Philosophical Knowledge of Order."

abolish or ignore the structure of reality, still maintain a belief in the possibility of human progress.[23] And how could it be otherwise if, at the level of "essence," all such movements are equivalent?

While Voegelin's thought may be open to criticism in this regard, it is not altogether clear that Arendt has adequately responded to *his* criticism. Voegelin maintained that "the true dividing line in the contemporary crisis does not run between liberals and totalitarians, but between the religious and philosophical transcendentalists on the one side, and the liberal and totalitarian immanentist sectarians on the other side."[24] His language is strong; but if he was correct in his understanding of humanity as constituted by its relationship to the divine ground, then does not liberalism's agnosticism on such questions of ultimate ends reveal a view of humanity as impoverished as that of totalitarianism, which, in the long term, will exact an equally terrible price? One wonders whether Arendt has seriously considered this point in her correspondence with Voegelin.

This is not in any way to suggest that Arendt is the liberal Voegelin apparently took her to be. First of all, she vehemently denies that such is the case; and in addition, her discussion of modern "masses" would seem to situate her well within the classical tradition of political philosophy:

> To me, modern masses are disintegrated by the fact that they are "masses" in a strict sense of the word. They are distinguished from the multitudes of former centuries in that they do not have common interests to bind them together nor any kind of common "consent" which, according to Cicero, constitutes *inter-est*, that which is between men, ranging all the way from material to spiritual and other matters. This "between" can be a common ground and it can be a common purpose; it always fulfills the double function of binding men together *and* separating them in an articulate way. The lack of common interest so characteristic of modern masses is therefore only another sign of their homelessness and rootlessness.[25]

Arendt's concerns here reflect an interest similar to Voegelin's in trying to ground political life in what is "common." As discussed in

23. Voegelin also believed in progress, but the only type of progress he was inclined to recognize was that pertaining to the movement in consciousness from compactness to differentiation. This matter will be explored more fully in Chapter 8.
24. Voegelin, "Origins of Totalitarianism," 75.
25. Ibid., 81.

Chapter 3, Voegelin also considered *xynon,* "the common," to be an indispensable element in constituting a good society. In this regard, both Arendt and Voegelin reflect the influence of classical political philosophy. However, at least in this exchange it seems as if it was Voegelin who pursued the question further as to what it was that is being articulated in the symbol. In doing so he discovered humanity's constitutive orientation toward the divine ground as the basis for what is common, leading him to draw the "dividing line" in political philosophy in a way that Arendt found perplexing. Had Arendt followed Voegelin's direction in her analysis, she may have found herself more willing to accept some of his conclusions, for Voegelin's project would seem to coincide in many respects with her own philosophical and political instincts.

Arendt's insistence that a liberal is not a totalitarian is a point well taken, but that does not mean that Voegelin's argument is without merit. Arendt argued that "phenomenal" differences were more important than Voegelin acknowledged. In her method she appealed to the concrete "phenomena" of history to substantiate her position. Yet Voegelin's insistence on transposing the issue to the level of essence might have been due in part to his realization that one must be very careful about generalizing from the data of history when that data itself is the product of disordered consciousness. Unintelligible situations can scarcely serve as the basis for an intelligible and intelligent theory. Thus Voegelin was concerned with recapturing the structure of reality and consciousness in order to provide a framework within which to distinguish order from disorder as it manifests itself in history. Both philosophers were in substantial agreement as to the dangers of totalitarianism and other mass movements. Voegelin saw his task as penetrating to the sources of such disorder, and to do so meant to plumb the depths of consciousness and reality. It was a task he pursued relentlessly—so much so that in attempting to recover the essential structures of reality and consciousness, his attention may have been diverted from the important particular and concrete differences between historical phenomena, regardless of their common source. Arendt, on the other hand, while not neglecting the problem of similarities among political phenomena, concentrated more closely on these differences. In doing so, Voegelin believed that she had not delved deeply enough into the sources of disorder.

WHAT CAN BE DONE?

None of my comments concerning the Voegelin-Arendt exchange are meant to suggest that Voegelin turned his back on social problems by explaining them away at a level of symbolic expression or "essence." While it seems to me that there are indeed some problematic areas in his approach, these do not stem from any lack of commitment to social and political issues. Like that of the classical philosophers he so admired, Voegelin's work was motivated by the need to resist social disorder. It would be difficult to find a more practical reason to engage in philosophy than that offered by Voegelin:

> I should perhaps say the strongest influence is my perhaps misplaced sensitivity toward murder. I do not like people just shooting each other for nonsensical reasons. That is a motive for finding out what possibly could be the reason someone could persuade somebody else to shoot people for no particular purpose. It is not simply an academic problem, or a problem in the history of opinion and so on, that evokes my interest in this or that issue in the theory of consciousness, but the very practical problem of mass murder which is manifest in the twentieth century.[26]

The philosophical enterprise, as he saw it, was always a practical one; not perhaps in the sense of instrumental practicality, but in the wider sense of *praxis* as that transforming knowledge that animates all of our action.[27]

Even on the matter as to what is possible in the social realm, Voegelin's caution should not be misconstrued as a recommendation for political or social quietism. His hard-headed political realism and attention to questions of social order and disorder belie any such assumption. On this score it is important to understand that Voegelin was critical not only of those whom he considered to be activist dreamers but also of those who wash their hands of any involvement in the social/political process. Indeed, he believed that the success of activist dreamers is attributable in part to the vacuum left by the failure of pre-modern traditions to deal adequately with the tension of existence.

The tendency toward apoliticism is most evident within the orbit

26. Voegelin, "Autobiographical Statement," 117.
27. On this understanding of *praxis,* see Bernard Lonergan, "Theology and Praxis," in *A Third Collection,* 184–201.

constituted by the pneumatic differentiation. Noetically oriented societies can also succumb to this temptation, but the balance inherent
to the noetic differentiation tends to prevent this from happening.[28]
With pneumatic differentiation, one can be so caught up in the
transcendent experience that one neglects life in the world. This is
one of the charges Voegelin leveled against the Israelite prophets.
For the most part his critique focuses on their inclination to expect
society to embody more of the truth of order than it can actually
bear. This constitutes flight from the world in the sense of ignoring
the laws that govern worldly existence. In Voegelin's view the prophets
refuse to compromise with the human condition. At the same time,
their refusal to acknowledge the limitations inherent to the pragmatic situation, coupled with their experience of rejection by their
own society, can lead to what Voegelin considered to be an unrealistic reliance upon God. In that case the prophet spurns any reliance
on human means and waits for God to intervene. As Voegelin inter-
prets Isaiah, this translates into doing nothing in the face of blatant
aggression because to act militarily would be to demonstrate a lack of
faith. From this point it is but a short step to apocalyptic vision and
gnostic salvation.

Although Voegelin found this tendency toward passivity to be
present in the prophetic movement, it is with the emergence of
Christianity that it begins to dominate the pneumatic response to
the tension of existence. In Voegelin's view, the teachings of Jesus
(especially the Sermon on the Mount) had effectively disengaged the
life of the spirit from the conditions of any particular society or
civilizational order. So effective was this separation that the earliest
Christians often seemed to be oblivious to the limitations and pragmatic problems of social order:

> While the Prophets had to struggle for an understanding of Yahwism
> in opposition to the concrete social order of Israel, a long series of
> Christian statesmen, from St. Paul to St. Augustine, had to struggle
> for an understanding of the exigencies of world-immanent social and
> political order. The Prophets had to make it clear that the political
> success of Israel was no substitute for a life in obedience to divine in-
> struction; the Christian statesmen had to make it clear that faith in
> Christ was no substitute for organized government. The Prophets had

28. Voegelin finds the tendency toward apoliticism to be more pronounced
in Aristotle than in Plato. See *Plato and Aristotle,* 161, 289, 304.

to stress that status in the social order of Israel did not confer spiritual status on a man before God; the Christian thinkers had to stress that sacramental acceptance into the Mystical Body did not touch the social status of a man—that masters were still masters, and slaves were slaves, that thieves still were thieves, and magistrates were magistrates. The Prophets had to explain that social success was not a proof of righteousness before God; the Christian thinkers had to explain that the Gospel was no social gospel, redemption no social remedy, and Christianity in general no insurance for individual or collective prosperity.

The prophets suffered under the mortgage of Canaan; in Christianity the order of the individual soul and its relationship to the divine Beyond disengaged itself from any particular society. Like the prophetic reaction to revelation, the Christian response could have moved in two directions. The transfiguring experience could have resulted in a downplaying of social and political concerns, an awaiting for the Parousia. Certainly Voegelin detected this attitude in the Pauline writings.[29] After all, humanity had been redeemed by Christ, and history was coming to its end! The other possibility was to imagine that the experience would effectively transform existing social structures. According to Voegelin, it was the former reaction that predominated in early Christianity. The balance was always precarious; the Christian development of the pneumatic differentiation could have led to a neglect of social and political duty or to the most dangerous revolutionary action, as the attempt was made to force transfiguration upon a resistant society.

With the development of the Church, the Christian tradition was able to control those impulses toward immediate transfiguration, and managed to relegate them to the status of fringe movements and sects. Much like Plato in the *Laws*, it was the Church's task to mediate between the truth of order and its social incarnation:

> Within the boundaries drawn by the myth of the cosmos, the position of Plato evolves from the *Republic* to the *Laws* in a manner that can be best elucidated by comparison with the evolution from the Sermon on the Mount to the function of the institutionalized Church. The counsels of the Sermon originate in the spirit of eschatological heroism. If they were followed by the Christian laymen to the letter among men

29. *Israel and Revelation*, 182–83; *Ecumenic Age*, 241, 246, 258, 271; "Gospel and Culture," 193–95.

as they are, they would be suicidal. . . . Since the Sermon is unbearable in its purity, the Church infuses as much of its substance as men are capable of absorbing while living in the world; the mediation of the stark reality of Jesus to the level of human expediency, with a minimum loss of substance, is one of the functions of the Church.[30]

Christian society (at least in the West) dealt with the tension between order and its social realization by distinguishing between spiritual and temporal orders, a *civitas Dei* and a *civitas terrena*. The Parousia did not come; but since the Beyond had been differentiated, there was no question of returning to a more compact formulation. The solution was the institutional Church, which, while existing in the world, represented human destiny beyond the world. The tension, then, was not resolved at all, but made into a "permanent structure of civilization."[31]

Such a solution, though, was not without ambiguities, and the uneasy relationship between spiritual and temporal orders as embodied in Church and State prepared the ground for modern derailments:

> The Christian compromise with reality has assumed the form of the Church which is neither an empire nor a community living in expectation of the imminent end of the world, but an institution representing the eschatological *telos* within the world. The Christian answer . . . was thus the separation and balance of spiritual and temporal powers within the order of a society. Whatever the shortcomings of the solution proved to be in practice, the construction at least held fast to the insight that the end of society in history is a question of eschatology. If the solution proved unstable nevertheless, the fundamental reason must be sought in the inadequacy of the compromise. For the Church never quite disengaged itself from its apocalyptic origin—its apocalyptic unconcern about mankind in history narrowed its intellectual horizon so badly that it never developed an adequate philosophy of history. By the eighteenth century, finally, the gulf between our knowledge of historical reality and the limited understanding provided by the Church had become so wide that the gnostic movements could pour into the vacuum with a vengeance. The long-neglected reality of mankind in historical existence came into more than its own when the new movements, while taking their stand firmly within this world, denied the reality of the world beyond and consequently replaced the es-

---

30. *Plato and Aristotle*, 226.
31. *New Science of Politics*, 158–59.

chatological by an intramundane *telos*. . . . Two factors stand out in
the West as responses to the Christian *contemptus mundi*, to the neglect
of the structure of this world: (1) the revolt of the individual and the
release of its forces—which has derailed into the *libido dominandi* of
the gnostics: and (2) the revolt of society and the release of its forces
in history—which has derailed into the intramundane apocalypse.[32]

Christian failure to deal adequately with the problems of mundane
existence thus helped to create a civilizational context in which disordering social and political movements could flourish.

The reason for my digression on Christianity and the Church is to
reinforce the point that, whatever his reservations concerning the
extent to which social change is possible, Voegelin was also highly
critical of those who, confronted with social disorder, opt for apoliticism and disengagement from the public life of society. For those
confronted with social chaos, he did not advocate withdrawal into the
academy or into a "spirituality" that simply blocks from view the
surrounding disorder. Those who would enlist Voegelin in the cause
of defending the status quo will be disappointed; for he was rather
forthright in denouncing various conservatisms and traditionalisms
as obstacles in the recovery of reality. With regard to student radicals,
he remarked: "Every leftist student is as much against the Communist establishment as against our establishment. They are against
doctrine. Their solutions are wrong but their revolution is right."
And in another place he wrote: "It will be sufficient to state that the
students have good reasons to revolt; and if the reasons they actually
advance are bad, one should remember that the educational institutions have cut them off from the life of reason so effectively that they
cannot even articulate the causes of their legitimate unrest."[33]

In addition, Voegelin had nothing but contempt for intellectuals
who refuse to speak out in the face of social corruption, and who
assuage their consciences by claiming that, since people will never be
completely good, it is better to lower one's horizon concerning what
is possible. While at first this attitude might seem to resemble Voegelin's own position, he would make a careful distinction between his
analysis and the "polite philosophy" of modern humanists:

32. Voegelin, "World Empire," 185–87.
33. Voegelin, "German University," 18, 31; *Anamnesis*, 188–89. See also Germino, *Beyond Ideology*, 176; Voegelin, *Conversations*, 107; and Voegelin, "On Classical Studies," in *Collected Works*, vol. 12, 261.

"Polite philosophy" knows its place, does not abstractly hold a truth to be opportune in every situation, does not talk out of turn and does not, like a bad actor, disturb the play at hand. One cannot root out bad opinions and traditional vices at a moment's notice—but that is no reason for deserting the commonwealth like a ship in a storm. One must not pester people with strange notions, but use the arts and tricks of persuasion so that "if you cannot turn things to the good, at least you can make them less bad". "For all things cannot be well, as long as all men are not good. . . ." The answer is not impressive. It is neither Platonic, nor otherwise profound. It is persuasive common sense for a man who wants to play a role in politics, who is intelligent and sensitive enough to feel the responsibilities which he may incur, and who needs a little opiate to overcome his scruples. Today we call it the argument of a "collaborator". . . . One can, indeed, not root out traditional vices at a moment's notice; but there is a limit beyond which delay is impermissible. And that all men are not good and therefore all things cannot be well, is sound admonition to a perfectionist; but it easily can become a cover for condoning crimes. What makes this argument so flat is the renunciation of the spirit as the ultimate authority beyond the temporal order and its insufficiencies. The commonwealth tends to acquire an ultimacy which properly belongs to the spirit.[34]

Voegelin's views on the possibility of creating a good society escape categorization. As discussed earlier in this chapter, his insistence that the structure of reality does not change and the epistemological/ontological framework within which he operated led him to make certain statements indicating that most attempts to insure a more equitable and just social order are at odds with the "laws of mundane existence" and are therefore a revolt against the order established by God. At the same time, Voegelin clearly believed the state of social disorder in which he found himself to be unacceptable

---

34. Voegelin, "More's *Utopia*," 456. Compare this passage with the passage from "The Nature of the Law," 61 (quoted above in Chapter 3), where Voegelin seems to make an argument similar to that he dismisses in the passage quoted here. There he argues that, human nature being what it is, a certain degree of injustice must be tolerated. Now this is not necessarily inconsistent with what he says in the present selection, for here he admits that such cautions are quite appropriate when directed to the "perfectionist." Once again, though, a question may be raised: By what criteria does one distinguish between the "collaborator" and the realist, or between the "perfectionist" and the realist? One person's "realist" may be another's "collaborator." When does the toleration of "gross injustices" become "a cover for condoning crimes"?

and he strongly desired that it be improved. He was committed to fighting such disorder. A problem arises, however, from within his philosophical perspective, where that dimension of being that is humanly constituted is not always clearly distinguished from human life as conditioned by the operation of lower manifolds. This tension lends to Voegelin's writings on these matters a sense of poignancy, not unlike that found in the later writings of Plato, whom he so admired.

These tensions in Voegelin's account are reflected in his statements concerning the possibility of the good society ever becoming a reality. As might be anticipated, his reactions ranged from a somber pessimism to a guarded optimism.[35] For the most part, though, he assumed an attitude of cautious hopefulness toward the contemporary situation. The essential nucleus of a good society, according to Voegelin, is the life of reason. If reason, understood as conscious participation in the ground, is not made socially effective in a given society, then that society cannot be considered good. Within these parameters Voegelin offered his reflections as to what can be done to transform society, drawing upon the Western philosophical traditions:

> What do we have to offer by way of guidance or leadership in this world-wide transformation of society? The answer is: everything and nothing. We know what the life of reason and the good society are; we can cultivate the former and try, by our actions, to bring about the latter. We can restate the problem: the formation of the psyche by encouraging participation in transcendent reason. . . . And that is all one can do; whether or not this offer is accepted depends on the Spirit that blows where It pleases. Collectively, as a society, there is at the moment little, if anything, we can do. . . . To be sure, the ideologies have not been able to destroy the life of reason in the West, but the damage is serious—even though we hide it under the euphemism of "pluralistic society."[36]

35. Voegelin's article "The Origins of Scientism" finds him at his bleakest. More often, though, he expresses the opinion that contemporary ideologies have had their day and that now restoration can begin. See Voegelin, *Conversations*, 30–31; *Autobiographical Reflections*, 100–101, 118–19; "Immortality," 57; "Industrial Society in Search of Reason," 41–45; and "On Readiness," 283–84. Voegelin also speaks about these matters as part of his contribution to a series of discussions transcribed in E. Cahn and C. Going, eds., *The Question as Commitment: A Symposium*, 97–98.

36. Voegelin, "Industrial Society in Search of Reason," 45–46; *World of the Polis*, 283.

The ideologies have done their work; Voegelin was under no illusions as to the difficulties involved in restoring rational discussion:

> Rational discussion on questions of social order is possible; and in a complicated modern society it is an essential condition of the social order. . . . But the discussion is possible only between men capable of using their powers of reason; a fool, as here defined in the technical sense, has lost this ability. . . . The decisive manifestations of this loss have been the mass and intellectual movements of our age. In this jungle of irrationality, rational discussion is confined to important but socially comparatively ineffectual enclaves. After centuries of systematic confusion of reason, it will not be easy to render these enclaves once more effective. But that is the task that lies before us.[37]

While it is essential that the life of reason become socially effective if society is to attain any substantial order, Voegelin held out little hope that a large number of people would be attracted to this life: "There is no expectation or reason to expect, in any visible future or at any time in history we know of for the future, that there will be human beings of whom a considerable percentage will not be fools. That will be a constant problem in every society and in every social order. You can't get rid of it." Potentially, all are equal in regard to the life of reason, "but empirically (for whatever reason) they are unequal in the application of their potentiality." As he explained in an article written twenty years before these comments, "The psychic tension of the life of reason is difficult for the majority of the members of a society to bear," and because of this, "any society in which the life of reason has reached a high degree of differentiation has a tendency to develop, along with the life of reason, a 'mass belief.' By sheer social expansion, mass belief may reduce the life of reason to socially meaningless enclaves or even forcefully suppress it."[38]

Confronted with such prospects, how is one to proceed in making reason socially effective, and what are the resources at one's disposal? For Voegelin, the beginning of a solution lay in critically clarifying the present disorder and bringing to consciousness the true structure of reality. A first step toward creating order is to reconstruct a climate where rational discourse is possible. The eclipse of reality

37. Voegelin, "On Readiness," 283–84.
38. Voegelin, *Conversations*, 128; "Industrial Society in Search of Reason," 34–35. See also Voegelin, "Autobiographical Statement," 116–19; Cahn and Going, eds., *Question as Commitment*, 97; and Aron, *World Technology*, 171.

through ideological deformation has made rational discussion impossible; the work to be done includes not only "a careful analysis of the noetic structure of existence," but "an analysis of Second Realities, with regard to both their constructs and the motivating structure of existence in untruth." It is not the philosopher's task to engage in revolutionary action or even to take an active role in formulating specific economic, legislative, and social policies. Rather, his or her task is to penetrate to the truth of order and to convey as well as possible "the types of conduct that would be adequate optimally to translate the truth about order, as it lives in the soul of the philosopher, into the practice of society. The weight of the work lies, therefore, in the inquiry into the nature of true order." Recovering reality, though, is an arduous task:

> Recapturing reality in opposition to its contemporary deformation requires a considerable amount of work. One has to reconstruct the fundamental categories of existence, experience, consciousness, and reality. One has at the same time to explore the technique and structure of the deformations that clutter up daily routine; and one has to develop the concepts by which existential deformation and its symbolic expression can be categorized. This work, then, must be conducted not only in opposition to the deformed ideologies but also to deformations of reality by thinkers who ought to be its preservers, such as theologians.[39]

The ultimate goal of such a project is persuasion with an eye toward social transformation: "Political science goes beyond the validity of propositions to the truth of existence. The opinions for the clarification of which the analysis is undertaken are not merely false: they are symptoms of spiritual disorder in the men who hold them. And the purpose of the analysis is to persuade—to have its own insights, if possible, supplant the opinions in social reality. Analysis is concerned with the therapy of order."[40] Such persuasion, if it is to be genuinely effective, must be the fruit of meditation. Without a recovery of participatory experiences, the philosopher will have nothing of substance to offer. It is for this reason that much of Voegelin's later work was taken up with "meditative exegesis." For Voegelin this shift

39. Voegelin, "On Debate and Existence," 51; "The Nature of the Law," 53; *Autobiographical Reflections,* 97. See also Germino, *Beyond Ideology,* 171.
40. *Science, Politics, and Gnosticism,* 19.

did not signify a movement away from political philosophy, but rather deeper probing into the sources of order.

The philosopher, then, is involved in articulating his or her experience with the intention of persuading others to join in the quest, thus forming communities of the spirit that may, in time, achieve some degree of social effectiveness. The creation and reinforcement of a "substantial public," that is, a public guided by the life of reason, is the aim of the philosopher. This is especially difficult when the socially dominant public is estranged from reality, but one must still try to create communities with sufficient persuasive power to shift social dominance from a condition of estrangement to the life of the spirit. If this occurs, public opinion would then compel reform. It is to the public, not its leaders, that one must appeal, because those in positions of leadership are not likely to respond favorably to calls for reform, imprisoned as they are by their interest in preserving their own positions.[41]

At a certain level Voegelin believed the ideologies that have marred modern civilization have exhausted themselves; nothing new could be said. While this may be the case, their actual pragmatic influence in the world may continue long after their intellectual capital has been spent.[42] I have already noted in Chapter 4 that, in order to understand this phenomenon, Voegelin distinguished between the "primary process," in which the deforming ideologies emerge, unfold, and expire, and the "secondary movements" deriving from the primary process, which may continue to shape the climate of the age long after the ideologies have expired.

There is, then, cause for hope and cause for concern. Because the

41. Voegelin, "German University," 34–35; Cahn and Going, eds., *Question as Commitment,* 97–98.

42. Voegelin, following Toynbee and Spengler, estimates that it takes about 250 years for civilizational establishments to run their course. Voegelin presciently suggested that the process would move more rapidly in the case of Russian communism: "There is, however, one point to be noted that may speak in favor of a shorter period, especially in the Russian case. Russian communism takes place on the general background of philosophical and Christian tradition. If there is established publicly a highly defective conception which neglects the life of reason, which doesn't permit you to find sense in your life by reflecting on problems of life and death—especially of death—then you get, sooner or later, disappointment that the things promised, like a perfect Communist realm, never come, and the restlessness of this defectiveness. There is no sense in life because indefinite progress doesn't work" (*Conversations,* 16–19).

eclipse of reality is just that, the ideologies and movements to which it gives rise eventually collapse; the constant need to project second realities takes its toll as the true structure of reality refuses to conform to the dreamers' whims. The ideologies, insofar as they exist in constant friction with reality, contain within themselves their own future destruction. On the other hand, Voegelin was not optimistic when considering the secondary effects of these movements. The ability of these secondary movements to stifle the life of reason and to create a climate of opinion where questioning unrest has been largely submerged led Voegelin to conclude, sadly, that the damage to society may already be irreparable and the process of social decline irreversible:

> And there are social processes that have to run their course; there's nothing you can do about it. You can try, of course, to impress individuals, but you can't do more; you can't influence the social process as a whole; that probably has to go through all the misery of revolutions and world wars until even the most stupid person understands that he doesn't get anywhere that way. It is our critical situation today that these revolutionary communal experiences which started in the eighteenth century have run to their death now.

And in answer to a question about the efficacy of intelligent people in persuading the unintelligent, Voegelin replied that "results come when murderous excesses have gone far enough to make even an idiot see that he is not getting anywhere. But that can go very far."[43]

Despite these warnings, it remains the responsibility of philosophers, and all those in whom the life of reason has not been eclipsed, to create a climate in which rational discussion on social and political matters is possible. Concretely, Voegelin saw a role for the universities in helping to form people in the life of reason. Unfortunately, these institutions have far too often abdicated their responsibility. The university, as Voegelin saw it, does not exist to indoctrinate; as we well know, Voegelin saw doctrine in any form as part of the problem. What the university can do, however, is allow students' questioning unrest to unfold and expose them to texts that can serve as pathways to the underlying experiences of which they are literary symbols. Voegelin found the possibility of exposure to such texts becoming increasingly frequent with the contemporary revival and expansion

---

43. Voegelin, *Conversations*, 109; "Autobiographical Statement," 130.

of those disciplines that study humanity and its symbols, for example, classical, patristic, and scholastic philosophy; classical philology; and comparative religion:

> On the one hand, the spiritual disease has manifested itself massively in bouts of global war and revolution; on the other hand, the experiences of transcendence are being recaptured in a peculiarly backhanded manner. For the experiences which had been reduced to shadows by dogmatic incrustations, and seemed to be removed from the land of the living by the successive attacks of antitheologism and antimetaphysicism, have returned from limbo by the back door of historical knowledge. To a field that apparently had been cleared of them so they would not disturb the futuristic dreams of *paradis artificiels*, they are being reintroduced as "facts of history"—through the exploration of myth, of the Old and New Testament, of apocalyptic and Gnostic movements, through comparative religion, Assyriology, Egyptology, classical philology, and so forth. This renewed knowledge about experiences on which depends the order in personal and social existence makes itself felt even now in an increasingly accurate diagnosis of the contemporary disorder and its causes; and it would be surprising if it did not become a living force, sooner or later, in the actual restoration of order.[44]

The role of the university is to aid in this effort. The university exists to enable people to recapture reality by helping them to recover and articulate transcendent experience. People so transformed will not easily succumb to the lure of ideologies. At the heart of social transformation, then, is mystagogy.

Another factor that contributes to the restoration of order is the cultural context in which such an effort occurs. Voegelin believed that the societies existing within the Anglo-Saxon orbit are best prepared to resist disorder. Part of the reason for this is the conservative nature of the English and American revolutions; in neither case do we find a wholesale rejection of the classical/Christian tradition.[45] The preservation of these traditions, coupled with the Ameri-

---

44. Voegelin, "Immortality," 57. See also "On Classical Studies," in *Collected Works*, vol. 12, 261–62; *Autobiographical Reflections*, 95; "Autobiographical Statement," 105–6.

45. Voegelin, *Autobiographical Reflections*, 115; "Industrial Society in Search of Reason," 37. "The English Revolution, in the seventeenth century, occurred at a time when gnosticism had not yet undergone its radical secularization. . . . The left-wing Puritans were eager to present themselves as Christians, though of an

can and English power, represent the greatest hope for the eventual return of reason to social and political life:

> Western society as a whole, thus, is a deeply stratified civilization in which the American and English democracies represent the oldest, most firmly consolidated stratum of civilizational tradition, while the German area represents its most progressively modern stratum.
>
> In this situation there is a glimmer of hope, for the American and English democracies which most solidly in their institutions represent the truth of the soul are, at the same time, existentially the strongest powers.[46]

Voegelin's praise for American and English democracy must be qualified, however, by the recognition that his attitude toward the Anglo-American political tradition was more ambivalent than this quotation would indicate. Consonant with his understanding that the truth of order is never experienced as a set of self-evident propositions, Voegelin maintained that there is no "best" form of government. Instead, what is required is the flexibility to develop and institute those political structures that will best serve to embody the truth of order. The "goodness" of a society resides in the presence or absence of a socially effective life of reason, not in the form of its government. Voegelin points out:

> In the West, constitutional democracy as a constitutional form is so closely allied with the notion of the good society that we must note a strong tendency to forget, both in theory and in practice, that 'goodness' is the quality of a society and not of governmental form. When society is good it can function under the form of a constitutional democracy; when it is not good, it cannot. Thus a society which is not qualified for this governmental form can easily start down the road to disaster if it adopts a Western-type constitution. Unconscionable damage to millions of people throughout the world has resulted from ill-considered constitutional experiments modeled after the West. . . .
> We must admit that constitutional democracy may be a terrible form of government for an Asian or African country, whereas some form of

---

especially pure sort. When the adjustments of 1690 were reached, England had preserved the institutional culture of aristocratic parliamentism as well as the mores of a Christian commonwealth, now sanctioned as national institutions. The American Revolution, though its debate was already strongly affected by the psychology of enlightenment, also had the good fortune of coming to its close within the institutional and Christian climate of the *ancien regime*" (*New Science of Politics*, 187–89).

46. *New Science of Politics*, 189.

enlightened despotism, autocracy, or military dictatorship can be the best if we believe that the rulers are using this means to create a good society.

In this regard Voegelin takes to task the English belief in the self-evident superiority of constitutional democracy by suggesting that, far from being fundamental principles whose presence or absence mark a political order as good or bad, rights such as the "free pursuit of truth, religious freedom according to conscience, and civil liberties" are simply prudential devices appropriate to particular historical circumstances, not "inalienable, eternal, and ultimate" truths. In making this point, Voegelin's view seems to have been shaped by his experience with National Socialism in Germany and Austria, where the Nazis made use of democratic process to further their quite undemocratic aims. Perhaps as a result of these experiences, Voegelin developed a certain skepticism toward democratic institutions as *the* solution to the problems of political and social order. He decried the lack of distinction between formal and substantial democracy, and felt that Western democracies were in danger of allowing their own relatively successful social/political orders to be undermined by a naive adherence to the letter of the democratic process while allowing its "substance" to be eroded by antidemocratic groups.[47]

It remains the case, though, that the pragmatic political configurations of Anglo-American societies make them social fields in which resistance to disorder is possible. In addition, the English and American traditions of commonsense philosophy also contribute to the creation of a climate where threats to order can be dealt with effectively and where ideologies find no foothold. In the ability of commonsense traditions to resist ideological deformations, Voegelin perceived a "great cultural advantage" for Anglo-American civilization.[48]

What does Voegelin mean by "common sense"? He borrows the term from Scottish philosophers, especially Thomas Reid. As understood by Voegelin, common sense is a "compact form of rationality" found in all people who are able to carry out their ordinary, daily tasks:

47. Voegelin, "Industrial Society in Search of Reason," 41–42; "Oxford Political Philosophers," 103–4; "Extended Strategy," 194–95.
48. *Conversations,* 65; *Autobiographical Reflections,* 29.

Common sense means the same as "a branch or degree of *ratio*" for which a separate name is justifiable in "that in the greatest part of mankind no other degree of reason is to be found. It is this degree that entitles them to the denomination of reasonable creatures." Common sense, therefore, does not connote a social deadweight of vulgar ideas, nor any *idees recues* or "relatively natural world view," but rather it is the habit of judgment and conduct of a man formed by *ratio:* one could say, the habit of an Aristotelian *spoudaios* minus the luminosity of his knowledge of the *ratio* as the source of his rational judgment and conduct. Common sense is a civilizational habit that presupposes noetic experience, without the man of this habit having himself a differentiated knowledge of *noesis*. The civilized *homo politicus* need not be a philosopher, but he must have common sense.[49]

Common sense, then, is noetic in character, but without a reflexive understanding of *noesis*. If people wish to sustain a workable social order, it is not necessary that they all be philosophers, but they, or at least their leaders, must possess a sufficient openness toward Nous to enable them to manage the affairs of society intelligently. The relationship between the order of consciousness and the level of common sense is not that of general principles to their specific applications. While the order of consciousness is the ground for common sense, it must be emphasized that what is present at this higher level is not a set of more general truths from which the more specific commonsense insights are deduced, but an experience of transcendent order to be mediated in social form. Voegelin maintained that there were neither principles nor propositions in political science.[50] People in possession of common sense have a share in the truth of order, but without the luminosity characteristic of the philosopher. For whatever reason, they are not as permeable to the fullness of transcendent experience. It seems as if common sense is very similar to that rationality required of the citizens described in Plato's *Laws;* they need not possess a vision of the Good, but they must be capable of recognizing the wisdom of laws and intelligent enough to follow them. From Voegelin's perspective, even this level of response presupposes some participation in Nous.

Voegelin believed that most political and social matters can be dealt with on the level of common sense, because common sense,

49. *Anamnesis*, 211–12.
50. Ibid., 210–11.

like the *phronesis* it resembles, has a flexibility enabling it to adapt to changing circumstances and conditions: "There are no principles of political science, because there are no propositions. Rather, the 'propositions' of political science are common-sense insights into the correct modes of action concerning man's existence in society, from insights concerning the organization of government, to insights into the requirements of domestic and foreign policy, finance and military policy, down to concrete decisions."[51] Unlike ideologies, which block reality, common sense is able to deal effectively with the exigencies of pragmatic existence:

> You don't need an ideology. Most of the problems you have to handle are commonsense problems on the pragmatic level within the contexts about which you perfectly well know what pragmatically can be done. . . . One can do on the commonsense level (say, within a framework of the next ten years) all sorts of things. As soon as you have ideologies you usually obfuscate the structure of reality within which you have to move. That is the problem. Ideologies are highly dangerous because they make you lose contact with reality.

Common sense and its accompanying pragmatic outlook are largely responsible for the stability of social/political order in the Anglo-American social field; its importance can hardly be overestimated.[52]

Yet if the practicality of common sense is its greatest strength, it is at the same time the source of its weakness; and if there exists a danger to the Anglo-American cultural area, it lies in its inability to meet the ideologies at their own philosophical level:

> The ideologies, in spite of their dogmatic derailments, constitute an explicit coming-to-grips with the order of consciousness. Common sense may insist on its self-assuredness to "judge of things self-evident" but it cannot meet the ideologies on their level of argumentation, since it does not have an explicit noesis. The remarkable power of resistance of the Anglo-American social field against the ideologies of which we just spoke, must not obscure the just as remarkable sterility of the philosophical contention with the ideologies.

51. Ibid., 61–70, 210, 212. In Voegelin's interpretation of Aristotle, *phronesis* is a virtue and a power that mediates between the truth of order and its embodiment in society. In order to mediate, it must possess a degree of luminosity not found in common sense. Both *phronesis* and common sense deal with practical matters; as a result, both are flexible and adaptable. *Phronesis*, though, is characteristic of the *spoudaios*, while common sense is found in nearly everyone.

52. *Conversations*, 65–66; *Anamnesis*, 212–13.

If common sense, thus, is a pragmatic factor of highest importance for the stability of political order in the West, it still is no substitute for differentiated noesis, in our historical situation. The desire for "principle" of political science, however, which I characterized above as a potential source of social disorder, seems to me also to express a genuine desire to go beyond the relative inadequacy of common sense and to attain again the luminosity of noetic consciousness.[53]

While Voegelin is lavish in his praise of common sense, the passage just quoted serves as a reminder that such praise is not without qualification. As an aid in resisting ideologies and dealing effectively with pragmatic concerns, common sense is invaluable, but it remains a relatively inadequate solution to the problem of social/political order: it is incapable of addressing the issue on the level of consciousness. Those social fields in which commonsense traditions predominate are certainly better off than those possessing a climate of opinion in which ideologists and activist dreamers can gain a foothold. But from Voegelin's perspective, it would seem that, despite their many strengths, Anglo-American political forms, such as constitutional democracy, would still fall into the Platonic category of a "second-best polis," since they represent the best possible solution in the present situation and not an embodiment of the truth of order.[54] Nor should this be surprising, considering that from Israel through Plato and Aristotle, through the emergence of Christianity and the development of the ideologies, the tension between the truth of order and its social embodiment has remained permanent and unresolved. It is this acute consciousness that the truth of order *ought* to be embodied in society, joined to the belief that human nature and pragmatic exigencies *prevent* this from happening, that account for the paradoxical combination of fervor and resignation that marks Voegelin's thinking on the good society. In this he once again mirrors Plato.

In many ways Voegelin's approach to social and political problems reflects the influence of Plato;[55] among the notable similarities are the conception of philosophy as a response to social disorder, the

---

53. *Anamnesis,* 213.
54. Voegelin, "Industrial Society in Search of Reason," 36–37.
55. An important question, but one that would require extended treatment, is whether Voegelin's thought had really been profoundly influenced by Plato (as he himself claimed), or whether the Plato that Voegelin presents is a creation and a reflection of his own philosophical position.

experienced tension between the truth of order and its social incarnation, the realization that the truth of order is not in the least diminished by its failure to be embodied in society, the focus on the incarnation of order in individual souls, the ambivalence concerning the use of persuasion and force, the pragmatic adaptation of the truth of order in conformity with what society can realistically be expected to bear, a sense that the structure of the cosmos we inhabit is bound by inexorable and unchangeable laws, and finally, as we shall examine in the following chapter, a looking beyond the tension of existence to a vision of ultimate transfiguration.

The following passage from an early article on Nietzsche captures the Platonic tone of Voegelin's reflections on social order. Reflecting upon the crisis of the twentieth century, Voegelin considers the possibilities for response:

> We have analyzed four positions which can be assumed towards the crisis and the challenge of Nietzsche: (1) The position of the Last Man who lives totally in the crisis and meets the challenge with derision; (2) the suppression of the consciousness of crisis through the projection of evil into the German character; (3) the recognition of the crisis and the undaunted faith in the survival value of the Liberal Tradition; and (4) the profound understanding of the Nietzschean problem and the resignation in spiritual solitude. The last of these positions . . . is ultimate in the sense that it reflects an immediate mystical experience beyond the crisis. It is not ultimate, however, in the sense that no other fundamental position is possible. Man has to die alone and the experiences of intellectual mysticisms have their truth in that they anticipate the last solitude of existence. But man has to live in society, and the spiritualization of the life in society has inevitably to grapple with the spirit of the institutions; in this condition of our finite existence originate the experiences which lead to the Platonic attitude.[56]

While this may be the language of the early Voegelin, many of the most important concerns of his later writings are present here. For we find in this passage the tensions which appear throughout the development of Voegelin's work, and which characterize his reflections on the good society. There is the acknowledgment that the truth of order abides in individual souls through transcendent expe-

56. Voegelin, "Nietzsche, the Crisis, and the War," 197–98.

rience. In addition, there is the recognition that human existence is inherently social and that one must strive to incarnate the truth of order in society. And finally, we have the profound sense that the ultimate resolution of the problem lies somehow beyond the present situation, in transcendent mystery.

EIGHT

BEYOND ORDER
Vision and Transfiguration

The tension between the truth of order as it emerges in consciousness and its attempted incarnation in social form remains a permanent feature of human existence. Such existence is always existence in the metaxy. In approaching the question of whether or not the good society is possible, Voegelin was especially concerned with preserving this insight into the structure of reality. He was very critical of those thinkers whom he considered to have ignored this structure. This criticism, however, represents only one dimension of Voegelin's thought on society, for he was equally emphatic in stressing the need to recover the life of reason and to render it socially effective. The truth of order may never be adequately embodied in any society, but the insight into the structure and movement of reality must still be communicated, for it is only in relationship to the ground that our humanity is fully constituted.

It was the conjunction between the realization that no society is an adequate vessel for the truth of order and the knowledge that humanity is constituted through its relationship to the transcendent ground that would move Voegelin to consider the problems of society and history in terms of the movement of reality beyond order. His "resolution" of the problem will be our concern in the present chapter. This will involve a further examination of the relationship between order and history, as expanded and reformulated in *The Ecumenic Age,* the fourth volume of *Order and History.* From within the context of the epoch identified as the Ecumenic Age will arise the notion of universal humanity, opening onto questions of vision and the ultimate transfiguration of reality.

THE ECUMENIC AGE

Far from abandoning the concerns that animated his earlier work, Voegelin was in *The Ecumenic Age* once again reflecting upon the relationship between spiritual and pragmatic order. Indeed, this relationship might be said to constitute the central theme of the book and of the age it attempts to describe.[1]

Nonetheless, it is clear that there has been a shift in perspective. Voegelin's original plan for *Order and History* envisioned six volumes, which would trace the important differentiations of consciousness as they unfolded through successive civilizational periods. While not rejecting the idea of meaningful advance in differentiation, Voegelin moves in *The Ecumenic Age* away from conceiving those differentiations as being neatly arrangeable on a time line. For Voegelin discovered that the notion of history as a linear development, which he originally believed to be an idea stemming from the Israelite orbit, was actually present in cosmological societies as well. This discovery of historiogenesis disturbed the original program: "For the very unilinear history which I had supposed to be engendered, together with punctuations of meaning on it, by the differentiating events, turned out to be a cosmological symbolism. Moreover, the symbolism had remained a millennial constant in continuity from its origins in the Sumerian and Egyptian societies, through its cultivation by Israelites and Christians, right into the 'philosophies of history' of the nineteenth century A.D."[2]

No longer could differentiations be understood as simply following one another in successive fashion. In addition, the tenacity and endurance of cosmological symbolism had to be acknowledged. The absence of meaningful linear patterns in history did not mean, however, that history was senseless. Rather, for Voegelin it meant the discovery of a new historical intelligibility.[3] Instead of a series of societies succeeding one another in time and advancing in differentiation of consciousness, we find lines of meaning emerging from all directions, cutting horizontally across societies and civilizations. No longer speaking about the *meaning of* history, which was nothing

---

1. *Ecumenic Age,* 197.
2. Ibid., 1–8.
3. *Anamnesis,* 203–4.

more than an attempt to impose one's own perspective on the historical data, one could more accurately speak of *configurations* of history.

The difference between a configuration and a supposed meaning of history is that a configuration emerges as a meaningful pattern to be found within the empirical data—that is, societies, their institutions, and the meanings that inform those institutions—rather than as a pattern imposed upon the data from an ideological perspective, for example, positivist, progressivist, or Marxist interpretations of history. Such emergent patterns are far more than an account of institutions and their interrelationships; the constitutive meanings and the self-interpretations of a society are an essential dimension of any configuration.[4]

While configurations include societies and are in a sense constituted by them as the underlying empirical manifold to be understood, they cannot be said to be circumscribed by any particular social, or for that matter, civilizational form: "The transcendental texture of history thus is richly structured by various patterns into which the single phenomena combine to form phenomena of a higher order. Furthermore, the patterns, as we have just seen, do not remain isolated from one another. Periods can form chains of periods; periods of several societies can interlock; and so forth. The aggregate of these patterns I shall call the *configuration of history*."[5] One can speak, then, both of *configurations* of history and of *the configuration* of history, depending upon how widely encompassing the pattern under consideration is. For Voegelin, perhaps the most crucial period of configuration was that which he referred to as the Ecumenic Age.

Chronologically, the Ecumenic Age extends from the rise of the Persian to the fall of the Roman Empire. What is it, though, that characterizes this period and enables it to be recognized as a decisive configuration? To answer this question we must begin by speaking briefly about those epochal events whose impact has been so great as to raise the very question of an ecumenic age.[6]

In earlier chapters we followed the struggle for order as it unfolded in Israel and Hellas, the societies in which originated the pneumatic and noetic differentiations, respectively. Ultimately these

---

4. Voegelin, "Configurations of History," 96–98.
5. Voegelin, "What Is History?," 38.
6. *Ecumenic Age*, 114.

two societies were to fall victim to the imperial drive for conquest. Their conquerors, however, differed in several respects from the older Near Eastern empires against whom Israel and Hellas contrasted themselves by virtue of their differentiated understanding of reality. First of all, the new empires were not societies in the same sense that the earlier cosmological empires had been:

> The new empires took their names from the comparatively small societies on the outskirts of civilization who, at intervals of about two hundred years, conquered the vast Near Eastern-Aegean civilizational area. . . . In none of these cases did the conquerors belong to the societies organized by them; in none of them did the resultant empire organize a Persian, Macedonian, or Roman society. On the contrary, the conquerors were spread fairly thin over the vast territorial expanse and could keep their empires in being only with the aid of the subjects. . . . The empire as an enterprise of institutionalized power, thus, had separated from the organization of a concrete society and could be imposed as a form on the remnants of societies no longer capable of self-organization.

The earlier cosmological empires had been held together by their self-understanding as cosmic analogues. This was not the case with the new empires, whose territorial expansion was not supported by any such underpinning meaning. Instead, there was little more than a power field comprising several societies. Nor was it possible to simply return to cosmological form. A second difference to be noted concerning the new empires has to do with the fact that they emerge at a time when the differentiations have already occurred; the truth of order can be disengaged from pragmatic existence. Within this context it became possible to distinguish between conquests devoid of spiritual meaning and spiritual movements in search of a people to be formed.[7]

Originally, *ecumene* meant no more than the inhabited world as understood by the Hellenes, or "contemporaneous cultured humanity as a field of potential organization." But under the pressures of

7. Ibid., 115–17, 145. See also pages 202–3, 308 for Voegelin's discussion of the compact symbol *oikumene-okeanos* and its disintegration in the Ecumenic Age. In cosmological societies, *oikumene* represented the human habitat in the cosmos, while *okeanos* was the horizon of *oikumene*, marking the boundary between heaven and earth. In the Ecumenic Age this symbolism was threatened, but not completely replaced, by the triad of spiritual outburst, ecumenic empire, and historiography. This triad will be discussed below.

imperial expansion it came to mean the entire power field into which a number of organized societies were unwillingly drawn. As such the ecumene could expand and contract according to the reach or limit of imperial power. The ecumene, then, encompasses the entire power sphere dominated by the imperial conquerors, and does not require that all those conquered be brought under the jurisdiction of any single empire at any specific time.[8]

In coming to understand the configuration that is the Ecumenic Age, Voegelin discerned three predominant factors: (1) spiritual outbursts, (2) the founding of ecumenic empires, and (3) the emergence of historiography.[9] He would insist that such a pattern does not represent an artificial construct forced upon historical data but rather that it is more respectful of and sensitive to the data than other interpretations; both those of an ideological stripe and those that take "axis time" or "civilization" as the basic unit of meaning in history.[10]

The three factors do indeed constitute a "configuration"; they cannot be separated from one another. The isolation of any single factor as the criterion for historical meaning leads to a distorted view of history. A narrow focus on parallel spiritual outbursts as constituting an axis time or an "absolute epoch" means having to contend with those uncooperative outbursts which refuse to fit themselves into the designated time of parallels. Exclusive attention to empire ignores important societies that are not empires. A concentration on the occurrence of historiography is forced to deal with the question of how it is that certain phenomena are judged to be historically important. It would appear, then, that the three factors must be understood as constituting a complex interrelationship:

> On the one hand, neither the ecumenic empires nor the spiritual outbursts alone can mark the "absolute epoch," because there is no ep-

8. *Anamnesis,* 203–4; *Ecumenic Age,* 133, 145, 313; *Autobiographical Reflections,* 103–4.

9. *Ecumenic Age,* 312–13; *Autobiographical Reflections,* 104; "Configurations of History," 98; "World Empire," 171.

10. Voegelin's problem with the idea of an "axis time" is that it tends to focus almost exclusively on spiritual outbursts as constituting a historical epoch, without relating such outbursts to other accompanying factors. The term *civilization* may be helpful, but it is not able to deal adequately with those configurations whose intelligibility transcends civilizational boundaries. See *Ecumenic Age,* 2–6, 311–13; *Autobiographical Reflections,* 103–5; and "Configurations of History," 101–2.

och without historical consciousness. On the other hand, history as the horizon of divine mystery that surrounds the spatially open ecumene can hardly emerge unless the ecumene actually opens under the impact of concupiscential expansion, and the expansion is no more than a senseless rise and fall of peoples and their rulers unless the consciousness of the historians can relate the events to the truth of existence that emerges in the spiritual outbursts.[11]

From the very start, the symbolism of a pragmatic ecumene to be gained by conquest was beset with problems. To a large extent this had to do with the fact that the horizon of the ecumene, which expanded and contracted along with the vicissitudes of imperial power, could never be reached. Every conquest revealed that there was yet more to be conquered.[12]

What made ecumenic expansion unique was that it occurred in a context in which the transcendent and immanent poles of reality had been differentiated. With this differentiation came the realization that human beings were interpreters of an order that was universal. Once human beings became aware of themselves as the source of conceptions of order, a myriad of such conceptions could arise, reflecting the various drives and desires of the psyche in both their benign and dangerous forms.[13]

Among the numerous unbalanced conceptions was one whose goal was to conquer all the known world. This ecumenic drive for conquest was thus motivated by a perverted desire to achieve an immanent universality by means of pragmatic power:

> The extreme of pragmatism, culminating in the conception of world dominion, is related, as its immanentist counterpart, to the conception of a society whose order is informed by orientation toward transcendent being. The "world" that can be conquered is an aggregate of world-immanent objects endowed with a universality for which the conception of ecumenic rule had to draw on the other pole of the Within-Beyond tension—that is, transcendent being. The Alexandrian or Caesarian desire holds its peculiar fascination, not only for the actors but even for the victims, because it heightens the splendor of strength and power by endowing it with the illusionary aura of universality. Ecumenic desire is the ontologically perfect response to the appeal for order going forth from a world that experientially has become

11. Voegelin, "Configurations of History," 101–3; *Ecumenic Age*, 313.
12. *Ecumenic Age*, 206–11.
13. Voegelin, "What Is History?," 30.

immanent. Hence, an ecumenic empire can go far by way of expansion and duration before the illusion of universality is shattered and the tedium of senselessness compels a restoration of balance by accepting transcendental orientation nevertheless.[14]

We have, then, a situation in which there is an attempt to create by conquest the universality discerned by philosophers in understanding their experiences as representatively human. Such an effort can have limited success as more and more peoples and lands are brought under the conqueror's jurisdiction; but ultimately the enterprise is doomed to failure, "for the concupiscence of conquest cannot reach the horizon beyond which lies the divine source of human universality."[15] The horizon constituted by the Beyond cannot be brought under the control of imperial ambition.

This literalism that would create a universal ecumene by force of arms has been a recurrent problem in history. Yet the limitations imposed on ecumenic expansion by the structure of reality do not always put an end to the desire for mastery. Imperial speculators are not necessarily deterred by the *de facto* limitations of their situation. If there is no more land on earth to be conquered, there is always the unbounded space discovered by modern science. Voegelin viewed contemporary science fiction, space exploration, and notions of other inhabited worlds within the cosmos as in some sense indicators of a human desire not only to dominate the earthly ecumene but to "conquer space."[16]

Voegelin found such musings to be relatively harmless phenomena; far more dangerous are the modern attempts to dominate the pragmatic ecumene. Whether in the form of progressivism, communism, or Western colonialism, we find the same tendencies to domi-

14. Ibid., 31–32.
15. *Ecumenic Age,* 208.
16. Voegelin, "World Empire," 174–76. See also Voegelin, "The Mongol Orders of Submission to European Powers, 1245–1255," 378–413; *New Science of Politics,* 56–59; and *Ecumenic Age,* 210–11. In the case of the Mongol empire, the fact that the societies conquered were not yet coextensive with the entire ecumene did not alter the view that, jurisdictionally, all lands remaining to be incorporated by force were *already* part of the empire. According to Mongol theorists, "all lands under heaven" fell within the boundaries of their empire. Hence, any territorial expansion was merely a reincorporation of rebellious subjects into the empire. According to Voegelin, much the same can be said for the Communist attitude, where people who are made subject to Communist rule have not been conquered, but "liberated."

nate humanity and to bring the known inhabitable world under the sway of one's own ideology. The pathological character of the contemporary situation is evident in the dangerous constellation that has developed, as Voegelin details in his essay "World Empire and the Unity of Mankind":

> (i) the existence of an ecumene; (ii) the feeling that the ecumene, though it is not a world, should be one; (iii) the 'co-existence' of rival worlds within the ecumene; (iv) the absence of symptoms to show that one of the rival worlds was persuasive enough to capture the ecumene and become its only world without violence; (v) the absence of symptoms that a new world was in the making which could capture the ecumene and replace the present manifold of worlds; (vi) the apparently insoluble bond between the conception of a world and dominion in the instrumentalist sense; and (vii) the consequent threat of a destructive conflict of arms.

The language of this passage is not that of *The Ecumenic Age* (which appeared twelve years later); but what is at issue is essentially the same. "World" in this context means both the inhabited world and world in the sense of "different conceptions of existence, each trying to incarnate itself in visible dominion over territory and people." When "world" in the latter sense is merged with the former sense we arrive at a situation in which various power blocks compete with one another for influence in an attempt to dominate the ecumene, if not by military means, then by economic power. At the root of the problem lies a crude immanentization of the universality experienced in the great differentiations of consciousness. Compounding the dilemma in the contemporary context is the loss of spiritual substance. The earlier ecumenic empires existed in a world in which spiritual order of some sort was understood to be a reality—a reality that might set at least some limits to imperial hubris. The new empires, however, often start from a position of revolt against any notion of spiritual order. Lacking any spiritual standard of restraint, and possessing impressive technological/material power, they constitute a particularly lethal form of imperial aggression.[17]

Ultimately the "ecumene" fails as a symbol, because it is impossible to organize humanity by pragmatic means. Humanity is constituted by its orientation toward the divine ground, not by being incor-

---

17. Voegelin, "World Empire," 175–76, 180, 179–80; *Ecumenic Age*, 211.

porated into the political or jurisdictional reach of an empire. Ecumenic conquest is self-defeating; there are always new areas and peoples to be conquered, and in conquering other societies the conqueror must be aware at some level that the fate he inflicts upon others may one day fall upon his own people. In addition, the simple corralling of human beings within a field created by raw, external power does not form them into a "humanity" or a people; that is solely a function of their transcendent orientation. "Philosophically," Voegelin states, "the ecumene was a miserable symbol."[18]

SPIRIT AND EMPIRE

The effect of conquest upon the organized societies can best be described as traumatic:

> This pragmatic impact of conquest on the traditional forms of existence in society is abrupt; and its abruptness is not matched by an equally sudden spiritual response to the situation. The divine authority of the older symbols is impaired when the societies whose reality of order they express lose their political independence, while the new imperial order has, at least initially, no more than the authority of power. Hence the spiritual and intellectual lives of the peoples exposed to the events are in danger of separating from the reality of socially ordered existence. Society and the cosmos of which society is a part tend to be experienced as a sphere of disorder, so that the sphere of order in reality contracts to personal existence in tension toward the divine Beyond. The area of reality that can be experienced as divinely ordered thus suffers a severe diminution.[19]

Of course the question that immediately arises is whether the older symbols that evoked the truth of order were ever fully integrated into the societies in which they arose. If we focus on Israel and Hellas as we have done in Chapters 5 and 6, the question would have to be answered negatively. In neither case did the truth of order become fully socially effective. Neither revelation nor philosophy had ever truly penetrated these societies. Their more insightful members realized this and withdrew into circles of like-minded individuals, biding their time until that day when a society formed by the truth of order would be possible. At the same time, the suspicion also began

18. *Ecumenic Age,* 171–72.
19. Ibid., 21–22.

to emerge that no concrete society could ever be the adequate bearer of transcendent order.[20]

Imperial expansion, then, was not a matter of voracious conquerors putting an end to societies in which the truth of order had flourished and become the standard for social existence. On the contrary, the empires simply engulfed social orders already weakened from within, social orders whose inability to embody the truth of order was becoming increasingly apparent. What was becoming clear to philosophers and prophets was the insight that *no* society could adequately incarnate transcendent order. The empires did not put an end to the glorious and successful wedding of transcendent truth with institutional order; they simply compounded the unintelligibility of the situation by attempting to create universal order through pragmatic conquest. The shortsightedness of the organized societies was replaced by the foolishness of imperial designs. The new empires simply provided a new stage upon which the struggle for order could continue to unfold.[21]

The new pragmatic scene thus created was experienced by the participants as senseless. To conquered peoples, history now seemed to be without meaning, since their very existence as a society was jeopardized. And among the more prescient conquerors there arose the sickening realization that, eventually, they too would go the way of all other empires.[22] History, then, became a cause for despair, since it seemed to consist of little more than a meaningless succession of empire after empire. The ground was thus prepared for apocalyptic and gnosis, in which the present history would be brought to a close through a cataclysmic act of God or through a knowledge that would abolish history altogether by offering a means of escape from its apparent senselessness.

The social chaos engendered by conquest leads to a situation in which spiritual order, that is, the truth of order discovered in the great differentiations of consciousness, becomes disengaged from the organized societies that gave it birth. In addition, there are the empires who are responsible for the demise of these organized societies, but who themselves are lacking in a spiritual substance that

20. Ibid., 115–16.
21. Ibid., 116.
22. Ibid., 126, 172.

would give meaning to the imperial enterprise. We have, then, a pragmatic shell in need of transcendent meaning, coupled with spiritual outbursts in need of a social carrier. According to Voegelin, "The universality of spiritual order, at this historical epoch, meets with the indefinite expansion of a power shell devoid of substance." Universal spiritual movements may come to see in the organizational structure of the ecumenic empire the means by which their universal message may be spread; and empires may find in such spiritual movements their unifying principles.[23]

The tension between the truth of order and its concrete realization, which had been at the heart of the Israelite and Greek struggle for order, is, if anything, intensified in the Ecumenic Age. The destruction of these organized societies severs the insights into humanity's transcendent orientation from their institutional moorings, while the raw exercise of power displayed by the conquerors brings into stark relief the utter senselessness of founding a social order by pragmatic means alone. The events of the Ecumenic Age bring the question of the relationship between spirit and society into sharp focus.

Nor was the "solution" to this problem without its own ambiguities. Voegelin could appreciate this solution while, at the same time, understanding its dangers:

> That is a problem, both theoretical and practical, of the first magnitude indeed. It is a theoretical problem for every philosophy of history, since the universal order of mankind can become historically concrete only through symbolic representation by a community of spirit with ecumenic intentions—that is the problem of the Church. And it is a practical problem in politics and history, since the attempt at representing universal order through a community with ecumenic intentions is obviously fraught with complications through the possibility that several such communities will be founded historically and pursue their ecumenic ambitions with means not altogether spiritual.

Understanding the problem in this fashion led Voegelin to distinguish between *ecumenicity* and *universality*. Ecumenicity is the tendency of a community claiming to represent the divine source of order to embody the universality of its claim by making itself coextensive with the ecumene, while universality simply means the experi-

23. Ibid., 117.

ence of the divine Beyond as the source of order that is universally binding for all people.[24]

The failure to take seriously these distinctions has been a recurring source of disorder in history. Spiritual communities in search of effective social carriers, have, at times, been all too willing to enter into an alliance with ecumenic conquerors. And the empires have often been most eager to appropriate spiritual movements in an attempt to legitimize and give meaning to an otherwise senseless drive for ecumenic domination. Even where there is no explicit association of spiritual and political power, the founders of religious communities may interpret imperial expansion as a providential movement clearing the field for the triumph of their religion. The resulting arrangement granted meaning and legitimation to empire, but its effect on the universality of order was rather ambiguous. If the legitimacy of empire was enhanced, the bearer of spiritual order, the church, found itself in the problematic role of an ordering force in society.[25]

The association of empire and spirit ultimately fails, because as each empire declines, its claims to embody universality are revealed as illusion. Likewise, those who would see in the expansion of empire a providential movement insuring their religious ascendancy are sure to be disappointed when it turns out that the divine intention is not to be confused with their own. Voegelin notes that history is filled with examples that undermine the claim to identify the workings of providence with any particular, historical association of spiritual and pragmatic power. Indeed, the very repetition of the rise and fall of empires, each claiming to represent the final truth, ought to give one pause when one is tempted to find the meaning of history in one's own time and place.[26]

Whereas the earlier organized societies had to contend with the "mortgages" that prevented them from understanding that the dif-

---

24. Ibid., 137.
25. Ibid., 142. In this regard one might consider Voegelin's treatment of Deutero-Isaiah (*Israel and Revelation*, 504–15; *Ecumenic Age*, 26, 212–14), Paul (*Ecumenic Age*, 256–60, 266–71, 300–303; "World Empire," 185), and Matthew ("World Empire," 184). In each case he finds important insights coupled with great ambiguities as to the relation between the truth of order and the meaning of empire.
26. *Ecumenic Age*, 214.

ferentiations of consciousness that emerged in their midst had implications for human existence far beyond the confines of their own
particular societies, the ecumenic variation of the problem consisted, as we have seen, in a confusion of the universality gained in
differentiation with the pragmatic expansion of empire. The earlier
societies were perhaps not as aware of the universal implications
contained in the differentiations; by the time of the ecumenic empires universality was better understood, but it had come to be associated with the scope of ecumenic conquest. In both cases the same
immanentizing tendencies are at work.

The problem stems in large part from a failure to adequately
understand both the meaning and the limitations of exodus. Whether
one means by *exodus* both a pragmatic and a spiritual movement
from cosmological empire, as in the case of Israel, the exodus of the
conqueror from his own organizing center into the wider ecumene,
or the spiritual exodus of prophets and philosophers from their own
societies, there always exists the danger that the liberation and en-
thusiasm experienced in exodus will be derailed by dreams of permanently realizing the truth of order in the world. Such dreams are at
odds with the structure of reality:

> No imperial expansion can reach the receding horizon; no exodus
> from bondage is an exodus from the *condicio humana;* no turning away
> from the Apeiron or turning against it, can prevent the return to it
> through death. . . . Conquest and exodus symbolize enterprises of par-
> ticipation in the directional flux of reality. Note: Enterprises of par-
> ticipation, *not* autonomous human actions that could result in the
> conquest of, or exodus from, reality. . . . Conquest and exodus, thus,
> are movements *within* reality.[27]

Properly understood, conquest and exodus are symbols that point
to the movement of reality as a whole; they are seriously misleading if
taken to mean that the truth of order could be realized in history. At
the same time, though, the inevitably frustrated attempt to establish
a universal dominion by human effort is not without its positive
consequences. As misguided as such efforts may be, it is their very
failure that leads the more insightful citizens of the age to understand that "the end of all human action does not lie within this world
but beyond it." It is for this reason that "the symbolism of a move-

27. Ibid., 215–16.

ment which transcends reality while remaining within it is not sense-less."[28]

There is a sense, then, in which one can say that the impasse created by the failure of ecumenic conquest to achieve universality has been responsible for the development of a more authentic under-standing of history. Having been conquered by the destructive new empires, organized societies were "forced" to look beyond the pres-ent order to find meaning. And as the newly ascendant empires came to see their own dreams of permanency and finality evaporate, their more astute citizens came to realize that, paradoxically, histori-cal finality lies somehow beyond history. The pragmatic events of the Ecumenic Age forced those affected by the events to reflect upon the true source of order. As noted earlier, certain members of the orga-nized societies had already come to understand that no particular society could ever fully embody order, but the conquest of these societies by ecumenic empires focused the question in a radical manner.

Voegelin was emphatic, however, in maintaining that the relation-ship between pragmatic events and spiritual advance is not a simple matter of direct causality. Ecumenic expansion does not mechanisti-cally "cause" spiritual outbursts. While it is apparent that certain social and civilizational contexts seem to be more favorable to the emergence of the great differentiations of consciousness, the differ-entiations are not the product of nor are they reducible to material or technological advances. Rather, Voegelin would insist that it is only in light of the insights gained in the differentiations of consciousness that historical events can be understood as meaningful. Spiritual outbursts and imperial expansion are related to one another as a configuration, not in terms of efficient causality. Writing twelve years before the publication of *The Ecumenic Age,* Voegelin would speak of this relationship as an "ontological connection":

> The parallelism of the two phenomena suggests a connection between them. Not, to be sure, a connection on the level of causality, for asser-tions that the spiritual openings were caused by imperial expansion or that the founders of empire were inspired by prophets and philoso-phers would be simplistic generalizations to be quickly falsified by ref-erence to historical facts. It is rather an ontological connection, inasmuch as the parallel phenomena in the areas of power and orga-

28. Voegelin, "World Empire," 184; *Ecumenic Age,* 215–16.

nization and of spiritual penetration display a parallelism of meaning. For the empires were world-empires, not by arbitrary declaration of the moderns, but by their own self-interpretation as attested by the literary texts; and the outbursts of the spirit were accompanied by the consciousness of achieving a new truth of human existence. An affinity of meaning subtly connects a creation of empire which claims to represent mankind with a spiritual efflorescence which claims representative humanity. The parallel phenomena, while not causing one another, are parts of a configuration of history by virtue of the adumbrated connection. Moreover, the *dramatis personae* of history were well aware of the affinity and acted upon their knowledge. Within the meaningful configuration, which as a whole is beyond causality, there run the motivations of pragmatic history, resulting in associations between imperial order and spiritual movements.[29]

The configuration, then, is not constituted by cause and effect, but rather on the basis of parallel yet common claims to universality. Within the configuration, though, one has to take into account "the motivations of pragmatic history" that somehow link spiritual and imperial advances.

From the travails of the Ecumenic Age, from the misguided and misdirected attempts at achieving universality, from the complex interaction between pragmatic existence and spiritual order there emerges the notion of universal humanity, or universal mankind. The repeated and frustrating non-finality of every empire raises serious questions as to history's meaning and moves certain thinkers toward a more profound reflection on precisely what it is that constitutes the meaning of human life. From within the messiness of history there emerges the insight that universal humanity is not the object of pragmatic organization, but the common human orientation toward the divine Beyond. While all people are conditioned by space and time, they also participate in the same "flux of divine presence." Far from being a mere "aggregate of members of a biological species," universal humanity is rather an "eschatological index" indicating that our commonality lies in our shared constitutive relationship to transcendent reality.[30]

Universal humanity has never existed in the world, nor is it a reality that could ever be created in this world. Voegelin rejected the

29. *Ecumenic Age*, 306; "World Empire," 171.
30. *Ecumenic Age*, 304–5.

dangerous dreams of those who would try to organize humanity through the imposition of an ideology or who would justify the annihilation of thousands as a necessary sacrifice in the progressive development of the *masse totale*.[31] Universal humanity is a symbol, an index, cutting across all ages and times. It is nothing other than human beings as oriented to the mystery that is the Beyond. Thus there is no "subject" of history other than those people who respond or fail to respond to the divine appeal and in so doing create history.

While it would be senseless to conceive of universal humanity apart from those concrete societies in which the struggle for order takes place, it would be no more accurate to conceive of universal humanity as an "abstraction" derived from the data constituted by all the concrete societies that have ever existed. Universal humanity is not some transcendent common denominator obtained by generalizing from the experiences of particular societies. It has far more to do with the realization that all humanity participates in reality's movement toward more eminent Reality. As such it cannot be circumscribed, for this movement originates in mystery and has no foreseeable end:

> Universal humanity is a symbol rather than a field of potential organization. Further, it is not a framework of a process of power, as are the civilizations and ecumenes, for besides the now living persons it also embraces all men of the past and the future. The experience of essential humanity rather is the point at which concrete men experience their concrete consciousness as the place at which man, even though existing in time, participates in the eternal being of the ground. The consciousness of the existential tension toward the ground, i.e., man's center of order, ontically rises above all immanent-temporal processes of history.

Every society shares in the mystery of the ground, and can, to a greater or lesser extent, illuminate that process. Universal humanity, then, is not an existing entity, but symbolizes "the historical equivalence of the plural modes of man's participation in the one reality."[32]

This participation is, however, a participation in tension. Yet even though the tension between the truth of order and the order of society remains a permanent feature of the human condition, this

---

31. Voegelin, "World Empire," 180–83.
32. *Anamnesis,* 204; Jurgen Gebhardt, "Toward the Process of Universal Mankind: The Formation of Voegelin's Philosophy of History," 85.

need not be taken as an indication that such tension represents the final word on our existence. The tension points past itself toward a transfiguration beyond space and time. To have grasped the direction in which this tension points, to be aware of its structure as operative in all societies at all times, is to understand the symbol "universal humanity" and its meaning as an eschatological index. In the final section of this chapter we will examine Voegelin's notion of transfiguration. Before doing so, however, let us conclude our discussion of spirit and empire with some observations concerning the relationship between history and differentiation.

When the symbol of universal humanity has been articulated, it is accompanied by the realization that history is not simply "a stream of human beings and their actions in time, but the process of man's participation in a flux of divine presence that has eschatological direction." Indeed, if this insight into the process were to remain a constant in human consciousness, then "what happens on the spatio-temporal level of existence would be of little relevance." While Voegelin insisted that there is no flux of presence in the metaxy without the concrete existence of human beings in the biophysical universe, he also maintained that there is no "length of time" in which "history" happens. Instead, time is a function of the lasting and passing characteristic of the "things" comprising the various strata of being. Time is defined implicitly in terms of the relations between the "things," while the process of the Whole, in which the things come into existence and fade away, is beyond time. As Voegelin put it, "Things do not happen in the astro-physical universe; the universe, together with all things founded in it, happens in God."[33]

While it may be the case that history does not consist in a sequence of events "in time," it is equally clear that Voegelin acknowledged the existence of meaningful advances in the differentiation of consciousness which do, indeed, constitute epochs whose importance can be recognized as "historical." These epochal advances may not be arrangeable in a linear chronological sequence from lesser to greater differentiation, but the fact remains that there are advances, and that these advances, in creating consciousness of a "before" and an "after," do constitute history. Although it is always the nature of humanity to be oriented toward the divine ground, this awareness

33. *Ecumenic Age*, 6, 305, 333–34.

unfolds only gradually. It is for this reason that Voegelin rejected what he considered to be the ahistorical existentialism of Heidegger and Bultmann:

> Above all we can recognize the technique of identification, familiar from Hegel's gnosis, by which historical phenomena are transformed into states of consciousness. We start from the Law, which in historical concreteness is the Torah. Through identification, not formal but in substance, the Torah changes into the "thou shalt" that is alive in everyman's conscience. And the "thou shalt" as pre-apprehension of faith becomes identical with unbelieving existence in freedom as interpreted by the philosopher. The historical relation between Law and Gospel, between the Old and New Testament, is thus transformed into the ontological tension between the natural existence of man and the Christian existence in faith. History in the sense of the *progressus* of mankind, shrouded in the mystery of a meaning incompletely revealed—the history we have in mind as long as we are not existentialists—has somehow disappeared. Moreover, with the transformation of history into ontology the relation between Bultmann's theology and Heidegger's existentialism comes into better view.[34]

At first glance, one might be tempted to assign this passage to that period in Voegelin's intellectual development in which he still conceived of history as a meaningful course of events to be arranged on a time line. But such is not the case. The article from which this passage is taken, "History and Gnosis" (1969), appeared one year after "Configurations of History" and one year before "Equivalences of Experience and Symbolization in History." Thus, at the time of its publication, Voegelin was very much aware of the notion of "configuration" as giving meaning to history. Rather than representing a return to an earlier way of conceiving history, what we find here is evidence of Voegelin's struggle to do justice to the idea of meaningful advance as embodied in particular concrete societies, while simultaneously acknowledging the atemporal, ahistorical mystery from which history derives its meaning.

Having said this, I would go further to assert that while Voegelin acknowledged the emergence and decline of particular societies and civilizations as integral to the historical process, the emphasis, particularly in *The Ecumenic Age* and the works that followed, is clearly on those events as they serve to illuminate the process of the Whole.

---

34. "History and Gnosis," 69.

History is primarily the history of differentiation: "The 'thing' that is called man discovers itself as having consciousness; and as a consequence, it discovers man's consciousness as the area of reality in which the process of reality becomes luminous to itself. A mute process about whose meaning one could be in doubt becomes a process increasingly articulate about its meaning; and what is discovered as its meaning is the emergence of noetic consciousness in the process." In another place Voegelin writes:

> What becomes visible in the new luminosity, therefore, is not only the structure of consciousness itself (in classical language: the nature of man), but also the structure of an "advance" in the process of reality. Moreover, the site of the advance is not a mysterious entity called "history" that would exist independent of such advances; the site rather is the very consciousness which, in its state of noetic luminosity, makes these discoveries. The theophanic events do not occur in history; they constitute history together with its meaning. The noetic theophany, finally, reveals consciousness as having the structure of metaleptic reality, of the divine-human Metaxy. As a consequence, "history" in the sense of an area of reality in which the insight into the meaning of existence advances is the history of theophany.

If there was any doubt as to what Voegelin means in these passages, he aimed to dispel it by stating clearly that "there is no history other than the history constituted in the Metaxy of differentiating consciousness, as the analysis of the noetic field has made clear."[35]

Advances in the differentiation of consciousness do not occur *in* history; rather history emerges as that dimension of the Whole in which its structure and movement become ever more luminous through a process of increasing differentiation of consciousness. History is the realization of eternal being in time, where "in time" must be understood not as "within" some sort of boundary or enclosure known as "time," but rather as an expression of the fact that history has to do with the relation of transcendent being to those embodied spirits known as human beings. While the process encompasses the emergence and decline of concrete societies, it is the increase in luminosity concerning the structure and movement of reality that is the real focus of history, for history is nothing other than "the process in which the differentiations occur," a process in which "reality becomes luminous for the movement beyond its own structure." In

35. *Ecumenic Age*, 177, 252, 243.

Voegelin's view, "The historical dimension of humanity is neither world time nor eternity but the flux of presence in the Metaxy."[36]

The significance of a given social order is determined primarily by its ability to articulate its response to theophany and thereby further illuminate the process of the Whole. The advance in differentiation is an end in itself. History is essentially the history of consciousness.[37] To pose the issue differently, might it not be the case that what distinguishes the earlier from the later volumes of *Order and History* is that in the first three volumes the emphasis was on how differentiations or leaps in being might transform the societies in which they occurred, whereas in the last two volumes societies are evaluated in terms of how well they serve to further the advance of differentiation?

There is a sense, when reading Voegelin's later writings, that the pragmatic events in which individuals, peoples, and nations are embroiled serve almost as a backdrop for the "real" history that is unfolding in consciousness, albeit through these particular events.[38] Indeed, Voegelin makes distinctions concerning the structure of history that indicate such an attitude. We recall his notion of a double constitution of history, where there exists a phenomenal strata of historical facts accessible to the methods of "objectifying science." This level of history, however, is "a secondary stratum within the comprehensive phenomenon that also carries the index of transcendence." There is a definite hierarchy among historical phenomena:

36. *Anamnesis,* 124–34; "What Is History?," 35; *Ecumenic Age,* 304.

37. *Anamnesis,* 153, 155, 158, 178, 204; *Ecumenic Age,* 8, 177, 185, 188, 243, 251–52, 304–6, 314–15; "Wisdom and the Magic," 372.

38. I find this stance in Voegelin's attitude concerning the Incarnation; he has little patience with discussions concerning the historicity of Jesus Christ. Questions as to whether or not the Incarnation is "historically real" turn "the structure of reality upside down; it flies in the face of all our empirical knowledge about history and its constitution of meaning. The misunderstandings arise from the separation of a 'content' from the reality of the experience, and from the treatment of the content as an object of propositional knowledge. In its metaleptic context, Incarnation is the reality of divine presence in Jesus as experienced by the men who were his disciples and expressed their experience by the symbol 'Son of God' and its equivalents" (*Ecumenic Age,* 242–43). My point here is to call attention to Voegelin's tendency to treat the Incarnation as an advance in the differentiation of consciousness rather than as an event occurring in history, and to identify history with such advances. In Voegelin's reading, the Son of God does not so much enter into human history as it is a matter of the meaning of history coming into view through the differentiation of consciousness in the man Jesus Christ.

> Historical phenomena do not all belong to the same class. The first rank among them is occupied by the experiences of transcendence because a) they raise the realization of eternal being in time to the level of consciousness and because b) they discover in these vicissitudes of consciousness the substance of history and thereby establish the criteria of historical relevance. . . . In general, one may say that an indefinite range of events belonging to the economic, social, governmental, intellectual, and spiritual order of society can acquire historical relevance because closely or distantly—as causes or effects, as social settings, as conditions or consequences—they are related to the central phenomenon, that is, to the experience of transcendence. Moreover, since all these events, as well as their personal and collective carriers, are rooted in the external world, their space and time data will enter the sphere of historical relevance.[39]

It is this conceptual framework that lends *The Ecumenic Age* its peculiar cast. History, in *The Ecumenic Age*, is a strangely divided, curiously disembodied affair. While dealing with pragmatic events, that is, with the rise and fall of empires, the emergence and decline of organized societies, the relationship between these events and the encompassing movement of Reality is never clearly articulated. Pragmatic conquest and spiritual exodus are said to be "so closely related in forming new social fields that the border line between them tends to lose its sharpness."[40] At the same time, history would seem to be characterized by the same "split" that we noted in earlier chapters. In the Ecumenic Age this split is intensified, as we are faced with a truth of order that has become disengaged from organized societies, confronting pragmatic "shells" in need of spiritual meaning. We are left with a two-tiered universe, with civilizational and societal clashes occurring on the phenomenal level, while history as meaningful unfolds on the level of consciousness. The two strata seem to be intertwined, but not fully integrated.

This becomes clear when considering the relationship between pragmatic events and spiritual outbursts. Voegelin maintains that the "phenomenal" events do not "cause" differentiations of consciousness. Imperial expansion does not serve as an efficient cause, generating differentiations of consciousness. Even before they were conquered, the more astute members of organized societies had realized

---

39. Voegelin, "What Is History?," 34, 35–36.
40. *Ecumenic Age*, 212.

that their societies were not adequate vessels for the truth of order. And yet, as we noted earlier, there is a strong sense in which clashes on the phenomenal level create such chaotic conditions that the historical participants are led to look beyond their present horizon toward the atemporal process of Reality in which the phenomenal events are but a secondary stratum. If not the cause of differentiations, pragmatic events would seem to be at least a significant catalyst in their emergence. Voegelin acknowledged that certain levels of social, political, and economic achievement are more favorable to differentiation than others, but he did not develop this theme much beyond this observation, and the relationship between the development that takes place on these levels is never really integrated with the emergence of the great differentiations. We are left with an acknowledgment that there is some connection between pragmatic conditions and the development of consciousness, but the stratification of reality reflective of the "double constitution of history" with which we have to contend makes it difficult to articulate what that connection might be. Discussing the experiential complex of spiritual outburst, ecumenic empire, and historiography, Voegelin seemed to recognize this tension:

> The experiential complex, though it is an integral unit, thus, suggests by its structure a split into subject and object of knowledge. If one yields to the temptation, empires and outbursts are liable to move into the position of events that happen in history, while the historiographer tends to become the recorder of a history that is structured by the events; and between the hypostatized subject and object of historical consciousness, the reality that has become luminous as a process of transfiguration will evaporate.[41]

While it is clear that Voegelin's purpose here is to caution against the reification of the poles within the experience, one still finds in this passage a tendency to contrast consciousness as intentional with consciousness as luminous, rather than to specify them both in terms of the Question.[42] Human understanding as operative in economy, society, and polity seems somehow discontinuous with that same understanding as operative in raising questions about our transcendent destiny. And since consciousness as luminous is clearly the favored

41. Voegelin, "What Is History?," 31–32; *Ecumenic Age*, 313.
42. *Ecumenic Age*, 316–35.

mode of cognition in apprehending the structure of Reality, we are left with a bifurcated history, in which phenomenal events have meaning only insofar as they are related to the process of the Whole grasped in luminosity. To attempt to deal with the problem by asserting that we must not hypostatize the two strata, and that both strata are encompassed by the process of the Whole, which, as mystery, is inaccessible to human knowing, is perhaps to situate history properly within Reality as a whole, but there still remains a discontinuity between history as phenomenal and history as differentiation. The discontinuity between the two has simply been projected onto a larger canvas.

The tension between the truth of order and its historical incarnation in society has thus been resolved by allowing the emphasis to shift decidedly toward the articulation of transcendence in the differentiation of consciousness as the primary criterion for determining historical relevance. And this articulation takes place through a process in which the structure and movement of Reality become increasingly lucid in the luminosity of differentiating consciousness. The derailment toward which intentional consciousness is inclined can only be avoided "if one acknowledges the process of differentiation itself as the exclusive source of our knowledge concerning the unit of experience that understands itself as historically epochal when it differentiates."[43] History has come to be understood not so much as a struggle to incarnate order in society, but as the unfolding of differentiated consciousness in and through particular societies. The philosophy of history and society described in *The Ecumenic Age* is, I believe, not so much a break with Voegelin's earlier conception as it is a thoroughly consistent development and working out of social and political problems within his ontological/epistemological framework. That framework had itself to be clearly articulated; but having done so, Voegelin, with notable consistency, drew out its implications for a philosophy of history and society.

Those implications, however, give rise to further questions, one of which is whether the "transcendental index" ought to be the sole or even the primary source of historical meaning. While acknowledging our ultimate orientation toward mystery, might not the restriction of historical relevance to those events associated with advances in differ-

---

43. Ibid., 314.

entiating consciousness ignore other levels of human development not so explicitly tied to these crucial insights? Can we not go beyond the broad claim that "the structure of man's earthly existence in society is somehow involved in the process of differentiating consciousness," without necessarily operating with a "Marxian consciousness" determined by a "Marxian Being"? Is there no middle ground between insisting, on the one hand, that consciousness is determined by technology, economy, or society, and maintaining, on the other hand, that these areas of human life derive their meaning primarily from their relationship to differentiations of consciousness? Is it possible that in rejecting immanentist derailments, and in emphasizing humanity's transcendent orientation, Voegelin perhaps devalued the operation of human intelligence in technology, economy, society, and polity as independent sources of meaning in history?[44] Concerning the discrepancy between transcendent and mundane order, it would seem as if the tension has been resolved by identifying the meaning of history with those differentiations of consciousness that point beyond this world toward a resolution of the tension.

VISION AND TRANSFIGURATION

These criticisms are not meant to call into question what, in many ways, could be considered Voegelin's most profound contribution to social and political theory; that is, his recovery of the transcendent dimension of political/social life and his restoration of political *philosophy* as a genuine love of that wisdom which reveals itself in the structure and movement of Reality. As we have noted, his exploration of the relationship between transcendence and social order was at the center of his project. In his later writings there develops, I believe, an increased attention to the transcendent pole of this relationship as it becomes more fully articulate in consciousness. Indeed, there is a sense in which this process comes to be identified as history. Reflections upon the structure of Reality and its movement toward the divine Beyond become the focus of Voegelin's final work, and "meditation" becomes the preferred mode of analysis.[45] Refer-

44. Voegelin, *Ecumenic Age,* 306. See also Doran, "Theology's Situation," 80–81; Douglass, "Voegelin's Program," 20–21.

45. For example, "The Beginning and the Beyond: A Meditation on Truth"; "Wisdom and the Magic of the Extreme: A Meditation"; "The Meditative Origin of the Philosophical Knowledge of Order."

ences to particular societies and their struggles for order become far less frequent as Voegelin directs his attention to exploring the formative presence of the Beyond in the human soul. Thus it is that the symbol of "vision" or *opsis* comes to the fore.

To speak of vision is to have come full circle in our analysis. This study began by exploring Voegelin's understanding of reality, its structure, and its movement. And these topics could not be considered without also taking into account that human participation through which reality becomes luminous. Vision, for Voegelin, is nothing other than that encompassing cognition by which reality is known. The accent here falls on the adjective *encompassing:*

> To the old language of the Beginning and the Beyond, the *fides quaerens intellectum,* the presence of the divine reality, the divine appeal, and the human response, the divine-human movement and counter movement, the human quest and the noetic pull from the Beyond, the Parousia of the Beyond, the existence in the Metaxy, the existential *agon* of man in the Metaxy of mortality and immortality, we must now add the vision as the comprehensive mode of man's cognitive participation in reality.

Vision, or *opsis,* is a term borrowed from Plato. It is an event, a process within reality, and not, according to Voegelin, the intentional subject's apprehension of reality as an object. *Vision* is the technical term coined by Plato to describe "the experiential process in which the order of reality is seen, becomes reflectively known, and finds its appropriate language symbols."[46]

As comprehensive and as a process, vision ranges along the entire continuum from myth to noesis. Vision is operative whenever the divine Beyond exerts its appeal and finds a willing response from the human pole of the metaxy. While the symbol may have found its articulation in the work of Plato, Voegelin states clearly that, to the extent that earlier figures such as Hesiod, Isaiah, and Jeremiah were aware of themselves as heeding a "divine voice," they were indeed possessed of "vision," although perhaps in a less self-reflective form than that found in Plato. What is grasped in vision is the presence of the divine Beyond and the possibility of articulating the vision:

> (1) The Vision is man's participatory experience of "seeing" the paradox of a reality which depends for its existence, formative order, and

46. Voegelin, "The Beginning and the Beyond," 230, 229.

luminosity on the presence of "the god" who, as distinguished from the Olympian gods, is a non-present Beyond of the being things in which he is present.

(2) The Vision is the experienced possibility of raising the "seeing," which in various degrees of compactness is always present as the formative force in man's existence, from compactness to a state of reflective differentiation, as well as of finding the language symbols that will express the paradoxical structure of differentiated consciousness.

In the vision, history comes to be seen as a flux of divine presence in which human actions come to be "seen" in terms of either response or rejection of the divine appeal. The consciousness of divine presence characteristic of the vision marks every event with a sense of an "indelible present."[47]

It is through vision that the "indelible present" is apprehended, that is, in the vision one becomes cognizant of the timelessness that characterizes the Beyond and that encompasses the process of the Whole. The vision, as luminous to itself, is aware that its own occurrence is a dynamic event within the flux of divine presence, serving to further illuminate the structure and movement of reality: "In recognizing these structures, finally, the vision reveals their recognition as an event in the process of reality becoming luminous for its truth. The experiential variations do not proceed as a meaningless sequence; their process is intelligible inasmuch as it is internally cognitive."[48]

Vision includes, but is not limited to, noesis. As comprehensive, vision encompasses not only *cognitio rationis,* but also *cognitiones fidei, amoris, et spei.*[49] Within this broad range of cognitive activities, the activity of *fides quaerens intellectum* characterizes the philosophical enterprise; "in Plato's case, the *fides* has found its symbolic truth in the vision of love as the source of order in reality and by the vision of truth in human existence through the participation in the movement of reality toward the divine beyond." We are oriented in reality not only by means of noetic rationality, but through a knowledge constituted by faith, hope, and love. Voegelin's articulation of vision is an explication of his earlier insight that "philosophy is the love of being through the love of divine Being as the source of its order."[50]

---

47. Ibid, 228; Voegelin, "Wisdom and the Magic," 362, 346.
48. Voegelin, "Wisdom and the Magic," 347–48.
49. *Anamnesis,* 184.
50. "Wisdom and the Magic," 255; *Israel and Revelation,* xiv.

Noesis, then, while inseparable from vision, is that dimension of vision which enables vision to become explicit to itself and which helps to preserve the balance of consciousness that could so easily be lost in the intensity of the vision: "The *intellectus* is the noetic action of exploring the structures in a process of reality whose fundamental order and direction are revealed by the visions *(opsis)*. The philosopher's truth thus results from the interaction of noesis and vision; and the result must be carefully balanced so as to violate neither the truth of structural analysis nor the truth of the vision." Noetic inquiry emerges from within the wider vision:

> "Imaginative vision," emerging from reality in response to the appeal of reality, is the comprehensive event of experience and symbolization. The philosopher's meditation can operate only within the comprehensive vision and make it self-reflectively luminous for man's existence in tension toward the Beyond. Hence imaginative vision and noesis are not independent, rival, or alternative sources of knowledge and truth but interacting forces in the historical process of an imaginative vision that has noetic structure.[51]

While vision would seem to be operative at all levels of differentiation, one is also left with the impression that vision reaches its optimal clarity in articulating the Beyond and the movement of reality toward the Beyond. The cosmological *fides* is as much a dimension of vision as is noesis; differentiation never abolishes, but rather illuminates earlier truth. But it remains the case that there *are* advances in the differentiation of the truth concerning reality, and that the fullness of vision consists in an articulation of the Beyond and its parousia.[52]

It is here that the role of vision becomes clear in relation to the tension between the truth of order and its social incarnation. For what is revealed in the vision is the truth that the struggle for order is not the final word, and that one must look beyond order to discern the process of which the struggle is but a part:

---

51. "Wisdom and the Magic," 337–38; "The Beginning and the Beyond," 227. See also *Ecumenic Age*, 249–50. It is precisely this balance that Voegelin found lacking in the visions of pneumatic figures such as Isaiah and Paul. As vision, Paul's experience is equal if not superior to that of Plato; what is lacking in Paul's vision, according to Voegelin, is the noetic balance found in Plato.

52. Voegelin, "The Beginning and the Beyond," 218–32; *In Search of Order,* 76–81.

The Platonic Vision is so comprehensive, and its articulation so thorough, that its reality not only is luminous to itself but illuminates the structure and modality of visionary truth in general . . . . The noetic ascent reveals the truth of order, but the truth of order is not the whole truth. The truth of the Whole is the undying struggle *(mache athanatos)* between the Indestructible *(anolethron)* and the Eternal *(aionion)* in reality, the Indestructible being identified as body and soul, the Eternal as the immortal divinity (904a). The vision thus reveals the truth of reality as an undying struggle in which man is fated to participate by his existence. From this struggle there is no salvation *(psyches soteria,* 909a) other than the participatory noetic movement in existence from the mortal Beyond to the immortal Beyond.[53]

While we live, human existence is circumscribed by the structure of the metaxy; we are thus "fated" to exist in the tension between mortality and immortality, between society as it in fact exists and the truth of order emergent in consciousness.

And yet the vision reveals possibilities beyond this tension. For it points to the possibility of immortalization *(athanatizein)* to be gained through participation in the process of reality becoming luminous to itself for its structure and its movement toward an immortal Beyond. To immortalize is to respond to the appeal from the Beyond while living in this world, simultaneously understanding that one's ultimate destiny is part of a mystery only partially revealed by the parousia of the Beyond. As a composite of body and soul, human beings are subject to the tension of existence; yet by virtue of our orientation toward the Beyond we can be described as indestructible. As such, we share in the *mache athanatos,* the undying struggle that characterizes the process of the Whole in its immortalizing movement toward the divine Beyond. From this struggle there is salvation and redemption to the extent that we respond to the appeal through vision, a vision granted by the very same divine reality that has aroused the response: "When the presence of the Beyond is experienced in the noetic act, there reveals itself a Being that is neither the Apeiron nor one of the cosmic things but the immortally divine reality that will redeem its followers from their Apeirontic fate. The Beyond is indeed beyond the cosmos because the participation in its *parousia* permits the

---

53. "Wisdom and the Magic," 365.

soul of man to 'rise' from intracosmic mortality to transcosmic immortality."[54]

As human we remain beset by those evils that have afflicted people in every age—sickness, death, and the various social and political ills that result from the fact that not all will respond to the divine appeal and that even those who do can never fully incarnate the truth of order in social existence. In vision, however, we not only gain insight into our final destiny beyond the struggle to embody order, but the vision is itself an event in the process of immortalization and movement toward the Beyond. In the vision there is both revealed and constituted the immortalizing transfiguration that is the eschatological destiny of universal humanity:

> The Vision, while revealing the noetic truth of existential consciousness in opposition to the anoetic untruth of the Cave, reveals itself as an epochal event in the revelatory flux of presence; and the event is epochal because the visionary is conscious that the truth of immortalizing transfiguration through the divine-human movement in the *metaxy,* when "seen," transfigures. The saving tale is more than a tale of salvation; it is the tale that saves. Transfiguration in reality is real. Visionary revelation thus reveals revelation as an event of transfiguration; reality is really moving toward the eschaton of immortality.

The vision itself is an event of transfiguration; to the extent that the visionary apprehends the eschatological movement of reality in the direction of the Beyond, to that degree is reality indeed transfigured.[55] The saving tale that articulates the vision is more than a story *about* salvation; salvation can be said to have actually begun when one consciously participates in the movement of reality beyond itself. In this regard transfiguration is real; such visions do indeed occur. The process of differentiation is more than an advance of insight into the structure and movement of reality; it is the very process of transfiguration.

Transfiguration, then, has two meanings, which must not be separated. First, there is the ultimate transfiguration of reality that can be known only as the mysterious Beyond toward which history is moving. Inseparable from this final transfiguration is the transfiguring presence of the Beyond as it unfolds in the consciousness of the visionary, that is, the parousia of the Beyond in historical reality. It is

54. Ibid.; *Anamnesis,* 103–4; "The Beginning and the Beyond," 187–88, 224–25, 221–22.
55. "Wisdom and the Magic," 370; *Ecumenic Age,* 248.

important to emphasize this, because it is precisely the failure to make this distinction that has accounted for the emergence and growth of distorted social and political realities in the form of ideologies, utopias, second realities, and activist dreamers.

Here again we can appreciate Voegelin's caution when he is considering the advance constituted by the pneumatic differentiation. In terms of differentiating the Beyond, pneumatic visionaries (in particular, Paul) are superior even to Plato. But as discussed earlier, the very intensity of the experience can incline such visionaries toward imbalance; and this is exactly what Voegelin found to be the case with Paul. According to Voegelin, Paul wished to abolish the tension between our eschatological destiny and the mystery of transfiguration as it is occurring in the present. Rightly, Paul understood that reality is moving in the direction of the immortal Beyond. But in Paul, Voegelin detected a tendency to pull our immortalizing destiny into our mortal condition, a condition governed by the laws of genesis and perishing *(phthora)*.[56] Pneumatic visionaries like Paul may allow themselves to be so captivated by their experiences that they anticipate an imminent end to the tension of existence in the metaxy. With some this takes the form of an apocalyptic entry of the divine Beyond into history; with others it means the abolition of history through its absorption into the Beyond. And in the case of activist dreamers, for whom the divine Beyond is illusory, we find the attempt to pull the Beyond into history and create its secular equivalent on earth.

According to Voegelin, there *is* transfiguration in history, but this transfiguration has to do primarily with the differentiation of vision in which the eschatological dimension of human existence comes into view.[57] Transfiguration, understood as the transformation of social and political structures in light of the truth of order, has receded in importance. It is not that the struggle for order has been dismissed as misguided or meaningless; on the contrary, the human effort to embody order in society through the ages is the very process that gives rise to the vision in which it is understood that human destiny lies somehow beyond the struggle and that history can only be meaningful when understood from this perspective. Voegelin rec-

---

56. Ibid., 270–71.
57. *Autobiographical Reflections,* 122.

ognizes advances in history, but the predominant focus is on advances in the differentiation of consciousness.

According to Voegelin, eschatological vision in no way diminishes the importance of political and social life; it simply places these concerns within their proper context. Nowhere does he suggest that social and political life is unimportant; instead we find in his thought a growing emphasis on those transcendent sources of meaning from which the institutional life of society takes its bearings. I do not believe that he would understand his later work as in any way an abandonment of his earlier concerns. On the contrary, Voegelin would likely say that he had penetrated to the heart of the matter concerning politics and society.

With this discussion of vision and transfiguration we have returned to the place where we began in the first chapter, that is, the paradox of a reality that is engaged in a movement beyond its own structure. To understand Voegelin's thought concerning the possibility of creating a good society, one must understand this paradox, for society is a part of this all-encompassing It-reality. As such, the history of societies and their attempts to embody the truth of order are caught up in the process of the Whole. For just as reality as a whole is engaged in a movement beyond its structure, a movement whose end remains engulfed in mystery, so it is that societies, by reason of their participation in reality, come to understand that in apprehending the truth of order they discover that its source lies beyond order. Attempts to incarnate the truth of order in society, while not meaningless, can never fully succeed. For the more sensitive participants in this process, such knowledge can be a source of grief, but it can also serve as the catalyst for a broader vision. For out of this disappointment there arises the insight that this poignant spectacle occurs within an encompassing process headed toward redemption.

CONCLUSION

There is a sense in which the discussion of vision and transfiguration brings to completion this analysis of Voegelin's thought on the good society and its possibility. The first chapter began by providing a broad context within which to situate social reality. There we reflected upon Voegelin's conception of reality, its structure, its movement, and the human experience of participation. From a consideration of participation there arose the question of consciousness and its differentiations. Only then was it possible to properly discuss Voegelin's analysis of social reality, because in addition to the functioning institutions and practices of a society there exists also the crucial dimension of meaning constituted through each society's self-understanding in terms of the divine and human poles of reality; and this dimension could not be adequately articulated without some account of differentiation. From this discussion of social reality there followed in the fourth chapter a reflection on the possibility of derailment and disorder, once it became clear that attunement to the divine ground was always a precarious and hard-won achievement. The interrelationship between differentiations and the societies in which they took place occasioned the introduction of the question of history, for it was the gradual advance of differentiation through various societies that constituted history. Reflecting this notion of history, Chapters 5 and 6 were concerned with the struggle for order as it manifested itself in Israel and Hellas, the two societies in which the pneumatic and noetic differentiations emerged. From the failure of these societies to adequately embody the truth of order, there emerged the realization that perhaps no society could ever fully embody this truth. This insight led to the question as to what extent the good society is possible at all. Finally, in the eighth chapter, we considered Voegelin's "resolution" of the problem in *The Ecumenic Age* and other late writings. Here it was emphasized that history was primarily concerned with advances in consciousness and that transfiguration had to do with the granting of vision rather than with the transformation of the institutional structures of society. The possibility of such institutional change was not ruled out; but any human plans to alter social structures could easily derail into an immanentization of the divine Beyond, and must therefore be viewed with great caution.

For Voegelin, it was impossible to speak about the good society apart from the foundational human orientation toward the divine ground or It-reality as articulated in the symbols of the Beginning and the Beyond. To understand Voegelin's approach to this issue one must realize that his method involves above all an ever deeper probing of those experiences underlying the symbols and meanings expressing a given society's self-reflective orientation within reality. If there is anything that can be said to have remained continuous throughout his development as a thinker, it is his attempt to clarify these experiences of participation. What impresses many readers about Voegelin (and may perhaps drive others to distraction), is his willingness to abandon an earlier formulation or conceptualization in order to better explain the experiences upon which he is reflecting. Beginning with a typology of political religions, Voegelin moved on to a history of political ideas. Finding that analysis on this level did not probe deeply enough, he was moved by his own questions to reflect upon the structures of consciousness and reality. This involved a meditative exegesis of reality in which Voegelin came to understand the vision that had animated philosophers, prophets, and saints.

Whether Voegelin, in his later work, moved away from the more explicitly social and political concerns of his earlier writings remains, I believe, a valid question. Did he, through "meditation," move toward apoliticism when confronted with social disorder? Was it the realization that the truth of order stood little chance of becoming socially effective that served as the catalyst propelling him toward a withdrawal from the social/political sphere, and led him to solve the social issue through recourse to a vision transcending the historical struggle for order? Can the problem really be resolved on the level of consciousness?

When I began this study, my inclination would have been to answer "yes" to these questions. Now, however, it appears to me that Voegelin's position is more complex and nuanced than I had previously anticipated. What has emerged with greater clarity is that Voegelin advocated neither social quietism nor a withdrawal from public life. His goal was therapeutic—to recapture reality in the hope that such an enterprise would bear fruit in the creation of communities of discourse that might one day render the life of reason socially effective. To the extent that the life of reason came to characterize a given society, that society could be considered good. Voegelin challenged us to look beyond short-term pragmatic solutions to social problems, and he called those who would listen to nothing other than a total conversion. He came to appreciate that the key to social and political change lies in the transformation and conversion of human subjects, who are by nature social and political beings. If his suspicion of those who would create a heaven on earth made him overly cautious in recognizing or acknowledging human efforts to bring society into greater conformity with the truth of order, still, he was equally insistent that those in whom the truth of order has not been extinguished have a responsibility to speak out and to communicate their insights in the hope of reinvigorating enclaves of reason with an aim toward wider social transformation.

What may frustrate some readers is that Voegelin said so little about what such transformation might mean. Obviously those possessed of vision continue to exist as members of their respective societies. And, if Voegelin was correct, they have a responsibility to try and render the life of reason socially effective. The question that then arises is, What could be done if the life of reason *were* to become socially effective? Voegelin was very forceful in denouncing human pretensions to create a significantly better world, but he did not speak a great deal about the fact that those in whom reality has not been eclipsed continue to act in the world. Would they merely be content to be recipients of a vision pointing them toward an eschatological destiny beyond earthly limitations, or would they not be compelled by that very same vision to redirect their gaze toward the sufferings and disorder around them, and to pour themselves out in an effort to heal that suffering and reduce that disorder? And might they be able to do so precisely because they have been energized and transformed through the vision of the Beyond, enabling them to act tirelessly and without fear? Might not the vision itself be the source of that "peace which the world cannot give," freeing its recipients to reverse social decline through self-sacrificing love, confident that the victory has been won and that the *mache athanatos,* the undying struggle, is headed toward salvation? To raise such questions is not to suggest that Voegelin should have offered a blueprint for social change; rather, it is to ask whether or not he drew out the full implications of the vision he embraced.

With these questions in mind, we can briefly recall those areas already mentioned where Voegelin's thought on society might be open to further development. In the first place, there is his cognitional theory, which, I would argue, contributes to the tensions to be found in his account of society and history. In particular, his treatment of consciousness as intentional needs to be revisited. He rightly criticized an epistemological position that would discount or ignore any reality that was not accessible to the human knower in accordance with the method of the natural sciences. Yet when it came to discussing intentionality he seemed to have accepted the notion of an object as somehow "out there," waiting to be intuited by the human subject. Again, as noted earlier, this account of intentionality leads to a distinction between intentionality and luminosity that would seem to be mirrored in the reality known. This has unfortunate consequences for an account of society and history, for it is within social reality that we find the overlapping of reality as "noumenal," that is, as constituted by meanings expressing human orientation toward transcendent mystery, and reality as "phenomenal," as consisting of external objects to be studied in accordance with the methods of the natural sciences. In Voegelin's account of society and history these realms coexist ambiguously. The "laws of mundane existence" would seem to govern what it is that can be accomplished on the phenomenal or institutional level of society, while consciousness in the mode of luminosity advances in its apprehension of the structure and movement of reality, a reality of which the societies that give rise to the differentiations are but a part. These differentiations occur within the consciousness of certain individuals, whose responsibility it becomes to communicate these insights to a wider public, in the hope that this vision may become socially effective.[1]

---

1. Voegelin's approach to history, his employment of the language of "phenomena" and "noumena," and his overall epistemological stance reveal the in-

It is here, I believe, that we find a certain tension in Voegelin's thought. There is a sense in which Voegelin never abandoned his efforts to see the life of reason become socially effective. Yet what might this mean in a world in which the "laws of mundane existence," operative in social reality as phenomenal, restrict what can be accomplished politically and institutionally? Is social change to be limited to the communication of vision? Is this what Voegelin means when he hopes that reason may one day become socially effective? We find, then, in Voegelin's thought, the juxtaposition of tremendous caution as to what human beings can accomplish in the social sphere with a genuine concern that the life of reason be restored to society, without a great deal of consideration as to what that might mean concretely. I would suggest that part of this ambiguity stems from the two-tiered account of social reality with which Voegelin is operating, and that this account of social reality is reinforced by a cognitional position that offers a brilliant analysis of consciousness as luminous, but is in need of revision in terms of its account of intentionality. The resources for such a development are already present in Voegelin's thought in the attention that he gave to questioning unrest, wonder, and the Question as that by which human beings are oriented within reality. For here we find a way of speaking about intentionality in terms of questioning, rather than in terms of a subject/object split in which objects take on an aura of externality.

It is this problem of the implications of vision for social life that gives rise to further questions. Does Voegelin's understanding of vision and transfiguration allow sufficient room for a transformation of consciousness that not only results in a superior insight into the structure and movement of reality, but also leads to a concern to change social and political structures, a change that will not derail into metastatic dreaming precisely because it springs from a consciousness that is attuned to reality? Does the power of the vision lie simply in the fact that "the truth of immortalizing transfiguration

---

fluence of Kant. It would seem that many of the criticisms that could be leveled against Kant's cognitional theory and his philosophy of history would be equally applicable to Voegelin's approach to these matters. A study of the relationship between Kant and Voegelin would be an important contribution to Voegelinian scholarship, and it is something I hope to address in the future. At the risk of seeming evasive, I would simply note that, at the present time, such a study would take me beyond the boundaries of the topic at hand.

through the divine-human movement in the metaxy, when 'seen', transfigures"?[2] Or might the experience of transfiguration actually *empower* its recipients to act in ways that would go beyond what is commonly considered to be humanly possible? And if such experiences can result in new possibilities for human action, then is it not appropriate to speak of the possibility of new social realities?[3]

One might raise the question of whether Voegelin's use of the metaphor of "vision" is not itself significant. Does it make any difference that Voegelin, following Plato, employs the term *vision* rather than a more biblically oriented metaphor, such as "heeding" or "hearing"? The latter terms would seem to imply the possibility of human cooperation with the divine intention to transfigure creation, whereas *vision* does not suggest as strongly the same possibility for action.[4] In this regard it has already been noted that the phenomenon of classical Israelite prophecy poses problems for Voegelin, in that while he can praise the prophets for their extraordinary articulation of the experience of the divine Beyond, he is also deeply skeptical of their prescriptions for social justice. The same tension is evident in Voegelin's treatment of the teaching of Jesus, who announced to his audiences that those who could "hear" ought to heed his message (Matt. 13:43). For Voegelin, this message, if heeded too strictly, would lead to suicide.[5]

Another way of posing this question is to ask whether Voegelin has any notion of grace, a grace which, while going beyond the natural human capacity for performance, builds upon that capacity and elevates it to a higher level. Part of the problem in attempting to answer such a question in Voegelinian terms is his rejection of the natural/supernatural distinction. Voegelin was dissatisfied with the distinc-

2. "Wisdom and the Magic," 370.

3. Walter Brueggemann has addressed this issue in his book *The Prophetic Imagination*. For example: "Most of us are probably so used to these narratives that we have become insensitive to the radical and revolutionary social reality that emerged because of Moses. . . . And that new social reality drives us to the category of revelation. Israel can only be understood in terms of the new call of God and his assertion of an alternative social reality. Prophecy is born precisely in that moment when the emergence of social political reality is so radical and inexplicable that it has nothing less than a theological cause" (pp. 15–16).

4. For this insight I am indebted to the anonymous first reviewer of this manuscript.

5. *Plato and Aristotle*, 226.

tion between "natural" reason and revelation. For him, Plato was just as conscious of revelation as was Isaiah. Both men responded to a vision received; Plato did so without jeopardizing the balance of consciousness, whereas Isaiah to some degree succumbed to the metastatic temptation. But does not the biblical faith in the ultimate conquest of evil through the gift of redemptive love, as articulated by the prophets and embodied in the death and resurrection of Jesus, take us beyond a Platonic *opsis*, which views society and its problems with resignation, while those gifted with vision somehow rise above the travails of society by means of a consciousness that has been transformed? It does not seem as if Voegelin paid careful enough attention to this distinction, and part of the problem may lie in his antipathy toward distinguishing between reason and revelation, or between the natural and the supernatural.

For Voegelin, revelation was an occurrence *within* the experience; the distinction he preferred to draw was between noesis and vision, where both modes arise from within an experience whose poles must not be separated or even distinguished in terms of natural and supernatural. This may make it difficult for him to appreciate what it is that the pneumatic visionaries are trying to communicate. The religious experiences of an Isaiah, a Jesus, and a Paul point toward a higher integration of human subjectivity, and their symbolic language indicates, not a literal description of the future, but the anticipated supernatural solution to the problem of evil. Voegelin tended to view such language as evidence of a metastatic or apocalyptic disregard for the exigencies of human life in the metaxy. As Robert M. Doran has observed:

> Eric Voegelin would tend to place at least some anagogic symbols under the radical suspicion of being metastatic, of displacing the tension of existence in the Metaxy through an imbalance of consciousness. A distinction is in order here. The genuine anagogic symbol serves not to displace the tension of consciousness—though that is a danger if it is negotiated literally or "fundamentalistically"—but, *precisely as symbol,* to heighten the tension and release the psyche for cooperation with the divinely originated solution to the mystery of evil. Pertinent here is what Lonergan writes of the heightening of the tension of existence under the condition of a supernatural solution: " . . . when [the] problem of evil is met by a supernatural solution, human perfection itself becomes a limit to be transcended, and then, the dialectic is transformed from a bipolar to *a tripolar conjunction and opposition*" (In-

sight: 728; emphasis added). Voegelin, I think, rather consistently misses this point.[6]

To raise the issue of grace is to suggest that the vision of which Voegelin speaks can transfigure in such a way that a higher integration of human life in all its dimensions becomes possible. As the biological goes beyond but cannot do without the lower chemical level, and as the psychological integrates and goes beyond the biological, to speak of grace is to allow for the possibility that in response to the divine Beyond human life can be open to a deeper level of transformation on the levels of both thought and action. Grace, thus understood, builds on nature; not in the sense of some quality or "stuff" infused into an expectant or unsuspecting individual, but as an "elevation" and higher integration of already present human capacities under the influence of transcendent goodness. The uncompromisingness of the prophets concerning the fulfillment of the covenant and the admonition of Jesus, "Be perfect as your heavenly Father is perfect," only makes sense under these conditions. To say this is not to argue that because the biblical tradition speaks this way, therefore grace must be a reality; rather, it is to be faithful to the deepest insights of those religious traditions that, on the basis of the very sort of experiences to which Voegelin so often appeals, insist upon the transforming power of God.

Perhaps Voegelin's critical attitude toward the eschatological, pneumatic language of the biblical tradition and his wariness when considering the possibility of significant social transformation may stem, in part, from his emphasis on the permanency of the primary experience of the cosmos, an emphasis that became more pronounced in his later work.[7] Cosmological symbolism may be superseded, but the primary experience of the cosmos is never transcended. In *The Ecumenic Age* it is clear that while differentiation of consciousness does indeed represent an advance, the advance does not alter the structure of reality in the least.[8] The great Hellenic thinkers were very much aware of the abiding hold of the primary experience, even in those cases in which the thinker in question lived after the noetic differentiation of consciousness. Voegelin praised Plato for his ability

6. Robert M. Doran, *Theology and the Dialectics of History,* 272–73.
7. See "Equivalences," and *Ecumenic Age.*
8. *Ecumenic Age,* 8, 77.

to strike a "balance of consciousness," in which the vision of the Beyond is not allowed to disturb social processes unfolding in a world governed by cosmic rhythms and mundane laws.[9] As noted in Chapter 7, there is a certain inevitability to social process, an insight that Voegelin attributes to Thucydides.[10] One wonders if, in Voegelin's view, the cosmic flux described by Anaximander is ever overcome. One may ask whether, in emphasizing the durability of the primary experience of the cosmos, Voegelin perhaps also allowed himself to be influenced by the fatalism of these ancient thinkers. Voegelin saw the endurance of the primary experience of the cosmos as testifying to the fact that human life is always life in the metaxy, that human life is always imperfect, incomplete, and subject to the conditions of mortality. His caution here, in opposing those who would abolish life in the "in-between," is certainly reasonable. One wonders, though, whether acceptance of life in the metaxy necessarily entails a pessimism with regard to what is achievable by human means in the social realm.

The issues that have been raised here are intended to point out areas in which Voegelin's thought might have potential for further development; they are not meant to call into question the important contribution he made to political philosophy through his attention to those experiences of participation that underlie the social and political order. In particular, one can interpret the meditative exegesis of his later work not as a movement away from social and political concerns, but rather as a deeper penetration of social/political reality.

Again, Voegelin's approach to social and political problems remains eminently practical insofar as it concentrates on the conversion of human subjects who are also social and political beings. That is why the analysis of experiences such as faith, love, and knowing figure so significantly in his final writings. And this focus does not represent some sudden shift in approach. As early as *The New Science of Politics,* Voegelin spoke of Plato and Aristotle as mystic philosophers; and there is a sense in which through his own work Voegelin not only was appropriating what these philosophers *said,* but was engaged in an ever-deepening appropriation of the experiences they

9. Ibid., 218–38.
10. *World of the Polis,* 253–65.

articulated with such acumen.[11] Of course, this was not simply a matter of imitating Plato, for Voegelin was quite aware that advances in differentiation and the ideological eclipse of reality made a simple return to Plato both impossible and undesirable. Aware that the key to practicality lay not in temporary institutional solutions to social and political problems, but in the authentic subjectivity of society's members, Voegelin was involved in an attempt to recapture those foundational experiences of reality in which human authenticity has its origin. For Voegelin that meant recovering those experiences in himself, so that they might then be communicated to others—not as one passes on "information," but by opposing any obscurantism that would deny further questions, and by helping to point others toward reality through an encouragement of questions and an attention to those trans-cultural, trans-historical experiences of participation discoverable in one's own consciousness.

One can see this process at work in Voegelin's own writings as he moved from "ideas" to "experiences." Voegelin attempted to do for contemporary men and women what Plato had done in his time, that is, to follow his own questioning unrest and inquiring response toward the divine ground, and to engage others in this quest by articulating the experience. For Voegelin, there could be no social or political activity more practical than this:

> This eschatological tension of man's humanity, in its dimensions of person, society, and history, is more than a matter of theoretical insight for the philosopher; it is a practical question. As I have said, Plato and Aristotle were very much aware that the action of philosophizing is a process of immortalizing in this world. This action does not come to its end with Plato and Aristotle; it continues, though in every concrete situation the philosopher has to cope with the problems he encounters in his own position concretely. If the Classic philosophers had to cope with the difficulties created by a dying myth and an active Sophistic aggressiveness, the philosopher in the twentieth century has to struggle with the "climate of opinion," as Whitehead called the phenomenon. Moreover, in his concrete work he has to absorb the enormous advances of the sciences, both natural and historical, and to relate them to the understanding of existence. That is a considerable labor, considering the mountains of historical materials that have become known in our time.

11. *New Science of Politics,* 66–70.

A new picture of history is developing. The conceptual penetration of the sources is the task of the philosopher today; the results of his analysis must be communicated to the general public and, if he happens to be a professor in a university, to the students. These chores—of keeping up with the problems, of analyzing the sources, and of communicating the results—are concrete actions through which the philosopher participates in the eschatological movement of history and conforms to the Platonic-Aristotelian practice of dying.[12]

The philosophical enterprise remains a practical one—to foster the life of reason and to restore an awareness of reality in whatever situation philosophers find themselves. At the same time, Voegelin was also very conscious of the fact that such a project involves one in the practice of dying, through the realization that all of reality is engaged in a movement toward eschatological fulfillment beyond the world, beyond society, and even beyond the metaxy. In his deathbed meditation, "Quod Deus dicetur,"[13] Voegelin reflected upon the God beyond the gods, as this divine presence revealed itself to Hesiod, Anaximander, Plotinus, Plato, Paul, Thomas Aquinas, and Goethe. Voegelin speaks of the "prayers" uttered by these various figures as his language strains to articulate the mystery of love and awe in which he himself had come to be enveloped. Some would argue that there is no place for such reflections within a social or political philosophy, that such matters are strictly private and have no place in public discourse concerning the good society. Voegelin would disagree, and would insist that the good society can only come into existence when a significant number of its members have undergone the conversion entailed by responding in wonder to the drawing of the Beyond. If he did not deal extensively with the issue as to how such people might act to transform the societies of which they are a part, we might recall that for Voegelin, there could be no more practical contribution than to direct people's attention to that reality which underlies and sustains all knowledge and action. Nor is such an answer evasive, for Voegelin himself was very much aware that his contribution to social change lay not in specific solutions to concrete

---

12. *Autobiographical Reflections*, 123.
13. "Quod Deus dicetur," in *Collected Works*, vol. 12.

social and political problems, but in the recovery of those foundational experiences of transcendence that ground authentic humanity.[14] To understand this view of practicality is to understand Voegelin's lifework, and to realize that there is a sense in which to be an
authentic political philosopher one must also be a mystic.

14. Commenting on the differences between his own approach to social and
political change and that of Alfred Schutz, Voegelin remarked that he was "led
to the conclusion that, while classical politics is the basis of all philosophizing
about the order of society, it is by no means its last word on the subject. In the
first place there exists in fact the network of world-immanent behavior, particularly the whole area of goal directed rational planning behavior, the interpretation of which calls for a theory such as Schutz developed" ("In memorium,"
465).

BIBLIOGRAPHY

WORKS BY VOEGELIN

Anamnesis: Zur Theorie der Geschichte und Politik. Munich: Piper, 1966.

Anamnesis. Partial translation of *Anamnesis: Zur Theorie der Geschichte und Politik* (1966). Trans. and ed. Gerhart Niemeyer. Notre Dame, Ind.: University of Notre Dame Press, 1978; reprint, Columbia, Mo.: University of Missouri Press, 1990.

Autobiographical Reflections. Ed. Ellis Sandoz. Baton Rouge: Louisiana State University Press, 1989.

"Autobiographical Statement at Age Eighty-Two." In *The Beginning and the Beyond: Papers from the Gadamer and Voegelin Conferences,* Supplementary Issue of *Lonergan Workshop,* vol. 4, ed. Fred Lawrence, 111–31. Chico, Calif.: Scholars Press, 1984.

"The Beginning and the Beyond: A Meditation on Truth." In *The Collected Works of Eric Voegelin,* vol. 28, *"What Is History?" and Other Late Unpublished Writings,* ed. Thomas A. Hollweck and Paul Caringella. Baton Rouge: Louisiana State University Press, 1990.

The Collected Works of Eric Voegelin. Vol. 12, *Published Essays, 1966–1985.* Ed. Ellis Sandoz. Baton Rouge: Louisiana State University Press, 1990.

The Collected Works of Eric Voegelin. Vol. 27, *"The Nature of the Law" and Related Legal Writings.* Ed. Robert Anthony Pascal, James Lee Babin, and John William Corrington. Baton Rouge: Louisiana State University Press, 1991.

The Collected Works of Eric Voegelin. Vol. 28, *"What Is History?" and Other Late Unpublished Writings.* Ed. Thomas A. Hollweck and Paul Caringella. Baton Rouge: Louisiana State University Press, 1990.

"Configurations of History." In *The Collected Works of Eric Voegelin,* vol. 12, *Published Essays, 1966–1985,* ed. Ellis Sandoz. Baton Rouge: Louisiana State University Press, 1990.

"Consciousness and Order: Foreword to *Anamnesis* (1966)." Translation, by the author, of the "Vorwort" to *Anamnesis: Zur Theorie der Geschichte und Politik* (1966). In *The Beginning and the Beyond: Papers from the Gadamer and Voegelin Conferences,* Supplementary Issue of *Lonergan Workshop,* vol. 4, ed. Fred Lawrence, 35–42. Chico, Calif.: Scholars Press, 1984.

Conversations with Eric Voegelin. Ed. R. Eric O'Connor, S.J. Montreal: Thomas More Institute, 1980.

"The Eclipse of Reality." In *The Collected Works of Eric Voegelin,* vol. 28, *"What Is History?" and Other Late Unpublished Writings,* ed. Thomas A. Hollweck and Paul Caringella. Baton Rouge: Louisiana State University Press, 1990.

"Equivalences of Experience and Symbolization in History." In *The Collected Works of Eric Voegelin,* vol. 12, *Published Essays, 1966–1985,* ed. Ellis Sandoz. Baton Rouge: Louisiana State University Press, 1990.

"Extended Strategy: A New Technique of Dynamic Relations." *Journal of Politics* 2 (1940): 189–200.

Faith and Political Philosophy: The Correspondence between Leo Strauss and Eric Voegelin, 1934–1964. Trans. and ed. Peter Emberley and Barry Cooper. University Park: Pennsylvania State University Press, 1993.

"The Formation of the Marxian Revolutionary Idea." *Review of Politics* 12 (1950): 275–302.

From Enlightenment to Revolution. Ed. John H. Hallowell. Durham, N.C.: Duke University Press, 1975.

"The German University and the Order of German Society: A Reconsideration of the Nazi Era." In *The Collected Works of Eric Voegelin,* vol. 12, *Published Essays, 1966–1985,* ed. Ellis Sandoz. Baton Rouge: Louisiana State University Press, 1990.

"Gnostische Politik." *Merkur* 4 (1952): 301–17.

"Goethe's Utopia." In *Goethe after Two Centuries,* ed. Carl Hammer, 57–62. Baton Rouge: Louisiana State University Press, 1952.

"The Gospel and Culture." In *The Collected Works of Eric Voegelin,* vol. 12, *Published Essays, 1966–1985,* ed. Ellis Sandoz. Baton Rouge: Louisiana State University Press, 1990.

"The Growth of the Race Idea." *Review of Politics* 2 (1940): 283–317.

"History and Gnosis." In *The Old Testament and Christian Faith,* ed. Bernhard W. Anderson, 64–89. New York: Herder and Herder, 1969.

"Immortality: Experience and Symbol." In *The Collected Works of Eric*

Voegelin, vol. 12, *Published Essays, 1966–1985*, ed. Ellis Sandoz, 81–94. Baton Rouge: Louisiana State University Press, 1990.

"Industrial Society in Search of Reason." In *World Technology and Human Destiny*, ed. Raymond Aron, 31–46. Ann Arbor: University of Michigan Press, 1963.

"In memorium Alfred Schutz." In *The Philosophy of Order: Essays on History, Consciousness, and Politics*, ed. Peter J. Opitz and Gregor Sebba, 463–65. Stuttgart: Klett-Cotta, 1981.

"Kelsen's Pure Theory of Law." *Political Science Quarterly* 42 (1927): 268–76.

"Liberalism and Its History." Translation of "Der Liberalismus und seine Geschichte" (1960). *Review of Politics* 37 (1974): 504–20.

"Machiavelli's Prince: Background and Formation." *Review of Politics* 13 (1951): 142–68.

"The Meditative Origin of the Philosophical Knowledge of Order." Translation of "Der meditative Ursprung philosophischen Ordnungswissens" (1981). In *The Beginning and the Beyond: Papers from the Gadamer and Voegelin Conferences,* Supplementary Issue of *Lonergan Workshop*, vol. 4, ed. Fred Lawrence, 43–52. Chico, Calif.: Scholars Press, 1984.

"The Mongol Orders of Submission to European Powers, 1245–1255." *Byzantion* 15 (1941): 378–413.

"More's *Utopia*." *Oesterreichische Zeitschrift fuer Oeffentliches Recht* 3 (1952): 451–68.

"The Nature of the Law." In *The Collected Works of Eric Voegelin*, vol. 27, *"The Nature of the Law" and Related Legal Writings*, ed. Robert Anthony Pascal, James Lee Babin, and John William Corrington. Baton Rouge: Louisiana State University Press, 1991.

The New Science of Politics: An Introduction. Chicago: University of Chicago Press, 1952.

"Nietzsche, the Crisis and the War." *Journal of Politics* 6 (1944): 177–212.

"On Christianity" and "On Gnosticism." (Two letters to Alfred Schutz, 1953). In *The Philosophy of Order: Essays on History, Consciousness, and Politics*, ed. Peter J. Opitz and Gregor Sebba, 431–62. Stuttgart: Klett-Cotta, 1981.

"On Debate and Existence." In *The Collected Works of Eric Voegelin*, vol. 12, *Published Essays, 1966–1985*, ed. Ellis Sandoz. Baton Rouge: Louisiana State University Press, 1990.

"On Readiness to Rational Discussion." In *Freedom and Serfdom,* ed. Albert Hunold, 269–84. Dordrecht: D. Reidel, 1961.

Order and History. Vol. 1, *Israel and Revelation.* Baton Rouge: Louisiana State University Press, 1956.

Order and History. Vol. 2, *The World of the Polis.* Baton Rouge: Louisiana State University Press, 1957.

Order and History. Vol. 3, *Plato and Aristotle.* Baton Rouge: Louisiana State University Press, 1957.

Order and History. Vol. 4, *The Ecumenic Age.* Baton Rouge: Louisiana State University Press, 1974.

Order and History. Vol. 5, *In Search of Order.* Baton Rouge: Louisiana State University Press, 1987.

"The Origins of Scientism." *Social Research* 4 (1948): 462–94.

"The Origins of Totalitarianism." *Review of Politics* 15 (1953): 68–85. With a reply by Hannah Arendt.

"The Oxford Political Philosophers." *Philosophical Quarterly* 3 (1953): 97–114.

Political Religions. Translation of *Die politischen Religionen* (1938). Lewiston, N.Y.: Edwin Mellen Press, 1986.

"Political Theory and the Pattern of General History." In *Research in Political Science,* ed. Ernest S. Griffith, 190–201. Chapel Hill: University of North Carolina Press, 1948.

"Reason: The Classic Experience." In *The Collected Works of Eric Voegelin,* vol. 12, *Published Essays, 1966–1985,* ed. Ellis Sandoz. Baton Rouge: Louisiana State University Press, 1990.

Review of *On Tyranny: An Interpretation of Xenophon's Hiero,* by Leo Strauss. *Review of Politics* 11 (1949): 241–44.

Science, Politics, and Gnosticism. Translation of *Wissenschaft, Politik, und Gnosis* (1959). Gateway Edition. Chicago: Henry Regnery, 1968.

"Siger de Brabant." *Philosophy and Phenomenological Research* 4 (1944): 507–26.

"Some Problems of German Hegemony." *Journal of Politics* 3 (1941): 154–68.

Ueber die Form des amerikanischen Geistes. Tuebingen: J. C. B. Mohr, 1928.

"What Is History?" In *The Collected Works of Eric Voegelin,* vol. 28, *"What Is History?" and Other Late Unpublished Writings,* ed. Thomas A. Hollweck and Paul Caringella. Baton Rouge: Louisiana State University Press, 1990.

"Wisdom and the Magic of the Extreme: A Meditation." In *The Collected Works of Eric Voegelin*, vol. 12, *Published Essays, 1966–1985*, ed. Ellis Sandoz. Baton Rouge: Louisiana State University Press, 1990.

"World Empire and the Unity of Mankind." *International Affairs* 38 (1962): 170–88.

OTHER WORKS CONSULTED

Albright, W. F. "Eric Voegelin: Order and History." In *History, Archaeology, and Christian Humanism*. London: Black, 1965.

Anastoplo, George. "On How Eric Voegelin Has Read Plato and Aristotle." *Independent Journal of Philosophy* 5/6 (1988): 85–91.

Anderson, Bernhard W. "Politics and the Transcendent: Voegelin's Philosophical and Theological Exposition of the Old Testament in the Context of the Ancient Near East." In Stephen A. McKnight, ed., *Eric Voegelin's Search for Order in History*, 62–100. Exp. ed. Lanham, Md.: University Press of America, 1987.

Aristotle. *The Basic Works of Aristotle*. Ed. Richard McKeon. New York: Random House, 1941.

Aron, Raymond, ed. *World Technology and Human Destiny*. Ann Arbor: University of Michigan Press, 1963.

Berger, Peter, and Thomas Luckmann. *The Social Construction of Reality*. New York: Doubleday, Anchor Books, 1967.

Blumenberg, Hans. *The Legitimacy of the Modern Age*. Trans. Robert M. Wallace. Cambridge: MIT Press, 1985.

Booth, William James. *Interpreting the World: Kant's Philosophy of History and Politics*. Toronto: University of Toronto Press, 1986.

Brueggemann, Walter. *The Prophetic Imagination*. Philadelphia: Fortress Press, 1978.

Buber, Martin. "Plato and Isaiah." In *Israel and the World: Essays in a Time of Crisis*. New York: Schocken Books, 1963.

Cahn, E., and C. Going, eds. *The Question as Commitment: A Symposium*. Montreal: Thomas More Institute Papers 77, 1979.

Caringella, Paul. "Eric Voegelin: Philosopher of Divine Presence." *Modern Age* 33 (1990): 7–22.

Clements, R. E. *Isaiah 1–39*. The New Century Bible Commentary, ed. Ronald E. Clements and Matthew Black. Grand Rapids, Mich.: Wm. B. Eerdmans, 1980.

Cohn, Norman. *The Pursuit of the Millenium*. Rev. and exp. ed. New York: Oxford University Press, 1970.

Collingwood, R. G. *The Idea of History.* 1946. Reprint, London: Oxford University Press, 1956.

Cooper, Barry. "A Fragment from Eric Voegelin's History of Western Political Thought." *Political Science Reviewer* 7 (1977): 23–52.

———. *The Political Theory of Eric Voegelin.* Toronto Studies in Theology, vol. 27. Lewiston, N.Y.: Edwin Mellen Press, 1986.

Corrington, John William. "Order and History: The Breaking of the Program." *Denver Quarterly* 10 (1975): 115–22.

Dallmayr, Fred. "Postmetaphysics and Democracy." *Political Theory* 21 (1993): 101–27.

———. "Voegelin's Search for Order." In *Margins of Political Discourse.* Albany: State University of New York Press, 1989.

Dempf, Alois, Hannah Arendt, and Friedrich Engel-Janosi, eds. *Politische Ordnung and menschliche Existenz: Festgabe fuer Eric Voegelin zum 60. Geburtstag.* Munich: C. H. Beck, 1962.

Doran, Robert M. *Theology and the Dialectics of History.* Toronto: University of Toronto Press, 1990.

———. "Theology's Situation: Questions to Eric Voegelin." In *The Beginning and the Beyond: Papers from the Gadamer and Voegelin Conferences,* Supplementary Issue of *Lonergan Workshop,* vol. 4, ed. Fred Lawrence. Chico, Calif.: Scholars Press, 1984.

Douglass, Bruce. "The Break in Voegelin's Program." *Political Science Reviewer* 7 (1977): 1–21.

———. "The Gospel and Political Order: Eric Voegelin on the Political Role of Christianity." *Journal of Politics* 38 (1976): 25–45.

Dupre, Louis. "A Conservative Anarchist: Eric Voegelin, 1901–1985." *Clio: A Journal of Literature, History, and Philosophy of History* 14 (1985): 423–31.

Eliade, Mircea. *The Sacred and the Profane: The Nature of Religion.* Trans. Willard R. Trask. New York: Harcourt, Brace, and World, Harvest Books, 1959.

Faber, Richard. *Der Prometheus Komplex: Zur Kritik der Politotheologie Eric Voegelins und Hans Blumenbergs.* Wuerzburg: Koenighausen und Neumann, 1984.

Fallon, Timothy P., S.J., and Philip Boo Riley, eds. *Religion and Culture: Essays in Honor of Bernard Lonergan, S.J.* Albany: State University of New York Press, 1987.

Franz, Michael. *Eric Voegelin and the Politics of Spiritual Revolt.* Baton Rouge: Louisiana State University Press, 1992.

Gebhardt, Jurgen. "Toward the Process of Universal Mankind: The Formation of Voegelin's Philosophy of History." In *Eric Voegelin's Thought: A Critical Appraisal,* ed. Ellis Sandoz, 67–86. Durham, N.C.: Duke University Press, 1982.

Germino, Dante. *Beyond Ideology.* Chicago: University of Chicago Press, 1967; Midway Reprint, 1976.

———. "Eric Voegelin's *Anamnesis.*" *Southern Review* 7 (1971): 68–88.

———. *Political Philosophy and the Open Society.* Baton Rouge: Louisiana State University Press, 1982.

———. "The Primacy of Politics in the Understanding of 'Modernity'." *Modern Age* 31 (1987): 234–42.

———. Review of *The Ecumenic Age. Journal of Politics* 37 (1975): 847–48.

Hadas, Moses. Review of *Order and History,* vols. 1–3. *Journal of the History of Ideas* 19 (1958): 442–44.

Hanson, Paul. *The Dawn of Apocalyptic.* Philadephia: Fortress Press, 1979.

———. "Jewish Apocalyptic against Its Near Eastern Environment." *Revue Biblique* 78 (1971): 31–58.

———. "Old Testament Apocalyptic Reexamined." *Interpretation* 25 (1971): 454–79.

Havard, William. "The Disenchantment of the Intellectuals." In *Politische Ordnung und menschliche Existenz: Festgabe fuer Eric Voegelin zum 60. Geburtstag,* ed. Alois Dempf, Hannah Arendt, and Friedrich Engel-Janosi, 271–86. Munich: C. H. Beck, 1962.

———. "Voegelin's Diagnosis of the Western Crisis." *Denver Quarterly* 10 (1975): 127–34.

Heidegger, Martin. *Being and Time.* Trans. John Macquarrie and Edward Robinson. New York: Harper and Row, 1962.

———. *Discourse on Thinking.* Trans. John M. Anderson and E. Hans Freund. New York: Harper and Row, Harper Torchbooks, 1966.

Heilke, Thomas W. *Voegelin on the Idea of Race: An Analysis of Modern European Racism.* Baton Rouge: Louisiana State University Press, 1990.

Heschel, Abraham. *The Prophets.* Vol. 1. New York: Harper and Row, Harper Colophon Books, 1969.

Hesiod. *The Works and Days, Theogony, and The Shield of Herakles.* Trans. Richard Lattimore. Ann Arbor, Mich.: University of Michigan Press, 1959.

Hughes, Glenn. "Eric Voegelin's View of History as a Drama of Transfiguration." *International Philosophical Quarterly* 30 (1990): 449–64.

———. *Mystery and Myth in the Philosophy of Eric Voegelin.* Columbia: University of Missouri Press, 1993.

James, William. *Writings, 1902–1910.* N.p.: The Library of America, 1987.

Kant, Immanuel. *Perpetual Peace and Other Essays.* Trans. Ted Humphrey. Indianapolis: Hackett, 1983.

Keulman, Kenneth. *The Balance of Consciousness: Eric Voegelin's Political Theory.* University Park: Pennsylvania State University Press, 1991.

Kirby, John, and William M. Thompson, eds. *Voegelin and the Theologian: Ten Studies in Interpretation.* Toronto Studies in Theology, vol. 10. Lewiston, N.Y.: Edwin Mellen Press, 1983.

Kuhn, Helmut. Review of *Plato and Aristotle. Historische Zeitschrift* 141 (1960): 360–64.

Lamb, Matthew, ed. *Creativity and Method: Essays in Honor of Bernard Lonergan.* Milwaukee: Marquette University Press, 1981.

Lasch, Christopher. *The True and Only Heaven: Progress and Its Critics.* New York: W. W. Norton, 1991.

Lash, Nicholas. *A Matter of Hope.* Notre Dame, Ind.: University of Notre Dame Press, 1981.

Lawrence, Fred. "Political Theology and 'The Longer Cycle of Decline.'" In *Lonergan Workshop,* vol. 1, ed. Fred Lawrence, 223–56. Missoula, Mont.: Scholars Press, 1978.

Lawrence, Fred, ed. *The Beginning and the Beyond: Papers from the Gadamer and Voegelin Conferences,* Supplementary Issue of *Lonergan Workshop,* vol. 4. Chico, Calif.: Scholars Press, 1984.

Levy, David. *Realism: An Essay in Interpretation and Social Reality.* Manchester, England: Carcenet New Press, 1981.

———. "Voegelin as Philosopher." *Modern Age* 24 (1980): 47–54.

Levy, Guenter. *Religion and Revolution.* New York: Oxford University Press, 1974.

Lonergan, Bernard. *Caring about Meaning: Patterns in the Life of Bernard Lonergan.* Ed. Pierrot Lambert, Charlotte Tansey, and Cathleen Going. Thomas More Institute Papers 82. Montreal: Thomas More Institute, 1982.

———. *Collected Works of Bernard Lonergan.* Ed. Frederick E. Crowe and Robert M. Doran. Vol. 3, *Insight: A Study of Human Understanding.* 5th ed., rev. and augmented. Toronto: University of Toronto Press, 1992.

————. *Collected Works of Bernard Lonergan*. Ed. Frederick E. Crowe and Robert M. Doran. Vol. 4, *Collection*. Toronto: University of Toronto Press, 1988.

————. *Method in Theology*. New York: Herder and Herder, 1972.

————. *A Second Collection*. Ed. William F. J. Ryan, S.J. and Bernard J. Tyrrell, S.J. Philadephia: Westminster Press, 1974.

————. *A Third Collection*. Ed. Frederick E. Crowe, S.J. New York: Paulist Press, 1985.

Lowith, Karl. *Meaning in History*. Chicago: University of Chicago Press, Phoenix Books, 1949.

McCarroll, Joseph. "Man in Search of Divine Order in History." *Philosophical Studies* (Dublin) 31 (1986–1987): 15–24.

————. "Some Growth Areas in Voegelin's Analysis." *Philosophical Studies* (Dublin) 31 (1986–1987): 280–300.

McKnight, Stephen A. "Recent Developments in Voegelin's Philosophy of History." *Sociological Analysis* 36 (1975): 357–65.

————. "Understanding Modernity: A Reappraisal of the Gnostic Element." *Intercollegiate Review* 14 (1979): 107–17.

————. "Voegelin on the Modern Intellectual and Political Crises." *Sociological Analysis* 37 (1976): 265–71.

McKnight, Stephen A., ed. *Eric Voegelin's Search for Order inHistory*. Exp. ed. Lanham, Md.: University Press of America, 1987.

McPartland, Thomas J. "Historicity and Philosophy: The Existential Dimension." In *Religion and Culture: Essays in Honor of Bernard Loner-gan, S.J.*, ed. Timothy P. Fallon and Philip Boo Riley, 107–24. Albany: State University of New York Press, 1987.

————. "Meaning, Mystery, and the History of Consciousness." In *Lonergan Workshop*, vol. 7, ed. Fred Lawrence, 203–68. Atlanta: Scholars Press, 1988.

Meyer, Ben F. *The Aims of Jesus*. London: SCM Press, 1979.

Morrissey, Michael P. *Consciousness and Transcendence: The Theology of Eric Voegelin*. Notre Dame: University of Notre Dame Press, 1994.

Nieli, Russell. "Eric Voegelin's Evolving Ideas on Gnosticism, Mysticism, and Modern Radical Politics." *Independent Journal of Philosophy* 5/6 (1988): 93–102.

Niemeyer, Gerhart. "The Depth and Height of Political Order." *Review of Politics* 21 (1958): 588–96.

————. "Eric Voegelin's Achievement." *Modern Age* 9 (1965): 132–40.

————. "Eric Voegelin's Philosophy and the Drama of Mankind." *Modern Age* 20 (1976): 28–39.

————. "God and Man, World and Society: The Last Work of Eric Voegelin." *Review of Politics* 51 (1989): 107–23.

————. "The Order of Consciousness." *Review of Politics* 30 (1968): 251–56.

————. "The Order of History and the History of Order." *Review of Politics* 19 (1957): 403–9.

Nussbaum, Martha C. *The Fragility of Goodness: Luck and Ethics in Greek Tragedy and Philosophy.* Cambridge: Cambridge University Press, 1986.

Opitz, Peter J., and Gregor Sebba, eds. *The Philosophy of Order: Essays on History, Consciousness, and Politics.* Stuttgart: Klett-Cotta, 1981.

Pangle, Thomas. "On The Epistolary Dialogue between Leo Strauss and Eric Voegelin." *Review of Politics* 53 (1991): 100–125.

Plato. *The Collected Dialogues.* Ed. Edith Hamilton and Huntington Cairns. Bollingen Series LXXI. Princeton: Princeton University Press, 1961.

Porter, J. M. "A Philosophy of History as a Philosophy of Consciousness." *Denver Quarterly* 10 (1975): 96–104.

Rhodes, James M. "Philosophy, Revelation, and Political Theory: Leo Strauss and Eric Voegelin." *Journal of Politics* 49 (1987): 1036–60.

————. "Voegelin and Christian Faith." *Center Journal* 2 (1983): 55–105.

Rosen, Stanley. Review of *Order and History. Review of Metaphysics* 12 (1958): 257–76.

Sandoz, Ellis. "Eric Voegelin and the Nature of Philosophy." *Modern Age* 13 (1969): 152–68.

————. "The Foundations of Voegelin's Political Theory." *Political Science Reviewer* 1 (1971): 30–73.

————. *The Voegelinian Revolution: A Biographical Introduction.* Baton Rouge: Louisiana State University Press, 1981.

Sandoz, Ellis, ed. *Eric Voegelin's Significance for the Modern Mind.* Baton Rouge: Louisiana State University Press, 1991.

————. *Eric Voegelin's Thought: A Critical Appraisal.* Durham, N.C.: Duke University Press, 1982.

Schall, James. *Reason, Revelation, and the Foundations of Political Philosophy.* Baton Rouge: Louisiana State University Press, 1987.

Schram, Glenn. "Strauss and Voegelin on Machiavelli and Modernity." *Modern Age* 31 (1987): 261–66.

————. "Western Civilization in the Light of the Philosophy of History." *Modern Age* 34 (1990): 249–58.

Sebba, Gregor. "From Enlightenment to Universal Humanity." *Southern Review* 11 (1975): 918–25.

————. "Orders and Disorders of the Soul: Eric Voegelin's Philosophy of History." *Southern Review* 3 (1967): 282–310.

Snell, Bruno. *The Discovery of the Mind in Greek Philosophy and Literature.* New York: Dover, 1982.

Srigley, Ronald D. *Eric Voegelin's Platonic Theology: Philosophy of Consciousness and Symbolization in a New Perspective.* Lewiston, N.Y.: Edwin Mellen Press, 1991.

Tracy, David. *The Analogical Imagination: Christian Theology and the Culture of Pluralism.* New York: Crossroad, 1981.

————. "Theologies of Praxis." In *Creativity and Method: Essays in Honor of Bernard Lonergan,* ed. Matthew L. Lamb. Milwaukee: Marquette University Press, 1981.

Van Beeck, Franz Josef, S.J. *God Encountered: A Contemporary Catholic Systematic Theology.* Vol. 1, *Understanding the Christian Faith.* San Francisco: Harper and Row, 1989.

Von Rad, Gerhard. *Old Testament Theology.* Vol. 2, *The Theology of Israel's Prophetic Traditions.* Trans. D. M. G. Stalker. New York: Harper and Row, 1962.

Wagner, Helmut R. "Agreement in Discord: Alfred Schutz and Eric Voegelin." In *The Philosophy of Order: Essays on History, Consciousness, and Politics,* ed. Peter J. Opitz and Gregor Sebba, 74–90. Stuttgart: Klett-Cotta, 1981.

Wainwright, E. H. "Eric Voegelin: An Inquiry into the Philosophy of Order." *Politikon* 5 (1978).

————. "Political Gnosticism and the Search for Order in Existence." *Politikon* 6 (1979).

Walsh, David. "The Scope of Voegelin's Philosophy of Consciousness." *Philosophical Studies* (Dublin) 31 (1986–1987): 45–61.

————. "Voegelin's Response to the Disorder of the Age." *Review of Politics* 46 (1984): 266–87.

Webb, Eugene. *Eric Voegelin: Philosopher of History.* Seattle: University of Washington Press, 1981.

————. "In Memorium: Politics and the Problem of Philosophical Rhetoric in the Thought of Eric Voegelin." *Journal of Politics* 48 (1986): 260–73.

————. *Philosophers of Consciousness: Polanyi, Lonergan, Voegelin, Ricoeur, Girard, Kierkegaard.* Seattle: University of Washington Press, 1988.

Weiss, Raymond L. "Voegelin's Biblical Hermeneutics." *Independent Journal of Philosophy* 5/6 (1988): 81–84.

Wheelwright, Philip, ed. *The Presocratics.* Indianapolis: Bobbs-Merrill, Odyssey Press, 1975.

Wilhelmsen, Frederick D. "The New Voegelin." *Triumph* (1975): 32–35.

————. "Professor Voegelin and the Christian Tradition." In *Christianity and Political Philosophy.* Athens: University of Georgia Press, 1978.

Wiser, James L. "Eric Voegelin: A Study in the Renewal of Political Science." *Polity* 46 (1985): 295–312.

————. "Eric Voegelin and the Eclipse of Philosophy." *Denver Quarterly* 10 (1975): 108–14.

————. "From Cultural Analysis to Philosophical Anthropology: An Examination of Voegelin's Concept of Gnosticism." *Review of Politics* 42 (1980): 92–104.

Yovel, Yermiyahu. *Kant and the Philosophy of History.* Princeton: Princeton University Press, 1980.

INDEX

activist dreamers, 111–13, 228–29, 243; contrasted with philosophers, 106, 108–9, 121–22; effectiveness of, 113–14, 115–16, 117, 195

Anaximander, 72, 175, 180, 183, 186, 253

Anglo-American culture: strength of, 206–7, 206n45, 208, 210; Voegelin's ambivalence toward, 207, 208, 210, 211

anthropological truth, 56

apeiron, 12, 13, 72, 226, 241

apocalyptic: dangers of, 62–63, 65, 65n54, 198–99; causes, 64, 67, 223

apoliticism: Voegelin's criticism of, 195–96, 199; and pneumatic differentiation, 196–99

Arendt, Hannah: and Voegelin, 190–94

Aristotle, 95, 209, 253, 254–55; influence on Voegelin, 19–20; on *nous*, 33; and noetic differentiation, 49, 52, 176; balance, 68, 72; *Nicomachean Ethics*, 70; on good society, 80, 89; and polis, 159, 176; and *phronesis*, 210, 210n51

articulation. *See* social articulation

Augustine, 104, 196–97

authority of ignorance: result of deformation, 117–18

authority, political: and power, 82, 118, 166, 173, 184–86; and representative, 82, 100; and realization of "idea," 82–83; and revolution, 92, 118; challenged by differentiation, 100, 165–66; and philosophers, 159–64, 165, 166, 167–68, 172; and ethics, 184–86

Autobiographical Reflections, 17, 146

balance of consciousness, 68, 72; loss of, 105, 240. *See also* Plato

Beginning: symbol of, 13

Beginning and the Beyond: as apt symbols for reality, 14, 246; experience of, 105; and vision, 238

Beyond: symbol of, 14, 54, 135; differentiation of, 46, 72, 140, 143, 174n28, 237–38, 243; deformation of, 105, 112, 220; and vision, 237–39, 240, 241; and immortalization, 241–42, 255; and transfiguration, 242–43, 255

Brueggemann, Walter, 250n3

Bultmann, Rudolf, 146, 231

Canaan: symbol of, 143; as problematic, 144, 181; mortgage of, 145, 149, 159, 197

Christianity: and pneumatic differentiation, 55, 196; continuity with Israel, 55; distinctiveness, 55–56, 60, 61, 160, 197; and noetic differentiation, 55, 61; capacity for imbalance, 61–63, 67, 196–99; and human limitation, 74

Church, 160, 188, 197–99, 224, 225

Cicero, 107, 193

climate of opinion: creation of, 116, 254; effects of, 120

cognitional theory. *See* intentionality; luminosity

common sense philosophy, 208–11; and *ratio*, 209; and *noesis*, 209, 211; strengths of, 209–10; problems with, 210–11

community of being: partners, 8–11, 188; compactness, 35; consubstan-

eschatological perspective, 108*n12*,
197–98, 230, 242, 244, 252, 254;
eschatological index, 228
exodus: of Israel, 144; from itself,
154; proper meaning of, 226–27
experience, 1–2, 18–20, 127; recovery
of, 2, 97, 128, 192, 205–6, 246, 253–
54, 256; and participation, 9, 131,
238–39; "pure experience" (Wm.
James), 17; dynamic, 19; and consciousness, 19, 131; danger of hypostatization, 19, 27–28, 110–11, 128,
129, 235; metaleptic, 20; and luminosity, 23–24, 131; of whole, 35–37,
75, 238–39; relationship to political
philosophy, 192, 253–54; and vision,
238–39, 240; and revelation, 251

Fortescue, 82

Germino, Dante, 181
gnosis, 63–67 *passim*, 180; change in
Voegelin's treatment of, 65*n54;*
causes, 65–66, 223; ancient and
modern, 66, 76, 199; critique of
Voegelin's view, 76; and Isaiah, 147
good society: possibility of, 5, 6–7,
178, 195–213 *passim*, 244, 246;
problem of realization, 5, 92–93,
178, 200, 255; Aristotle on, 80; criteria for, 90, 194, 201, 207, 246,
247, 255; and democracy, 207–8
Gospel: and noetic differentiation,
62; Voegelin's interpretation of,
71–72, 196–97
grace, 56, 73, 73*n75,* 250–52
ground: as intended by questions, 3,
11, 52–53; as ontological hypothesis, 11, 78, 79, 123–24; and reality,
11; as symbol, 11; unknowable, 11;
and "things," 11, 78, 230; as "nonexistent," 12, 36–37, 238–39; as
divine ground, 14, 52–53, 246; as
basis for human nature, 79–80, 88,
90, 101, 118–19, 194, 221–22, 230–31,
246; constitutive of social/political
reality, 88–89, 90, 118–19, 120, 161–
62, 194, 246

Hegel, G. W. F., 231
Heidegger, Martin, 231

Hellas, 6, 157
Heraclitus, 79–80, 115, 158, 186
Hesiod, 238
hierarchy of being: emergence of,
36–38
historical index, 140
historiogenesis, 95, 215
historiography: as element of Ecumenic Age, 217*n7,* 218, 235
history: as response to truth of order,
123, 138, 139–42, 143, 180, 219, 229,
230, 232, 234, 236–37; change in
Voegelin's view, 137, 138*n1,* 138–43
passim, 140*n6,* 215, 230, 231; and
differentiations, 139–40, 215, 227,
230, 232, 233, 236, 237, 243–44;
double constitution of, 141, 142–43,
188, 233, 234, 235, 236, 248; in
Plato, 169–70; essence in, 191–92,
194; configurations of, 216, 218,
227, 228, 231
History of Political Ideas, 3–4
Hobbes, Thomas, 187, 187*n13*
Hitler, Adolf, 119
hypostatization of experience, 19, 28,
109–10

ideals: compared with utopias,
108*n12. See also* paradigm of order
ideas: inadequacy of in describing
reality, 3–4, 254; Platonic, 165–66.
See also social articulation
ideologies: problems with, 1, 98–99,
111, 120, 201, 202, 204–5; causes,
110–12, 243; as modern phenomena, 111–12, 202, 204; analysis of,
202–3; and common sense, 210
idiotes, 79–80, 115, 119
imagination: and experience, 105; as
structure of consciousness, 105*n5;*
as source of disorder, 105–6
imaginative oblivion, 106
imaginators. *See* activist dreamers
immanence (and transcendence): as
expressions of tension of existence,
14, 21; differentiation of, 46, 95,
219; and universality, 221
immortalization. *See* Beyond; vision
incarnation: and Jesus, 56–57, 61,
233*n38;* transfiguring, 57
intentionality: subordinate role in